CHRONICLE OF THE PHARAOHS

PETER A. CLAYTON

CHRONICLE
OF THE
PHARAOHS

THE REIGN-BY-REIGN RECORD OF THE RULERS AND DYNASTIES OF ANCIENT EGYPT

WITH 350 ILLUSTRATIONS
130 IN COLOR

For Janet,
in celebration of our heb-sed

© 1994 Thames & Hudson Ltd,
London
Text © 1994 Peter A. Clayton

First published in hardcover in the
United States of America in 1994 by
Thames & Hudson Inc.,
500 Fifth Avenue,
New York, New York 10110

Reprinted 2001

Library of Congress Catalog Card
Number 94-60269
ISBN 0-500-05074-0

Printed and bound in Slovenia
by Mladinska Knjiga

CONTENTS

Khafre
DYNASTY 4

Senusret III
DYNASTY 12

Tuthmosis III
DYNASTY 18

Psusennes I
DYNASTY 21

PREFACE: GOD-KINGS OF THE NILE

Copper alloy kneeling statuette of Amenemhet III (1842–1797 BC), part of a rare group of figures in this metal of the king, his wife and chief scribes (pp. 87–9). George Ortiz Collection, Geneva.

Egyptian civilization was one of the greatest in the ancient world, and certainly the most long lived, lasting for more than 3000 years. In the popular mind the immediate images are those of the pyramids, the great Sphinx at Giza, the enormous temples and the fabulous treasures that have been preserved in the dry sand of Egypt. But what of the people who were responsible for such splendours?

The ancient Egyptian pharaohs were god-kings on earth who became gods in their own right at their death. They indeed held the power of life and death in their hands – their symbols of office, the crook and flail, are indicative of this. They could command resources that many a modern-day state would be hard pressed to emulate. One has only to conjure with some statistics to realize this. For example, the Great Pyramid of Khufu (Cheops) at Giza, originally 481 ft (146 m) high and covering 13.1 acres (5.3 hectares), was the tallest building in the world until the 19th century AD, yet it was constructed in the mid-3rd millennium BC, and we still do not know exactly how it was done. Its base area is so vast that it can accommodate the cathedrals of Florence, Milan, St Paul's and Westminster Abbey in London and St Peter's in Rome, and still have some space left over.

The vast treasures of precious metal and jewellery that, miraculously, escaped the attentions of the tomb robbers are almost beyond comprehension. Tutankhamun's solid gold inner coffin is a priceless work of art; even at current scrap gold prices by weight it would be worth almost £1 million ($1.5 million), and his gold funerary mask £105,000 ($155,000). He was just a minor pharaoh of little consequence – the wealth of greater pharaohs such as Ramesses II, by comparison, is unimaginable.

The names of other great pharaohs resound down the centuries. The pyramid-builders numbered not merely Khufu, but his famous predecessor Djoser – whose Step Pyramid dominates the royal necropolis at Saqqara – and his successors Khafre (Chephren) and Menkaure (Mycerinus). Later monarchs included the warriors Tuthmosis III, Amenhotep III, and Seti I, not to mention the infamous heretic-king Akhenaten. Yet part of the fascination of taking a broad approach to Egyptian history is the emergence of lesser names and fresh themes. The importance of royal wives in a matrilineal society and the extent to which Egyptian queens could and did reign supreme in their own right – Sobeknefru, Hatshepsut, and Twosret to name but three – is only the most prominent among several newly emergent themes.

The known 170 or more pharaohs were all part of a line of royalty that stretched back to c. 3100 BC and forward to the last of the native pharaohs who died in 343 BC, to be succeeded by Persians and then a Greek line of Ptolemies until Cleopatra VII committed suicide in 30 BC. Following the 3rd-century BC High Priest of Heliopolis, Manetho – whose list of Egyptian kings has largely survived in the writings of Christian clerics – we can divide much of this enormous span of time into 30 dynasties. Egyptologists today group these dynasties into longer

The royal family: the 18th Dynasty king Akhenaten (1350–1334 BC) and his queen Nefertiti with three of their six small daughters. The intimacy of the scene is unprecedented in earlier Egyptian art. Berlin Museum.

eras, the three major pharaonic periods being the Old, Middle and New Kingdoms, each of which ended in a period of decline given the designation 'Intermediate Period'.

In *Chronicle of the Pharaohs*, that emotive and incandescent 3000-year-old thread of kingship is traced, setting the rulers in their context. Where possible, we gaze upon the face of pharaoh, either via reliefs and statuary or, in some rare and thought-provoking instances, on the actual face of the mummy of the royal dead. Across the centuries the artist's conception reveals to us the god-like complacency of the Old Kingdom pharaohs, the care-worn faces of the rulers of the Middle Kingdom, and the powerful and confident features of the militant New Kingdom pharaohs. Such was their power in Egypt, and at times throughout the ancient Near East, that Shelley's words, 'Look on my works, ye Mighty, and despair!', do indeed ring true as a reflection of their omnipotence.

Many books are published each year on ancient Egypt, on different aspects of its history and culture. Here, for the first time, an overall view is taken of those incredible people, the pharaohs who, although human after all, were looked upon by thousands as gods on earth and whose very achievements were, and even today still appear to be, the creations of the gods themselves.

Ramesses II (1279–1212 BC), in a typically aggressive pose, grasps a trio of Asiatic prisoners by the hair, ready to despatch them with the incongruously small axe held in his left hand. Cairo Museum.

Egypt and the Nile

Egypt is a land of extreme geographical contrasts, recognized by the ancient Egyptians in the names that they gave to the two diametrically opposed areas. The rich narrow agricultural strip alongside the Nile was called *Kmt*, 'The Black Land', while the inhospitable desert was *Dsrt*, 'The Red Land'. Often, in Upper Egypt, the desert reaches the water's edge.

There was also a division between the north and the south, the line being drawn roughly in the area of modern Cairo. To the north was Lower Egypt where the Nile fanned out, with its several mouths, to form the Delta (the name coming from its inverted shape of the fouth letter, *delta*, of the Greek alphabet). To the south was Upper Egypt, stretching to Elephantine (modern Aswan). The two kingdoms, Upper and Lower Egypt, were united in *c.* 3100 BC, but each had their own regalia. The low Red Crown (the *deshret*) represented Lower Egypt and its symbol was the papyrus plant. Upper Egypt was represented by the tall White Crown (the *hedjet*), its symbol being the flowering lotus. The combined Red and White crowns became the *shmty*. The two lands could also be embodied in The Two Ladies, respectively the cobra goddess Wadjet of Buto, and the vulture goddess Nekhbet of Nekheb.

(*Below*) Symbols of Upper and Lower Egypt

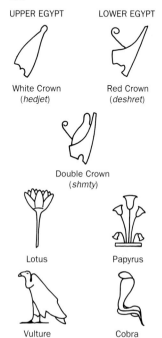

UPPER EGYPT   LOWER EGYPT

White Crown (*hedjet*)   Red Crown (*deshret*)

Double Crown (*shmty*)

Lotus   Papyrus

Vulture   Cobra

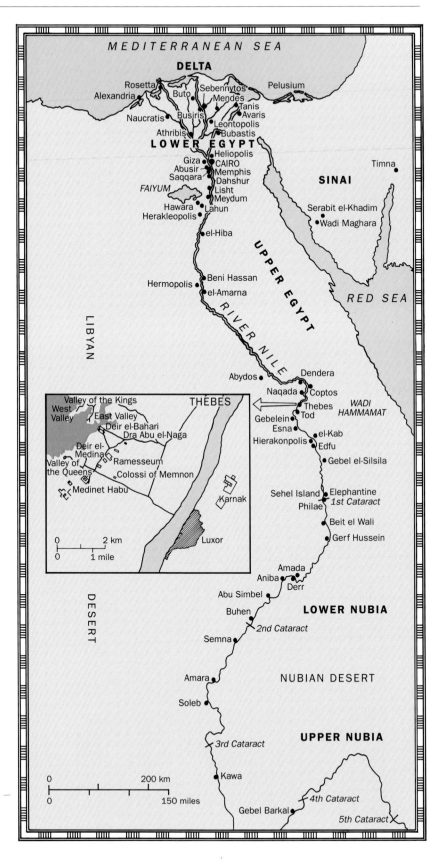

INTRODUCTION: THE CHRONOLOGY OF ANCIENT EGYPT

In the early 6th century BC Solon (c. 640–560 BC), the Athenian states-man and legislator, travelled to Egypt. There he visited the temple in the city of Naucratis in the Delta, a city recently settled by Greeks from Miletus. Solon, as a great statesman from a great city, was justly proud of Athens and its long history, but he was sharply put in his place by the priests of the temple with whom he was discussing history when they tartly reminded him: 'You Hellenes [Greeks] are but children.' They meant, and rightly so, that Greek history could not in any way equate in time and content with that of Egypt.

In this they were correct, but it is interesting to reflect that the priests themselves were only the inheritors of a long historical tradition that stretched back almost 3000 years. Whilst they obviously had sources to hand which are no longer extant today, they were living at a time when the grandeur of ancient Egypt was long past and we do not know exactly what historical records were then available to them. That some detailed records existed is proved by the fact that Manetho, a Graeco-Egyptian priest born at Sebennytos in the Delta, was able to write a detailed history of Egypt 300 years later in the 3rd century BC.

Manetho and the history of Egypt

Manetho's *Egyptian History* (also known as *Notes about Egypt*) gives us the basic structure or skeleton of Egyptian chronology that we use today. He divided Egyptian history into dynasties (essentially, ruling houses) and we recognize 30 of them from the unification of Egypt in c. 3100 BC down to the death of the last native Egyptian pharaoh, Nectanebo II, in 343 BC. Sometimes the last phase of ancient Egyptian history after this date has two dynasties added – the 31st and 32nd – which are the Second Persian Period, and the Macedonian rulers linked with the Ptolemaic Dynasty, which ends with the suicide of the last of the Ptolemies, Cleopatra VII, in 30 BC.

Curiously, although great reliance is placed on Manetho, no full text of his work survives. Perhaps one day a papyrus edition will be found, possibly coming from one of the cities of the Faiyum which have pro-duced so much literary and historical material on papyri from the Graeco-Roman period. Manetho's *History* is known to us only by chance since it was highly thought of in antiquity and several writers whose works have survived quoted extensively from it. Principal amongst these was Josephus (writing in the late 1st century AD), in his *Jewish Antiquities* and *Contra Apionem*, and the Christian chronogra-phers Sextus Julius Africanus, whose *Chronicle* comes down to c. AD 220, and Bishop Eusebius of Caesarea, whose writings add another 100 years into the early 4th century. Some 500 years later, the work of the last two writers was used as a basis for a history of the world by George the Monk who was secretary (hence his also being known as Syncellus) to the Byzantine Patriarch Tarasius (784–806). All these authors took what they wanted for their own purposes from their sources and so Manetho's account only exists in fragments within these later works.

MANETHO AND THE CULT OF SERAPIS

Manetho lived during the reign of Ptolemy I, Governor and Satrap of Egypt from 323 to 305 and king from 305 to 282 BC. Plutarch tells us that Manetho was one of the two priestly advisors to the king and that he had been concerned with the introduction of the cult of Serapis. This god, represented as a bearded man with a corn *modius* (measure) on his head, was a conflation of Egyptian and Greek ideas which had wide appeal and whose cult, under Rome, spread as far as Roman York (*Corpus Inscr. Lat.* VII, 240). Alexandria was noted for its temple to Serapis with the famous cult statue by the sculptor Bryaxis, introduced into the temple about 286 BC, as well as for its later Library and also being the burial place of Alexander the Great. Manetho's association with the foundation of the cult may be acknowledged by the appearance of his name on a statue base found in the temple of Serapis at Carthage (*CIL* VIII, 1007); it may have been a portrait bust of him, but we shall never know.

PT O LM Y S
K L E OP A T R A

(*Above*) The Rosetta Stone is perhaps one of the most famous antiquities in the world. It passed to Britain under Article 16 of the Treaty of Alexandria, 1801. By comparing the cartouche of Ptolemy on the Stone with the cartouche of Cleopatra on the Philae obelisk at Kingston Lacy, Dorset, Champollion was able to identify several coincidental letters, forming the basis of his decipherment. British Museum.

Manetho's sources were very mixed. He obviously had access to temple records, since we know that he was a priest in the temple at Heliopolis (the Biblical city of On). His name itself has overtones of learning because it appears to be associated with Thoth, the ibis-headed god of wisdom who invented hieroglyphs. It may mean 'Beloved of Thoth' or possibly 'Gift of Thoth'. He had sources such as the official papyrus histories, the sacred books in the temple and, not least, the historical inscriptions on the temple walls such as the king lists described below, Ramesses III's account of his battles with the Sea Peoples at Medinet Habu, and many more that have not been preserved. To all these possible sources, however, he added a lot of popular traditions and stories of the kings, some of which are far from credible. He was also, obviously, conversant with the writings of Herodotus, the Greek historian from Halicarnassus, who had visited Egypt around 450 BC and written much about the land and its history in Book 2 of his *History*.

Egyptian chronology: the evidence from inscriptions

From an incomplete and variously corrupt literary history it is possible to examine some of the actual written sources. Whilst these had survived from ancient Egyptian times, after about the end of the 4th century AD they could no longer be read. The latest dated inscription in Egyptian hieroglyphs occurs on the temple of Philae in AD 394. Thereafter the 'key' was lost although many scholars during the European Renaissance, and later the Jesuit priest Athanasius Kircher (1602–80), made valiant attempts at decipherment, often with incredible results. In 1761 another priest, the Abbé Jean Jacques Barthélemy, published a paper in which he suggested that the oval rings in which a number of the hieroglyphic signs occurred enclosed royal names. It was working from those 'ovals', now called cartouches, that Jean François Champollion was able to 'crack the code' of Egyptian hieroglyphs with the **Rosetta Stone**. This odd-shaped slab of black basalt was found by a French officer of engineers, Lieutenant P.F.X. Bouchard, serving with the Napoleonic Expedition in Egypt, at Fort Julien at the Rosetta mouth of the Nile in 1799. It is inscribed in three scripts representing two languages. The upper portion is written in Egyptian hieroglyphs, the centre in the Egyptian demotic script, and the lower section is in Greek. The latter was easily translated, revealing that the inscription, the Decree of Memphis, is a decree of Ptolemy V, dated to Year 9 of his reign, 196 BC. With this as a base Champollion was able to work toward his eventual epoch-making paper, *Lettre à M. Dacier*, in 1822 which opened the floodgates to the decipherment of Egyptian hieroglyphs.

Apart from priestly inscriptions such as the Rosetta Stone, the Shabaka Stone (p. 192) and others such as the Sehel boulder inscription No. 81 (p. 33), there are only a few sources with actual lists pertaining to Egyptian history and chronology. References to small, specific areas of chronology, often only reflecting an individual's part in it, occur, but the evidence is slight and often difficult.

(Above) A section of the Palermo Stone (17 inches high, 9¾ inches wide or 43.5 x 25 cm). It is thought that originally this monument was just over 6½ ft (2 m) long and about 23½ inches (60 cm) high. It is laid out in a series of boxes which give the king's name and then the events of that reign by numerical year (like the dating of laws by regnal year in England). Thus we find entries under a king's name, such as 'Year 4 First Occurrence of the Feast of Sokar'. Similar dating by year and events occurs on a number of the small ivory labels from Abydos and Saqqara that were tied to individual items such as sandals (pp. 22, 24). Palermo Museum, Sicily.

The earliest evidence surviving is the **Palermo Stone**, which dates from the 5th Dynasty (2498–2345 BC). One large section of this black diorite slab is in the Palermo Museum in Sicily and smaller fragments are in the Cairo Museum and the Petrie Museum, University College London. The Palermo fragment is inscribed on both sides and records some of the last Predynastic kings before 3150 BC followed by the kings through to Neferirkare in the mid-5th Dynasty.

The **Royal List of Karnak** (now in the Louvre) has a list of kings running from the first king down to Tuthmosis III (1504–1450 BC). It has an added advantage in that it records the names of many of the obscure kings of the Second Intermediate Period (Dynasties 13–17).

The **Royal List of Abydos** is still *in situ* on the walls of the corridor in the Hall of Ancestors in the magnificent temple of Seti I (1291–1278 BC). It shows Seti with his young son (later Ramesses II) before a list of the cartouches of 76 kings running in two rows from the first king to Seti I (the third row of cartouches on the wall beneath these merely repeats Seti's own). The kings of the Second Intermediate Period are not given (hence the value of the Karnak List, above), neither are there the cartouches of the kings at the end of the 18th Dynasty after Amenhotep III, who were not considered acceptable because of their association with the Amarna 'heresy' (Akhenaten, Smenkhkare, Tutankhamun and Ay: see pp. 120–139). A badly damaged duplicate of this list, but arranged in three rows instead of two, was found in the nearby temple of Ramesses II. Known as the **Abydos King List,** it is now in the British Museum.

(Right) The Abydos King list in the British Museum is a much inferior duplicate of the larger Royal List (p. 12) in the Hall of Ancestors or Records in the temple of Abydos.

Seti I and his young son, the future Ramesses II, worship the cartouched names of their ancestors in the Hall of Ancestors or Records in the temple of Abydos. Unacceptable ancestors such as Queen Hatshepsut and the 'Amarna' pharaohs (pp. 120–39) are conveniently omitted from the list.

One other list inscribed on stone is the **Royal List of Saqqara**, now in the Cairo Museum. It was found in the tomb of the Royal Scribe Thunery at Saqqara and has 47 cartouches (originally it had 58) running from Anedjib of the 1st Dynasty to Ramesses II, again omitting those of the Second Intermediate Period.

Egyptian chronology: the Royal Canon of Turin

The finest record of the chronology of the Egyptian kings is unfortunately the most damaged and now incomplete. It is a papyrus known as the Royal Canon of Turin, in which museum it is to be found. Originally the property of the king of Sardinia, tragically, it was badly packed and severely damaged during transportation. The list of the kings, originally over 300 of them, is written in a fine literate hand in the hieratic script on the back of a long Ramesside papyrus which has accounts on the front, or recto side. This dates it to having been written about 1200 BC. Like the scraps remaining from Manetho, and the first line of the Palermo Stone, it begins with dynasties of gods which are followed by those of earthly kings. A useful aspect is that it gives the exact lengths of each reign in years and even months and days. Its condition is such that piecing the fragments together is like solving a gigantic jigsaw puzzle with many pieces missing, so that what would have been the premier source for Egyptian chronology is an epigraphist's nightmare.

Fixing true dates by the stars

Even with the chronological information available, as outlined above, it may come as a surprise to realize that it is extremely difficult to fix true or absolute dates in Egyptian chronology. Most of the information given in the inscriptions mentioned is relative, in that it shows a sequence of kings relative to each other with sometimes a length of time between each reign, but to fix them in an absolute framework is a different matter altogether. Absolute dates from ancient Egypt rely on astronomical

dating. This is done by reference to the civil and astronomical calendars in a complicated calculation involving the Sothic cycle of 1460 years, based on the heliacal rising of Sirius, or Sothis, the 'dog star'. The ancient Egyptians knew that the year consisted of 365 days, but they made no adjustment for the additional quarter of a day each year – as we do with Leap Year every four years at the end of February. Hence their civil and astronomical calendars were gradually moving out of synchronization and could bring about extremes of dating between the two. Eventually, every 1460 years, the two calendars coincided and were correct for a short time, until they gradually became out of step again until the end of the next cycle.

The heliacal rising of Sirius was, ideally, supposed to coincide with New Year's Day in the civil calendar, but did so only every 1460 years. The 3rd-century AD grammarian Censorinus records that in AD 139 the first day of the Egyptian civil year and the heliacal rising of Sirius did actually coincide – this being the end of a Sothic cycle. This phenomenon is also confirmed by a reverse type on the billon tetradrachms issued at the mint of Alexandria with the standing figure of a haloed phoenix and the Greek word AION (indicating the end of an era); it is also dated by the characters L B to regnal year 2 of the emperor Antoninus Pius, which fell between 29 August AD 138 and 28 August 139. It is possible, working backwards, to deduce that comparable coincidences had occurred in 1317 BC and 2773 BC.

The occurrence of a heliacal rising of Sirius is recorded in the 7th year of the reign of Senusret III (1878–1841 BC) of the 12th Dynasty. The event is dated to the 16th day of the 4th month of the 2nd season in the 7th year of the king. (There were only three seasons, not four, in ancient Egypt: inundation, sowing and harvest; then the cycle started again.) By calculating from the 'coincidences' of 1317 BC and 2773 BC, this rising can be fixed at 1872 BC. Another such sighting recorded occurred on the 9th day of the 3rd month of the 3rd season in the 9th year of Amenhotep I (1551–1524 BC); this produces a date somewhere within a 26-year range in the second half of the 16th century BC, since it cannot be quite so closely tied as the Senusret date.

This shows just how fluid Egyptian chronology can be, essentially calculated on a structure of regnal years for each king (where known) and which, by counting backwards and forwards, are basically anchored to the three heliacal risings of Sirius mentioned. It is generally accepted that Egyptian chronology is on a firm footing from 664 BC, the beginning of the 26th Dynasty (Saite Period) and the reign of Psammetichus I. There are then outside links to the chronology of historical Mediterranean civilizations which become firmer as the full classical and Roman periods are reached. Margins of error in the dynasties prior to the 26th are variable; whilst in the New Kingdom 20 years might be acceptable, this will increase as earlier periods are reached so that dates around the unification and in the Early Dynastic Period (Dynasties '0'–2) could be subject to fluctuations of anything between 50 and 200 years.

DATES FOLLOWED IN CHRONICLE OF THE PHARAOHS

Some recent literature, both scholarly as well as 'fringe', has suggested outlandish and unacceptable changes in the chronology. Principal amongst the former is *Centuries of Darkness* by Peter James (1991), and amongst the latter the books of Velikovsky and Von Däniken. It is small wonder then that there is often such a variety in the dates suggested in much of the literature. In this book the dating followed is largely that put forward by Dr William J. Murnane in his *Penguin Guide to Ancient Egypt* (1983).

14

Narmer

1st Dynasty king

Khasekhemwy

DYNASTY 'O'
3150–3050

'Scorpion'

Narmer

DYNASTY 1
3050–2890

Hor-Aha

Djer

Djet

Den

Anedjib

Semerkhet

Qa'a

DYNASTY 2
2890–2686

Hotepsekhemwy

Raneb

Nynetjer

Seth-Peribsen

Khasekhemwy

PREDYNASTIC
PERIOD ENDS

EARLY DYNASTIC
PERIOD BEGINS

'Scorpion'
Narmer
(precise dates unknown)

Hor-Aha
Djer
Djet
Den
Anedjib
Semerkhet
Qa'a
(precise dates unknown)

DYNASTY 'O'

DYNASTY 1

3200   3150   3100   3050   3000   2950   2900

Narmer and standard bearers

THE FIRST PHARAOHS
The Early Dynastic Period 3150–2686 BC

THE EMERGENCE of civilization in the Nile Valley at the end of the 4th millennium BC was to affect, in one way or another, not only the following 3000 years of Egyptian history but also many of the subsequent civilizations of the ancient Near East. Prior to that date, prehistoric people had roamed the river swamps and the high desert gebel, but why, suddenly, should Egyptian civilization erupt almost like the lotus flower from the primeval waters in one of the old creation legends, and where did it come from? The full answers to these questions have yet to be found. Arguments still rage as to the origins of the first kings – were they from Central Africa or what was later to be known as the Fertile Crescent? What historical, though later, sources there are all seem agreed that the first kings came from This, an area somewhere near Abydos in middle Egypt, and were called the Thinite kings. Whatever their origins, they had the foresight, and the power to match it, to mould the first two dynasties. Such is the gap in time, that we can only speculate, in many instances, on the political and economic situations and high level of technology, artistic achievement and religious awareness which, within about 500 years, laid down many of the concepts that were to govern later thought in ancient Egypt.

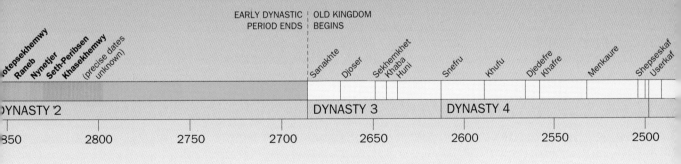

EARLY DYNASTIC   OLD KINGDOM
PERIOD ENDS   BEGINS

Hotepsekhemwy   Raneb   Nynetjer   Seth-Peribsen   Khasekhemwy   (precise dates unknown)

Sanakhte   Djoser   Sekhemkhet   Khaba   Huni   Snefru   Khufu   Djedefre   Khafre   Menkaure   Shepseskaf   Userkaf

DYNASTY 2   DYNASTY 3   DYNASTY 4

2850   2800   2750   2700   2650   2600   2550   2500

DYNASTY '0'
3150–3050

'Scorpion'   Narmer

DYNASTY 1
3050–2890

 Hor-Aha   Anedjib

 Djer   Semerkhet

 Djet   Qa'a

 Den

ROYAL NAMES	
'SCORPION' *Named after scorpion sign on macehead*	**DEN** *Horus name* Den ('Horus Who Strikes')
NARMER *Horus name* Narmer ('The Striking Catfish')	**ANEDJIB** *Horus name* Anedjib ('Safe is His Heart')
HOR-AHA *Horus name* Hor-Aha ('The Fighting Hawk')	**SEMERKHET** *Horus name* Semerkhet ('Thoughtful Friend')
DJER *Horus name* Djer ('Horus Who Succours')	**QA'A** *Horus name* Qa'a ('His Arm is Raised')
DJET *Horus name* Djet ('Horus Cobra')	

Egyptian civilization begins, according to Manetho, with the Unification of the Two Lands, namely Upper and Lower Egypt, under one king. A date often used is *c.* 3100 BC, largely arrived at by working backwards from known astronomical dates, tied in with such early regnal dates, or sequences, that are known (see above, p. 13). The essential question is, who was this first king who unified the two kingdoms? Tradition ascribes this feat variously to Narmer or Menes, who may well have been one and the same person. There is also a king 'Scorpion' who appears on the scene. Some would place him and Narmer sequentially in a 'Dynasty O', from *c.* 3150 to 3050 BC.

The physical evidence for this comes from the discoveries of J.E. Quibell, excavating at Hierakonpolis in Upper Egypt, in 1897–98. Hierakonpolis was the ancient city of Nekhen on the west bank of the Nile north of Aswan and dedicated to the falcon-headed god Horus. The site of the Early Dynastic town is known as Kom el-Ahmar, literally the 'red mound'. Excavations here produced some remarkable finds, includ-

PREDYNASTIC | EARLY DYNASTIC
PERIOD ENDS | PERIOD BEGINS

'Scorpion'
Narmer
(precise dates unknown)

DYNASTY '0'

3160   3150   3140   3130   3120   3110   3100

THE PREDYNASTIC PERIOD

At the end of the 4th millennium BC, Egyptian civilization entered the historical record. Prior to this there had been the so-called Predynastic Period, from around 5000 until c. 3150 BC. Its divisions are generally named, in archaeological fashion, after their eponymous sites, that is, where they were first recognized, and the essential framework is that of Upper Egyptian sites. In broad dates, the Badarian (named after el Badari) began around 5000 BC, the Amratian (el Amra) about 4000 BC (its chronology having now been refined as Naqada I), Early Gerzean (Gerzah) c. 3500 and Late Gerzean c. 3300 BC (the last two periods falling into the Naqada II).

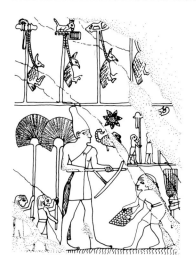

Detail from the 'Scorpion' Macehead. Before the king stands a diminutive retainer holding out a basket, ready to receive the earth which the king has turned with his mattock. Behind the king are small figures holding a pair of tall fans and in front of him, above the basket carrier, a file of people carrying upright standards. Ashmolean Museum.

ing a gold-headed hawk representing the town deity Horus, and an almost life-size, hollow-cast copper statue of Pepi I and his son Merenre of the 6th Dynasty (p. 66). The major find in relation to the Early Dynastic Period was made in a pit, labelled the 'Main Deposit', located between the walls of an Old Kingdom and a later Middle Kingdom temple. In the pit, Quibell found objects which have since proved to be the most important 'documents' of the Early Dynastic Period. The principal objects consisted of sculpted palettes and maceheads, although it is not totally clear from the excavator's accounts whether the major piece, the Narmer Palette, was found here or in a level nearby. Representations on the pieces, and also early-style hieroglyphs, identified 'Scorpion' and Narmer. The objects had been deposited long after the period in which they were made, possibly over 1000 years later towards the end of the Old Kingdom.

'SCORPION' AND NARMER

On the fragmented so-called 'Scorpion' Macehead, a king is seen in full ritual dress with the ritual bull's tail hanging from the back of his belt, wearing the tall White Crown (*hedjet*) of Upper Egypt and performing a ceremony using a hoe or mattock. Possibly he is opening the dykes ritually to begin the flooding of the fields; or he could be cutting the first furrow for the foundation of either a temple (here at Hierakonpolis) or of a city (as Roman emperors more than 3000 years later are depicted on coins ploughing the outline of a city at its foundation). Before the king's face, and therefore presumably signifying his name, is a scorpion with a seven-petalled flower above it. The decorative frieze around the remaining top of the macehead has lapwings hanging by their necks from vertical standards. This little bird, *rekhyt* in hieroglyphs, means 'common people' and their fate would seem to indicate that they have been overcome by the victorious King 'Scorpion'.

Whatever the ceremony being performed, two things seem clear: King 'Scorpion', wearing the White Crown, is king only of Upper Egypt (unless the missing side of the macehead depicted him with the Red Crown, i.e. as king of Lower Egypt as well); and there has been a battle and the lapwings have been conquered. The interpretation must be, therefore, that the event is taking place before the unification of Egypt, placing 'Scorpion' before Narmer.

Two major pieces from the 'Main Deposit' at Hierakonpolis refer to Narmer: the Narmer Palette and the Narmer Macehead. The Palette, a

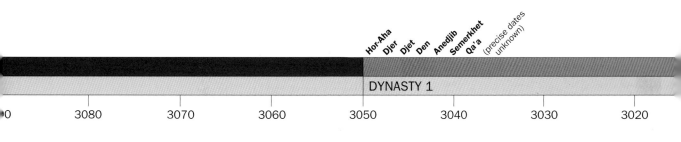

Hor-Aha Djer Djet Den Anedjib Semerkhet Qa'a (precise dates unknown)

DYNASTY 1

3080   3070   3060   3050   3040   3030   3020

(Above left) The principal scene on the Narmer Palette, described in the text.

(Above right) On the obverse of the Narmer Palette the king walks behind a procession of four standard-bearers towards two vertical rows of decapitated captives, five in each row, above whom there is a schematic boat with a cabin amidships and an apparent falcon standard on board as a totem. The central panel shows what is usually interpreted as evidence of early Mesopotamian art in Egypt, two four-legged serpopards, their necks entwined to form the cosmetic scoop, and held on leashes by two small retainers. Below all this, the lowest scene shows the king as a rampaging bull (one of the later royal titles was 'Strong Bull of Horus'), breaching the walls of a fortified town and a stricken enemy being crushed beneath his hooves. In a similar position on the other, reverse, side, two close-bearded foes are shown apparently drowning. Cairo Museum.

monumental piece of dark green slate, is the earliest historical record from Egypt. It shows a victorious king whose name appears within a *serekh* – the early form of presenting royal names – at the head of both sides between facing heads of the cow-faced goddess Hathor. The hiero-glyphs of the royal name are a mud fish depicted horizontally above a vertical chisel, read as the name of Narmer. Narmer is shown in two aspects, wearing respectively the White Crown of Upper Egypt (the *hed-jet*) and the Red Crown of Lower Egypt (*deshret*), implying that he is now king of both lands. Later, the dual monarchy was to be shown by both crowns being worn together (p. 8), one inside the other, and forming the Crown of Upper and Lower Egypt (the *shemty*). The principal scene, i.e. the more dominant artistically, has a large figure of Narmer wearing the White Crown and smiting with upraised mace a prisoner whom he grasps by the forelock. This is the earliest occurrence of what was to become an 'icon of majesty' throughout the rest of ancient Egyptian his-tory, right down to Roman times (pp. 24, 217). However, this side of the Palette should be the reverse since, on the other side, is cut a shallow depression that indicates the humble antecedents of this magnificent

Hor-Aha
Djer
Djet
Den
Anedjib
Semerkhet
Qa'a
(precise dates unknown)

► DYNASTY 1

3010   3000   2990   2980   2970   2960   2950

Evidence for a jubilee or renewal ritual (the *heb-sed* festival) first occurs on the Narmer Macehead (detail, below; Ashmolean Museum, Oxford). The king is usually represented wrapped in a tightly fitting cloak (on an ivory statuette

from Abydos it has a pattern of lozenges) and wearing either the Red Crown (as here) or the White Crown (pp. 26, 29). The purpose of the festival was to renew the king's potency and the fertility of the land. Initially celebrated every 30 years, later kings progressively shortened the intervals between the jubilees so that Ramesses II probably celebrated his 14th jubilee in Year 65/66 of his long reign. Part of the ritual involved the king running around a set course (the markers are seen on the Narmer Macehead as three vertical ellipses before the running figure). One of the finest representations of this occurs on a relief panel in the South Tomb of Djoser at Saqqara (p. 35).

piece: it is the scoop in which cosmetic powder, probably green eye paint, kohl, was crushed. This must then be the upper or obverse side. Here the king is shown in the Red Crown, in smaller stature but still the dominant figure, being larger than any of the other participants.

It is notable that on both sides of the Palette the king is shown barefoot, with his tiny sandal-bearer (who also appears to have been his seal-bearer, to judge from the cylinder seal suspended around his neck) following behind carrying a pair of sandals and what might be a small water jar. The king is twice represented in obviously symbolic and ritual contexts and it may be that the events are taking place in a sacred area, and the king is ritually barefoot, rather like Moses some 1800 years later (Exodus 3:5). Certainly the god Horus is the king's god, on his side, for as a falcon he holds an enemy, ready for the king's attention, by a rope uncomfortably threaded through the captive's nostrils.

The frontal face of the goddess Hathor is the dominant aspect of the top of both sides of the Palette, and must surely have deep significance in such a prime position. Although Horus was the god of Hierakonpolis (Nekhen), and it may be presumed that the principal temple was dedicated to him, it is possible that he is shown on the Palette as the younger Horus who was the son of Hathor, which would explain his mother's dominant role in the Palette's religious iconography. To draw analogies from much later in Egyptian history, the two finest remaining temples (both from the Ptolemaic period, pp. 215, 217) are built on much earlier foundations and are respectively dedicated to Horus (at Edfu) and Hathor (at Dendera), and their rituals involved an exchange of processions between them.

The Narmer Macehead also shows ritual scenes, principally the celebration of the *heb-sed* (jubilee) festival of renewal, where the king is seen seated, wrapped in the appropriate cloak (see left), within a pavilion. A cow (Hathor?) and her calf also have a prominent place in the iconography. The king here wears the Red Crown and his sandal-bearer is again in attendance, although the king's feet cannot be seen because of his ground-length ritual robe.

HOR-AHA

The name of Narmer occurs on other objects, generally scratched on potsherds and the like, and we can be sure that he was a historical personage. Hor-Aha, his successor, and therefore probably his son, possibly by Queen Nithotep, stood to inherit a unified kingdom, both by right and

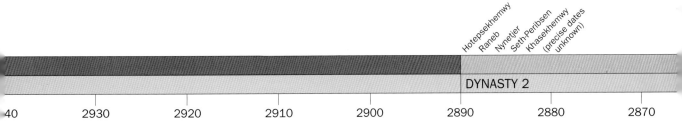

Hotepsekhemwy
Raneb
Nynetjer
Seth-Peribsen
Khasekhemwy
(precise dates unknown)

DYNASTY 2

2940 2930 2920 2910 2900 2890 2880 2870

Ivory label from the tomb of Queen Nithotep at Naqada which has in the top line the Horus name of Hor-Aha (second from right) and his *nebti* name, Men, in front of it. British Museum.

by conquest. He took the *nebti* name (the second royal name: p. 218) of Men, which means 'established', and this could be the origin of the later record of the first king as being called Menes. For present purposes we may look on Hor-Aha as the first king of the 1st Dynasty. An interesting piece of evidence is a small broken ivory label found in the tomb of Queen Nithotep at Naqada. Although schematically represented, the busy scene on this tiny piece seems to show two humans celebrating a ceremony called 'Receiving the South and the North' over an unidentified object (possibly the first representation of the later symbolic tying of papyrus and lotus stalks). The king's name, meaning 'Fighting Hawk' – an allusion again to Horus – indicates his Upper Egyptian origin and rule. His adoption of Men as his *nebti* name for ruling over both parts is indicated on the ivory label by the fact that his Horus name (his first and principal name, p. 218) Hor-Aha, and his *nebti* name, Men, appear side by side. Other similar small labels from Early Dynastic tombs indicate that his was not an easy reign. There were campaigns to be fought and rebels to be subdued in Nubia, recorded on a wooden label from Abydos, and another label records his foundation of a temple to the goddess Neith at Sais in the Delta. Her warlike aspect was signified by a pair of crossed arrows and her worship continued into Roman times when she was identified with Athena at Sais.

The founding of Memphis

Hor-Aha's greatest achievement was the founding of the capital city at Memphis, just south of the apex of the Delta. This was to endure throughout Egypt's history and become one of the greatest cities of the ancient world. The site was obviously chosen initially for its geographical and thus political importance in a newly unified country, rather than its situation as a good building site, which it was not. Herodotus records (Bk 2: 99) that Menes dammed the Nile just south of the future site of the city, diverting it so that he could build on the reclaimed land. A strict watch was kept on the dam – the Persians, he said, strengthened it every year because, should it be breached, Memphis would have been overwhelmed. Recent deep soundings taken by the Egypt Exploration Society expedition to Memphis have shown that the course of the Nile has been gradually moving eastwards in historical times.

(*Below*) Hor-Aha's Horus name, with the falcon Horus standing on a *serekh*, painted on a potsherd. British Museum.

According to Manetho, Hor-Aha (there called Menes) reigned for 62 years and met his end when he was carried off by a hippopotamus. He must have been of a great age and presumably out hippopotamus hunting. The Palermo Stone records a hippopotamus hunt in the reign of Udimu (Den), later in the dynasty, and their savage attacks on crocodiles are represented in a number of reliefs in later Old Kingdom, 6th Dynasty tombs.

After Memphis was founded the early Egyptian kings began to construct their tombs at the sacred site of Abydos in middle

Egypt and the nobles theirs on the edge of the desert plateau at Saqqara, overlooking Memphis. Controversy has raged as to whether the king built at both sites. Archaeological evidence is quite scarce with regard to specific attributions since the structures at both sites were badly damaged and heavily robbed throughout the ages. Those at Abydos were literally ransacked by the Frenchman Amélineau and much evidence destroyed at the end of the last century. Flinders Petrie took over the re-excavation and recording of the site, recovering plans of the early substructures and the meagre yet often important leavings of the earlier robbers, such as the wood and ivory labels referred to. Professor W.B. Emery excavated the Saqqara site, mainly between 1936 and 1956 (except for the war years). He, likewise, found only pitiful remains of once fine funerary provision.

The tombs at Abydos and Saqqara are not decorated, so evidence of their owners can come only from material remains, largely in the form of seal impressions, rolled out from cylinder seals on the wet clay stoppers of wine jars and the like. They may have the name of the high official responsible for the burial, on occasion a royal name, but it is not necessarily that of the tomb's occupant. In the light of recent analysis of the clay sealings, and the re-excavation of a number of the early tombs at Abydos by Professor G. Dreyer of the German Archaeological Institute, Cairo, Egyptological opinion now favours Abydos as being the site of the royal tombs. At Abydos there is also now recognized from the later Predynastic Period a sequence of tombs that leads into the early royal tombs and their evolution can be traced through the succeeding reigns. The large tombs at Saqqara are those of the nobles of the period; so mighty were some that it would seem they could, in several instances, emulate their royal masters and have satellite (sacrificial) burials associated with their tomb.

In the early cemetery at Saqqara, Emery located a large rectangular tomb (no. 3357) that he ascribed to Hor-Aha (but his tomb is now B 19 at Abydos). It had 27 storerooms at ground level for funerary equipment, and five rooms below ground. The mudbrick exterior was panelled all round in a style referred to as the 'palace façade', which it resembles. This was to be copied later as a decorative element in jewellery (it is the lower half of the *serekh*, p. 18) and for the first time in stone nearby in the 3rd Dynasty complex of Djoser (p. 34). On the north side of the structure, a brick-built pit had once held a wooden solar boat. At Abydos, in October 1991, a fleet of 12 boats dating from about 3000 BC were found buried side by side. The boats – the oldest surviving large-scale vessels in the world – were up to 100 ft (30 m) in length and their superstructures had been protected by mudbrick structures protruding slightly above the desert surface. Several individual, and now empty, boat pits were later provided around the Great Pyramid at Giza in the 4th Dynasty and one discovered there in 1954 was found still to contain a wooden boat (p. 49). All these boats and boat pits were presumably connected wih royal funerary ritual, although their precise function remains unknown.

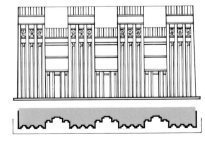

The *serekh* used for royal names represents the 'palace façade' system of panelled brickwork, seen here in elevation and plan views.

Hor-Aha's tomb at Abydos (B 19) is the largest in the north-western section of the cemetery, and another tomb close by produced small labels with the name Berner-Ib, literally 'Sweet-heart'. It is possible that the lady was Hor-Aha's queen, and her name also appeared on items from Naqada, the site of the great tomb of his possible mother, Queen Nithotep.

DJER, DJET AND DEN

Djer (probably Manetho's Athothis) succeeded Hor-Aha and is said to have reigned for 57 years. Once more, we rely on the evidence of the ivory and wood labels from Abydos and Saqqara for information. The hieroglyphs on all these labels are at an early stage in the development of writing and are often difficult to make out and prevent us from being positive as to their full meaning. One of these – an example in ivory from Abydos – has four lines of characters which include two ships, the sign for town and Djer's name in a *serekh*. It appears to record a visit to the northern Delta cities of Buto, one of the early capitals of Egypt, and to Sais, already noted for its temple to the goddess Neith. The other label bearing his name, which is wooden and comes from Saqqara, seems to record some kind of religious event that may have involved human sacrifice. In the early period of Egyptian history, sacrificial (satellite) burial occurred (as at the Royal Tombs of Ur in Mesopotamia), but this wasteful practice was soon abandoned and, much later, mummiform figures called *ushabtis* were provided to perform the necessary menial tasks required in the next world.

An ivory label of Djer from Abydos that apparently refers to a journey made to the Delta city of Buto, one of Egypt's early capitals. British Museum.

Around Djer's large tomb at Abydos (Tomb O) were over 300 satellite burials of retainers who had gone to the grave at the same time as the principal interment. Some of these were provided with simple wooden coffins and grave markers. Military expeditions were obviously still necessary since a schematic rock drawing near Wadi Halfa shows enemies cast into the water beneath the keel of a ship whilst another enemy is seen tied to the front of an Egyptian warship (just as Ahmose the admiral, son of Ebana, describes in his later tomb at el-Kab; below, p. 97). To one side Djer's Horus name is inscribed within a *serekh*.

Djer's successor is generally given as Djet (also referred to as Uadji) but it seems possible, to judge from the size (141 x 52 ft, 43 x 16 m) and location of a tomb at Saqqara (no. 3503) and a large tomb at Abydos (Petrie's Tomb Y), that there was a queen who either reigned alone between them or was later regent for a short period. The name on the large stone grave stele found at the Abydos tomb is Merneith, at first thought to be that of a king but later identified as a queen (consort of Djer). Her name has recently been found at Abydos on a clay seal impression that gives the names of the early kings in order from Narmer to Den, confirming her status and giving her the title of 'King's Mother', presumably of Den for whom she may have acted as regent during his minority. Around her Abydos tomb were 41 subsidiary burials of ser-

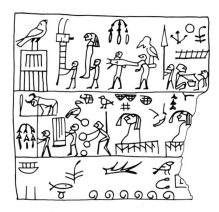

It is possible that the schematic drawings on this small wooden label of Djer from Saqqara represent some form of human sacrifice being carried out before the Horus-topped *serekh* in the first line. British Museum.

In Djer's tomb in 1901, hidden in a hole in a side wall, one of Petrie's workmen discovered a bandaged arm with four small bracelets still within the wrappings. The arm must have belonged to one of the royal women since Djer's queen, Merneith, had a large tomb nearby. It was probably ripped from the mummy by one of the early robbers, who then hid it and failed to collect it; subsequently, it was missed by later robbers and the Amélineau 'clearance'. Three of the bracelets were composed of gold, amethyst, turquoise and lapis lazuli beads; the fourth one, however, was particularly interesting. It consists of 13 gold and 14 turquoise alternating plaques with a pair of gold cone end pieces. The plaques are in the form of the king's *serekh*, representing both the façade and the ground plan of the royal palace (see pp. 20, 21), surmounted by the Horus falcon. Cairo Museum.

(*Near right*) Queen Merneith's stele from Abydos. The crossed arrows are the emblem of the goddess Neith, part of the queen's name. Cairo Museum.

(*Far right*) King Djet's stone funerary stele from Abydos, 4 ft 8 inches (1.43 m) high, has great strength and simplicity of design. The royal *serekh* contains a snake hieroglyph and is surmounted by the Horus falcon. The 'palace façade' design in the lower half of the *serekh* stands out clearly (p. 21). Louvre, Paris.

vants, the office of many of them in the queen's service being indicated by the grave's contents.

Djet's tomb at Abydos is Tomb Z. The one at Saqqara (no. 3504), formerly ascribed to the king and virtually twice the size of the Abydos structure, is now recognized as that of the noble Sekhem-kha, whose sealings were much in evidence in the debris. There was a number of subsidiary (sacrificial) burials made around both monuments, 174 at Abydos and 62 individual burials at Saqqara. Djet's great stone funerary stele from Abydos is a consummate piece of sculpture. The Saqqara tomb of Sekhem-ka (no. 3504) also produced surprises: running round the outer edge of the palace façade was a low bench with a series of about 300 clay bulls' heads modelled in relief, each provided with a pair of real bull's horns. As previously mentioned (cf. Palette of Narmer, above), the bull was a potent symbol of royalty and it seems curious for it to be found decorating the plinth around a noble's tomb.

With the next king, Den (or Udimu), the historical record becomes stronger. There are many labels and inscriptions on stone vases which cite this king and events in his reign. There is also an interesting correlation across to the Palermo Stone (p. 11). We can identify Den (Udimu) via his throne name, Semti, as king of the Two Lands (*nsw-bt*), with a king in the Abydos King List (p. 11) called Hesepti. From here we turn to Manetho for a correlation with his Usaphaidos with a reign of 20 years. On the Palermo Stone, with its annual records cited via principal events, there are several which tally with similar events known for Den from

Ivory label of Den from Abydos showing the king, with uplifted mace, smiting an Asiatic captive. He is identified by his Horus name in a *serekh* above the unfortunate foe. Note the Anubis-topped standard that precedes the scene. British Museum.

surviving labels. Those on the Palermo Stone relate to an unidentified king, but run sequentially for 14 years and appear to refer to the later years of the reign. There is a fair probability, therefore, that the Palermo Stone sequence relates to Den, and the subsequent listings to his successors. These we know to be Anedjib, Semerkhet and Qa'a in that order, for they appear thus following Den's (Udimu's) name on an inscribed stone vase from the galleries beneath the Step Pyramid at Saqqara. This sequence takes us to the end of the 1st Dynasty and has recently been confirmed by the sequence given on a clay sealing from Abydos.

A particularly interesting ivory label from Abydos, inscribed for Den, probably from a pair of sandals, records 'The first time of the smiting of the East' with Den shown, mace upraised in the classic pharaonic posture (p. 18), clubbing a foreign chieftain. This appears to correlate with the 'Smiting of the Troglodytes' recorded on the Palermo Stone, as the second year within a sequence of 14 years of an unidentified king.

Professor W.B. Emery found a tomb (no. 3035) at Saqqara in 1935 that, despite the numerous jar sealings present of Hemaka, the king's great chancellor, was at first thought by many to be the tomb of the king, Den, by virtue of its great size and the magnificent finds. The tomb has now been reassigned to Hemaka. Although much destroyed, the collection of objects recovered, the largest group of excavated Early Dynastic material, was of supremely high quality.

Den's Abydos tomb (Tomb Z, 62 x 49 ft/19 x 15 m) was much smaller than the Saqqara tomb previously ascribed to him (185 x 83 ft/56 x 25 m) and it had 174 satellite burials around it. On the grounds of architectural similarity, Emery considered that a badly destroyed tomb found at Giza, almost as large as Hemaka's at Saqqara, and which had the graves of sacrificed servants around it, might be the tomb of Den's queen, whose name is not known.

ANEDJIB, SEMERKHET AND QA'A

The next king of the 1st Dynasty reigned for 26 years, if we identify Anedjib with the Miebidos of Manetho. There is some evidence at this period of a dynastic struggle, of north versus south. Anedjib seems to have come from the area of Abydos known as This and is recorded as a Thinite king on the Saqqara King List from the tomb of Thunery (p. 12). Many stone vases bearing his name had their inscriptions erased under his successor Semerkhet, who was himself omitted from the Saqqara List. The Saqqara tomb of the noble Nebitka, previously ascribed to Anedjib (no. 3038), has an interesting architectural feature, also present in the earlier Saqqara tomb of Queen Merneith. Concealed within the normal rectangular palace façade *mastaba* was the base of a stepped structure, a curious juxtaposition of two quite different forms. (*Mastaba* is an Arabic word for 'bench', given to the early tombs since their low flat form resembled the bench found outside the door of village houses.) Possibly here, and in the tomb of Merneith, we have the beginnings of

(*Above*) Detail of a schist fragment inscribed with the names of Qa'a and Semerkhet, preceded by the sign *ntr* (god) within an enclosure fence. Cairo Museum.

(*Below*) The superbly carved limestone stele of Qa'a shows the king embraced by the falcon-headed god Horus. It probably came from Abydos since so fine a stele must surely have been associated with the king's tomb. Louvre, Paris.

the fusion of southern and northern styles that was to lead, ultimately, to the Step Pyramid (pp. 33ff).

Anedjib's tomb at Abydos (Tomb X) is one of the worst built and smallest amongst the Abydos royal tombs, a mere 53¾ x 29½ ft (16.4 x 9 m), although it had a burial chamber constructed entirely in wood. The surrounding 64 graves of retainers were also of low standard.

The next king Semerkhet, reigned for nine years according to the Palermo Stone, or 18 according to Manetho, who notes that there were numerous disasters during the reign. These may have been connected with the problems in relation to his predecessor, it having been suggested that Semerkhet was in fact a usurper because he erased the name of his predecessor from stone vases and was himself omitted from the Saqqara King List. His tomb at Abydos (Tomb U) measures 95 x 101¾ ft (29 x 31 m) and is vastly superior in size and quality to that of his predecessor, with its brick-lined burial chamber and the well-built servants' graves. Unusually, no large tomb has been identified at Saqqara to his reign.

The last king of the 1st Dynasty, Qa'a (Qa'a-hedjet), may have reigned for 26 years, but Manetho's name of Bieneches, whom he gives as the last king of the dynasty, hardly equates with Qa'a. A large tomb found at Saqqara by Emery in 1954 (no. 3505) was ascribed to Qa'a, but we now believe it to be that of a priestly noble, Merkha, whose large limestone stele giving his name and titles has one of the longest texts extant from the period. The size of the tomb, 213 x 121 ft (65 x 37 m), was such that it led Emery to suggest that Merkha had been granted the honour of burial close to his royal master.

The large tomb of Qa'a at Abydos (Tomb Q) was re-excavated in 1993 by the German Archaeological Institute, Cairo. They revealed that the tomb had been subject to numerous alterations and enlargements, starting from a simple brick-lined burial chamber. Small by Saqqara comparisons, only 98½ x 75½ ft (30 x 23 m), it also had a lesser number of satellite burials, only 26. It is notable that the practice of satellite (sacrificial) burials seems to have stopped in Qa'a's reign in the north, although some are still present, but not in such vast quantities, in the south at Abydos.

Petrie assigned the tomb at Abydos to Qa'a not only from the usual jar sealings but also from two fragmentary stele he found on the east side of the tomb that gave Qa'a's Horus name in a *serekh*. A superb limestone stele of the king acquired by the Louvre in 1967 shows him wearing the tall White Crown of Upper Egypt and embraced by the falcon-headed Horus. The White Crown also forms part of his name within the *serekh* above the two heads, possibly indicating the final triumph of the south, Abydos.

A change of dynasty normally indicates a break in the line of the ruling house, yet Manetho tells us that the kings of the 2nd Dynasty also came from This, being Thinite kings, from near Abydos, as were the last kings of the 1st Dynasty.

DYNASTY 2
2890–2686

 Hotepsekhemwy

 Raneb

 Nynetjer

 Seth-Peribsen

 Khasekhemwy

ROYAL NAMES	

HOTEPSEKHEMWY
Horus name
  Hotep-sekhemwy
  ('Pleasing in
  Powers')
 	
RANEB
Horus name
  Ra-neb ('Re is the
  Lord')
 	
NYNETJER
Horus name
  Nynetjer ('Godlike')
	SETH-PERIBSEN
	Originally called
	(Horus name)
	  Sekhemib
	  ('Powerful in Heart')
	*Later called (Seth
	name)*
	  Per-ib-sen ('Hope of
	  all Hearts')
	
	KHASEKHEMWY
	Horus name
	  Kha-sekhemwy
	  ('The Two Powerful
	  Ones appear')

Manetho tells us that the 2nd Dynasty consisted of nine kings, ruling for 302 years, but it is difficult to reconcile his statement with the surviving archaeological and written evidence. According to current thinking, six kings reigned in the 2nd Dynasty, which lasted little more than 200 years. The names and sequence of the first three rulers are inscribed on the back of a statue of a priest called Hotep-dif (opposite). The names are, right to left, Hotepsekhemwy, Raneb and Nynetjer.

Hotepsekhemwy is little known. Sealings with his name have been found near the later 5th Dynasty pyramid of Unas at Saqqara and may indicate that the remains of his tomb are nearby. There is no evidence of his having built at the southern site of Abydos like his predecessors. According to Manetho he had a long reign of 38 years, but there is little to show for it. His successor **Raneb** had a slightly longer reign, 39 years if Manetho is to be believed, but, once again, only the tell-tale sealings in the same area of the pyramid of Unas might point to the location of his tomb. There is a granite stele from Abydos with his name in the usual *serekh*.

An interesting point that Manetho adds about Raneb is that he introduced the worship not only of the sacred goat of Mendes but also of the sacred bull of Mnevis at the old sun-worship centre of Heliopolis, and

Hotepsekhemwy
Raneb
Nynetjer
Seth-Peribsen
Khasekhemwy (precise dates unknown)

DYNASTY 2

(*Left*) Portrait head detail of the limestone statue of Khasekhemwy from Hierakonpolis. The king wears the White Crown of Upper Egypt and is enveloped in his *heb-sed* festival cloak (p. 19). Ashmolean Museum, Oxford.

(*Left*) Kneeling statue of the priest Hotep-dif. His name appears in the inscription across the base of the statue together with a title that seems to read 'Great of incense in the Red House'. He was presumably a priest at Saqqara of the mortuary cult of the three dead kings recorded on his right shoulder (*above*): Hotepsekhemwy, Raneb and Nynetjer. Cairo Museum.

(*Below*) The two *serekh* names of Sekhemib. The *serekh* on the left is surmounted by a Horus falcon, but the king later changed his name to a Seth name and the falcon was replaced with a Seth animal. His name then read as Seth-Peribsen.

the Apis bull at Memphis. (In fact scholars now believe that an earlier king was responsible for founding the latter cult, which is attested on a stele dating from Den's (Udimu's) reign.)

The third king, **Nynetjer**, ruled for 47 years according to Manetho's calculations. Little happened during most of these: the Palermo Stone records events between Years 6 and 26 of his reign, including various feasts of gods; a 'running of the Apis bull' in Year 9; a military campaign in Year 13 when there occurred the 'hacking up of the city of Shem-Re' and the 'House-of-the-North'; and in Year 15 the birth of Khasekhemwy, next king but one. Manetho also adds that it was decided that women could occupy the throne, but Merneith had apparently pre-empted this in the previous dynasty.

The fourth king of the dynasty came to the throne under the name of Sekhemib and reigned for 17 years. During his reign, however, the simmering rivalry between north and south reached boiling point once more, and a period of internal unrest ensued. The conflict was of a politico-divine nature, legitimized in part by the mythological struggle between the two gods Horus and Seth, who fought for control of the kingdom of Egypt. It was of the utmost significance, therefore, that Sekhemib dropped his Horus name in favour of a Seth name, **Seth-**

Peribsen – indicating perhaps that the followers of Seth gained the upper hand. Peribsen's granite funerary stele from Abydos is clear evidence of this change in allegiance, since the falcon above the *serekh* of his Horus name has been replaced by the animal of Seth, with its pointed ears. A later king, Khasekhemwy, was obviously a religious diplomat because he incorporated the names of both gods with his, and apparently managed to mollify both factions.

Manetho inserts three kings between Peribsen and Khasekhemwy: Sethenes (Sendji), Chaires (Neterka) and Nephercheres (Neferkara), reigning respectively for 41, 17 and 25 years. The evidence for these kings is slight and archaeological remains are non-existent. **Khasekhemwy** was the last king of the dynasty, although some authorities suggest that he had an immediate predecessor with a very similar name, Khasekhem. Others opine that they are one and the same person who reigned for 30 years. According to this theory, Khasekhem changed his name to Khasekhemwy after he had put down various rebellions and thus united the land; meaning 'The Two Powerful Ones appear', the new name incorporated both the Horus falcon and the Seth animal on the *serekh*.

Prior to the restoration of peace, it appears that northern enemies struck south, since an inscription on a stone vase records: 'The year of fighting the northern enemy within the city of Nekheb.' The vulture goddess Nekhbet, shown in the inscription, was the patron deity of Nekheb (now known as el-Kab) – on the opposite, eastern, bank of the Nile to the ancient capital of the southern kings, Hierakonpolis (Nekhen) – and was much revered by the rulers of that city. The fighting must have been desperate if northerners could get so far south and into the capital city. The number of northerners killed is given as 47,209, represented as contorted bodies around the bases of two seated statues of Khasekhemwy. The statues, one of schist and the other of limestone, come from Hierakonpolis and show the king closely wrapped in his *heb-sed* cloak (p. 19). In both he wears the White Crown of Upper Egypt, indicative of his victory over northern Lower Egyptian enemies. They are each remarkable artistic studies at this early period.

Khasekhemwy died in about 2686 BC, and his huge tomb at Abydos is unique: it is trapezoidal in shape, 230 ft (70 m) in length and varying from some 56 ft (17 m) wide at one end to 33 ft (10 m) at the other, with a stone-built burial chamber almost in the centre. The robbers missed one prize item in their looting – the king's sceptre of gold and sard, as well as several beautifully made small stone pots with gold-leaf lid coverings.

(Below) The plan of Khasekhemwy's tomb at Abydos is unique amongst its contemporaries both in shape and for its huge size. Until quite recently its stone-built central burial chamber was considered the oldest masonry structure, but building in stone is now known from the 1st Dynasty.

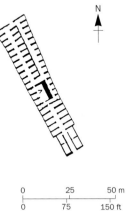

N

0	25	50 m
0	75	150 ft

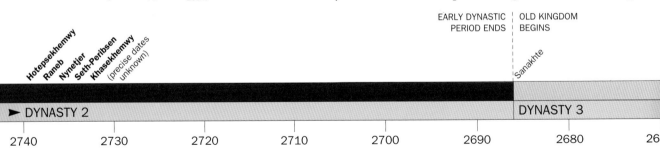

EARLY DYNASTIC | OLD KINGDOM
PERIOD ENDS | BEGINS

Hotepsekhemwy
Raneb
Nynetjer
Seth-Peribsen
Khasekhemwy
(precise dates unknown)

Sanakhte

► DYNASTY 2

DYNASTY 3

2740   2730   2720   2710   2700   2690   2680   26

(*Above*) Two of the small dolomite limestone pots with thin gold-leaf lids held by twisted gold wire from the tomb of Khasekhemwy at Abydos. British Museum.

(*Right*) One of a pair of limestone seated statues of Khasekhemwy from Hierakonpolis (shared between Cairo and Oxford, p. 26). The schematic hieroglyphic inscription around the base records his success as king of Upper Egypt (he wears the White Crown) over Lower Egyptian enemies. Cairo Museum.

(*Below*) Clay jar sealing, reading left to right, giving Queen Nemathap the title of 'King-bearing Mother'.

About 1000 yards from the tomb in the desert at Abydos is the Shunet el-Zebib, a vast rectangular mud-brick structure, 404 x 210 ft (123 x 64 m). Its walls, with their articulated palace façade, are up to 16 ft (5 m) thick and almost 66 ft (20 m) high; they are an incredible survival, being nearly 5000 years old. It is not known what the exact purpose of the building was, much as it may look like an impressive fort. Excavations revealed evidence of complicated internal buildings, and it may have been connected with the provision made for the king's *ka* (soul) in his tomb nearby.

As the dynasty ends with Khasekhemwy so, through him, the next one starts. He apparently married a northern princess to cement the good relations between the followers of Horus and Seth. She was called Nemathap and a jar-sealing gives her title as 'The King-bearing Mother'. Later ages saw her as the ancestral figure of the 3rd Dynasty, much as Queen Aahotep was regarded as ancestress of the New Kingdom.

Djoser

Khufu (Cheops)

Djedefre

Khafre (Chephren)

DYNASTY 3
2686–2613

Sanakhte
2686–2668

Djoser
2668–2649

Sekhemkhet
2649–2643

Khaba
2643–2637

Huni
2637–2613

DYNASTY 4
2613–2498

Snefru
2613–2589

Khufu
(Cheops)
2589–2566

Djedefre
2566–2558

Khafre
(Chephren)
2558–2532

Menkaure
(Mycerinus)
2532–2504

Shepseskaf
2504–2500

DYNASTY 5
2498–2345

Userkaf
2498–2491

Sahure
2491–2477

Neferirkare
2477–2467

Shepseskare
2467–2460

Neferefre
2460–2453

Niuserre
2453–2422

Menkauhor
2422–2414

Djedkare
2414–2375

Unas
2375–2345

DYNASTY 6
2345–2181

Teti
2345–2333

Pepi I
2332–2283

Merenre
2283–2278

Pepi II
2278–2184

OLD KINGDOM
BEGINS

Sanakhte Djoser Sekhemkhet Khaba Huni   Snefru   Khufu   Djedefre Khafre   Menkaure   Shepseskaf Userkaf Sahure   Neferirkare Shepseskare Neferefre Niuserre   Menk

► DYNASTY 2   DYNASTY 3   DYNASTY 4   DYNASTY 5

2750   2700   2650   2600   2550   2500   2450

Menkaure (Mycerinus)

Userkaf

Teti

Pepi I

THE PYRAMID BUILDERS
The Old Kingdom 2686–2181 BC

DURING THE OLD KINGDOM Egyptian civilization really came of age. The power of Egypt expanded considerably through the four dynasties it comprised, probably due in large part to the increasing centralization of government and the creation of an efficient administrative system. The concept of kingship changed too, with greater emphasis being placed on the divine nature of the office; the king was considered to be the incarnation of Horus and, from the 5th Dynasty, son of the sun god Re. At the same time, the advances begun in previous centuries – in building, technology, hieroglyphic writing and artistic representation – reached new heights in the Old Kingdom, nowhere more clearly than in the spectacular programme of pyramid construction, which reached its apogee in the 4th Dynasty. Djoser's Step Pyramid at Saqqara, the Great Pyramid of Khufu (Cheops) at Giza and the famous Sphinx, thought to represent the 4th Dynasty king, Khafre (Chephren), are among some of the most remarkable structures in the world.

This prosperity could not be sustained, however, and the 6th Dynasty saw the decentralization of power and an increase in the might of local officials. The Old Kingdom ended, around 2181 BC, in political fragmentation and anarchy.

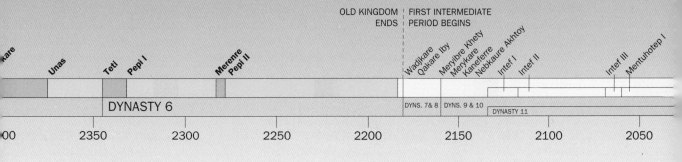

OLD KINGDOM ENDS | FIRST INTERMEDIATE PERIOD BEGINS

...kare — Unas — Teti — Pepi I — Merenre Pepi II — Wadjkare Qakare Iby — Meryibre Khety Merykare Kaneferre Nebkaure Akhtoy — Intef I — Intef II — Intef III — Mentuhotep I

DYNASTY 6 | DYNS. 7 & 8 | DYNS. 9 & 10 | DYNASTY 11

00 — 2350 — 2300 — 2250 — 2200 — 2150 — 2100 — 2050

DYNASTY 3
2686–2613

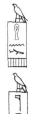

Sanakhte
2686–2668

Djoser
Netjerikhet
2668–2649

Life-size statue of Djoser, found in the *serdab* of his pyramid complex. His royal *nemes* headcloth is worn over a heavy wig which frames his strong face. The face is rendered even more remarkable by the depredations of the ancient robbers, who tore out the eyes of inlaid rock crystal, alabaster and obsidian which had given it an eerie life-like appearance. Cairo Museum.

ROYAL NAMES	
SANAKHTE	DJOSER
Horus name	*Horus name*
Sa-na-khte ('Strong Protection')	Netjeri-khet ('Divine of the Body')
Also known as	*Also known as*
Nebka	Zoser, Tosorthos (Greek)

Fragment of a sandstone relief from the Wadi Maghara in Sinai with Sanakhte's name in a *serekh* before his face. His smiting attitude closely parallels that of King Den (p. 24). British Museum.

SANAKHTE

The first king of the 3rd Dynasty, Sanakhte (also given as Nebka) is little known, despite a reign of some 18 years. Presumably the foundation of the dynasty was cemented by marriage with the female heir of the last king of the 2nd Dynasty, the matrilineal nature of ancient Egyptian society being evident from very early times. Sanakhte is thought to be the brother of his famous successor Djoser (or Zoser), who became the second king of the dynasty and built the Step Pyramid at Saqqara. Both these kings began the exploitation in earnest of the mineral wealth of the Sinai peninsula, which was particularly rich in turquoise and copper. A fragment of a large red sandstone relief from the Wadi Maghara, Sinai, shows the figure of the king wearing the Red Crown of Lower Egypt and about to smite a foe – a posture that was already well established by this early dynasty.

DJOSER

Both Sanakhte and Djoser, when he succeeded to the throne, apparently still had internal political problems to overcome. Djoser probably man-

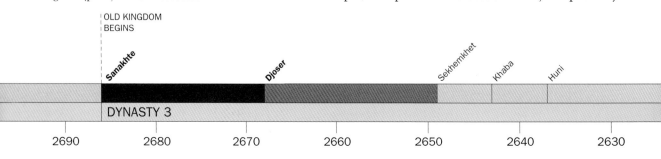

OLD KINGDOM
BEGINS

Sanakhte

Djoser

Sekhemkhet

Khaba

Huni

DYNASTY 3

2690   2680   2670   2660   2650   2640   2630

(*Above*) Inscription no. 81 is carved on the highest point of the island of Sehel. A Ptolemaic forgery purporting to be of 3rd Dynasty date, it shows the king, Djoser, before the triad of gods of Elephantine: Khnum, his wife Satet and their daughter Anuket. Interestingly, it makes an early reference to seven years of famine in Egypt.

(*Below*) Djoser's name and titles appear between the *djed* pillar and *tyet* amulet, followed by Imhotep's titles beginning 'The Treasurer of the King of Lower Egypt', on this broken-off statue base. Cairo Museum.

aged to extend his rule as far south as Aswan, the First Cataract, later the official southern boundary of Egypt. The name 'Djoser' in fact appears only in later records, and may have been his birth name. At the time he was known by his Horus name Netjerikhet, the name inscribed on all his monuments, including his Step Pyramid complex at Saqqara. While the two names are associated together at the Step Pyramid (New Kingdom graffiti there mention Djoser), the earliest proof that the names belong to the same king comes from a long inscription on a large rock on the island of Sehel at Aswan. The inscription is a Ptolemaic forgery cut by the priests of the god Khnum of Elephantine, and lays claim to some 85 miles (137 km) of territory south of Aswan known as the Dodekaschoinoi, 'in the god's name', it having been granted by Djoser. The priests of the goddess Isis on the nearby island of Philae, however, believed that Djoser had given the land to them. Both claims were probably untrue, but each side evidently considered that Djoser's promise had some ancient and lasting validity, endowing the king with substantial historical importance. The land grant was said to be in response to the local god Khnum terminating a seven-year-long drought, and associated famine.

The tombs of officials from the previous dynasties had lined the edge of the plateau at Saqqara, looking out over the cultivation towards the royal capital of Memphis. Being low *mastabas*, they appeared only as a series of low mounds on the skyline. Djoser decided to move his monument back from the escarpment edge by about a mile (1.6 km), and there commenced a grandiose complex that was to be an architectural first: the famous Step Pyramid.

The Step Pyramid of Saqqara

Today, Djoser's pyramid and its surrounding mortuary complex is recognized as the first stone building in the world. (Although stone had been used for certain features in earlier tombs, this was the first to be constructed entirely of stone.) The genius who produced this vast monument for Djoser was his vizier, Imhotep, who seems to have been a man of many parts. His high standing at court is indicated in the inscription on the base of a broken-off statue of Djoser where, after the name of the king, Imhotep's titles read: 'The Treasurer of the King of

(*Above*) The temenos wall surrounding Djoser's Step Pyramid complex can only be entered at one point: here. The other 13 doors around the pyramid are all dummies.

(*Below*) Replica of the statue of King Djoser which sits within the *serdab*, gazing out at curious visitors through a pair of small eyeholes; the original is preserved in the Cairo Museum (p. 32).

Lower Egypt, the First after the King of Upper Egypt, Administrator of the Great Palace, Hereditary Lord, the High Priest of Heliopolis, Imhotep the builder, the sculptor, the maker of stone vases...'

The whole concept of Djoser's funerary monument was that of an area for the spirit, focused on the pyramid itself. This began life as a normal *mastaba*, but was subsequently subject to several major enlargements, adding one *mastaba* upon another, until it consisted of six unequal steps rising to 204 ft (62 m). Its base area is 358 x 411 ft (109 x 125 m). The substructure is a honeycomb of shafts and tunnels, several of them dug by robbers which are difficult to distinguish from those original tunnels left unfinished. Vast quantities of stone vases were found beneath the pyramid, many of exquisite form and artistry, a number of them bearing the names of earlier kings. Perhaps Djoser added these vases to his monument as an act of piety towards his predecessors, to save their funerary goods as best he might. A mummified left foot found in one of the passages may be the only remains of the king. Other members of the royal family were buried in some of the shafts and tunnels, one being a young child of about eight years old found in a fine alabaster coffin. The various enlargements of the ground plan of the pyramid finally meant that these other tombs were all sealed beneath its expanding structure with no access. A new entrance to the king's actual burial chamber, cut from Aswan granite and plugged with a three-ton stopper after the burial, was dug from the north.

Close to this northern entrance stands the *serdab* (Arabic for 'cellar'), a box-like structure of finished Tura limestone with a pair of small holes pierced through its front-facing slope. This was found during the excavations of C.M. Firth and was a complete surprise. Within the

(*Right*) In one of the galleries deep below the South Tomb of Djoser's Step Pyramid complex the king, wearing the White Crown, runs eternally in the *heb-sed* festival ceremonies.

serdab was a painted limestone, life-size seated figure of Djoser, the oldest royal sculpture of this scale known from Egypt. It represents the king closely wrapped in a long white cloak, probably that used in the king's jubilee or *heb-sed* festival (p. 19). Food offerings and incense would have been placed on an altar before the two small eyeholes in the wall of the *serdab*, enabling the *ka* (the spirit of the king) to partake of the spirit substance – whilst, at the end of the day, the mortuary priests could enjoy the material substance of the offerings.

The mortuary complex

Facing the pyramid on the south side of the enclosure is the so-called South Tomb. Three carved relief panels set within the frames of its false doors show the king performing the *heb-sed* ritual, in which he re-affirmed his fitness to rule. On one panel he wears the tall White Crown and a ribbed ritual beard as he runs the requisite course. This also serves

THE GENIUS OF IMHOTEP

A Late Period seated bronze statuette of Imhotep, his papyrus scroll open across his knees. Cairo Museum.

Imhotep is most famous as Djoser's chief architect, and indeed is one of the few Egyptian architects to be known to us by name. He was also a man of great wisdom and scholarship, revered as a scribe, counsellor, doctor, priest and astronomer, and was later to be deified. In the Late Period and into classical times he was worshipped as a god of architecture and medicine, in the latter instance being assimilated with the Greek god of medicine, Asclepius. Devotees made pilgrimages to Saqqara where Imhotep must have been buried (although his tomb is not known) and left votive offerings, usually wrapped and mummified ibises – the bird associated both with him and Thoth, the god of wisdom, writing and learning. Ibises in their pottery containers were found in their thousands by Professor W.B. Emery in the sacred animal necropolis to the north-east of the Step Pyramid complex.

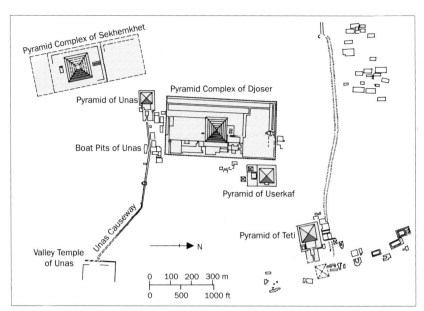

to underline the wholly ritualistic nature of the entire complex that Imhotep created for his master.

It is believed that the South Tomb also served as the burial place for Djoser's viscera, which were removed during the embalming process. With his mummy buried in the pyramid, the king thus fulfilled the requirement of having a northern and southern tomb, symbolic of the Two Lands of Upper and Lower Egypt.

Between the South Tomb and the pyramid lies a wide courtyard with a complex of buildings on the east side known as the *heb-sed* court; over the last 30 years in particular, this court has gradually been restored. Like everything else in the complex its structures are false, dummy buildings, which made perfectly good sense since it was intended as the place of the spirit. The whole complex was surrounded by a high temenos wall of white limestone blocks in the form known as the 'palace façade'; thirteen false or dummy doorways were set into it, while a fourteenth actually opened into the inner area. This doorway led into a long colonnaded hall of fluted columns, none of which were freestanding, all of them being engaged into a supporting wall behind them, exemplifying the initial, faltering steps of architecture in stone taking over from mudbrick and imitating the organic forms of earlier styles. The fine fluting on the columns immediately recalls the Greek Doric column, but that comes almost 2000 years later. This hall in turn opens on to the large court on the south side of the pyramid, containing two Jubilee festival altars whose bases only survive.

Along the east side of the court are a series of three *heb-sed* shrines or pavilions that face a narrower court which runs inside the eastern wall. Close to the southernmost *heb-sed* shrine is a large podium with a pair of round-fronted steps which was the base for the pair of back-to-back tents with curved roofs that were an integral part of the *heb-sed*

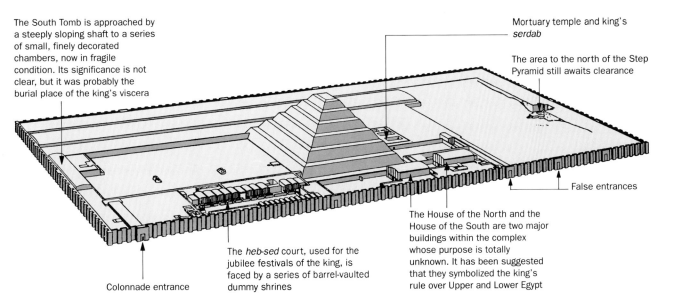

The South Tomb is approached by a steeply sloping shaft to a series of small, finely decorated chambers, now in fragile condition. Its significance is not clear, but it was probably the burial place of the king's viscera

Mortuary temple and king's *serdab*

The area to the north of the Step Pyramid still awaits clearance

False entrances

The House of the North and the House of the South are two major buildings within the complex whose purpose is totally unknown. It has been suggested that they symbolized the king's rule over Upper and Lower Egypt

The *heb-sed* court, used for the jubilee festivals of the king, is faced by a series of barrel-vaulted dummy shrines

Colonnade entrance

(*Above left*) Plan of the Saqqara necropolis.

(*Above*) Djoser's Step Pyramid complex at Saqqara.

(*Below*) The doorway, merely a shallow entry, to the House of the North is flanked by a pair of engaged Doric-looking columns and surmounted by a stylized *khekher* frieze that first appears as a fence delineating a sacred area on some of the small ivory labels from Abydos.

festival and which, in a schematic form, became the hieroglyph that stood for the festival. These pavilions all have doorways, but they only penetrate the façade for a short distance and lead nowhere. Three unfinished, roughly blocked-out standing statues of Djoser have been placed to one side of this court. They show the king in ritual pose wearing a *nemes* headcloth, long beard, and holding the flail and sceptre. To the north of this court is another, whose dummy buildings once again reflect the division of the Two Lands. The first structure is known as the House of the South and has a stylized *khekher* frieze over its doorway – a stylized protective fence motif which, like so many that first appeared in the early periods, continued to be used for centuries, if not millennia. The *khekher* frieze is particularly noticeable in the tombs of the 18th Dynasty pharaohs in the Valley of the Kings.

The House of the North is noted for its papyrus columns with large umbels, all of which are engaged in the supporting wall, but which also have the triangular-sectioned papyrus stems reproduced correctly in the small limestone blocks; later, in the New Kingdom, this accuracy is lost in favour of large, heavily rounded columns.

The death of Djoser

Djoser was succeeded by Sekhemkhet in about 2649 BC, after a reign of roughly 19 years. This scarcely seems long enough for the construction of a monument as remarkable as the Step Pyramid, but it is powerful testimony to the authority of the king. To build such a structure would have required a vast workforce, not to mention a strong government to organize and feed the workers. Djoser's funerary complex stands at the head of a long line of Egyptian stone architecture. Within it many of the later building forms and styles are first seen, admittedly in an experimental stage, to be copied or refined over the next 2000 years.

DYNASTY 3
2686–2613

Sekhemkhet
2649–2643

Khaba
2643–2637

Huni
2637–2613

(*Right*) Red granite head attributed to Huni. Brooklyn Museum.

ROYAL NAMES	

SEKHEMKHET
Horus name
  S-ekhem-khet
  ('Powerful in Body')
	HUNI
	Horus name
	  Huni
	  ('The Smiter')

KHABA
Horus name
  Kha-ba
  (The Soul Appears')	

Relief in the Wadi Maghara with three representations of Sekhemkhet proceeding to the right. Two of them wear the tall White Crown and have their names in a *serekh* before their faces; the middle king wears the Red Crown.

SEKHEMKHET

According to Manetho, the remaining six kings of the 3rd Dynasty were of no account, although he gave them a combined total of around 157 regnal years. Little is actually known of these kings, now generally thought to have been only three in number and with a joint reign span of about 36 years.

Prior to 1951 virtually nothing was known of Djoser's successor, Sekhemkhet. A relief in the Wadi Maghara in Sinai bears his name (although it had formerly been mistakenly attributed to Semerkhet, last but one king of the 1st Dynasty) and evidences the military interest of the 3rd Dynasty pharaohs in the area. The last king in the relief is engaged in the age-old motif of grasping foes by the hair with his left hand and bringing a pear-shaped mace crashing down on them with his upraised right hand. The 'icon' of 'smiting' the dwellers in the desert, the *bedu*, had already appeared in the 1st Dynasty and this is just one more instance of it (p. 24).

Information about Sekhemkhet increased dramatically, however, in 1951, when an Egyptian archaeologist named Zakaria Goneim discovered an unfinished step pyramid at Saqqara attributed to the king.

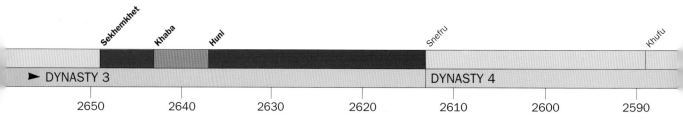

The buried pyramid

In March 1951, Goneim was appointed Chief Inspector of Saqqara. Intrigued by the fact that there was apparently only one 3rd Dynasty monument here (Djoser's Step Pyramid), he carefully surveyed the site and its ground features. To the south-west of Djoser's enclosure wall lay an oblong plateau or terrace recorded on the maps as a natural feature. Goneim was suspicious of the quantity and distribution of fragments of worked stone (granite, limestone and alabaster) lying about on it: there was too much for the terrace to be natural, added to which there were occasional small outcrops of rubble masonry.

So in late September 1951, Goneim began to investigate one of these outcrops. His efforts revealed a rubble-coursed masonry wall which, when cleared, was found to be 27 ft (8.2 m) deep, sitting on bedrock. Eventually an enormous platform was identified, roughly 1700 ft (518 m) on its long axis (north–south), and 600 ft (183 m) wide. This had formed a base upon which an enclosure wall of the 'palace façade' type, similar to Djoser's, had been built. This great work had been left unfinished, presumably because Sekhemkhet died after a reign of only about six years – shortly after construction had begun. Had it been completed, it would probably have risen in seven steps to a height of around 230 ft (70 m) – taller by one step and c. 16 ft (4.9 m) than Djoser's Step Pyramid.

The pyramid platform was especially well preserved on the north side, and it was from here that a deep, sloping rock-cut trench was located which led down to an entrance, a sealed doorway, that was opened in March 1954. Large areas of the entrance passageway were blocked by rubble debris which was extremely unstable, dangerous and difficult to clear. At the base of the blocking to the passage was found a small cache which included 21 gold bracelets and armlets, a hollow gold tube and an exquisite small gold box in the shape of a bivalve shell, all apparently having been deposited together in a now perished wooden box. A large diorite bowl was nearby. The group seems to have been deliberately placed where it was found, rather than abandoned or dropped as robber's booty.

The name of the owner of the complex was revealed when five small clay jar sealings were found, impressed by a cylinder seal with the name of Sekhemkhet. Eventually – after clearing more of the dangerous blocking – a large, cavernous, unfinished burial hall was reached in the centre of which stood a rectangular sarcophagus of translucent alabaster cut from a single block. Close examination of the area and various passageways nearby showed no evidence of robbers' intrusions after the tomb had been sealed.

In June 1954, almost three years after work had begun, the sarcophagus was carefully opened, the sliding panel raised with difficulty because the original gypsum mortar sealing held it tight in place. To the great astonishment of the invited audience of scholars and journalists, the interior was completely empty and a shock to which there was no ready answer. The sarcophagus had definitely not been robbed; the only expla-

(*Below*) The deep sloping trench on the north face of the unfinished pyramid of Sekhemkhet that leads down to the pyramid entrance.

(*Above*) The pyramid of Meydum, looking up its causeway from the east with the small mortuary temple at the foot of the pyramid's face.

(*Below*) Sekhemkhet's sarcophagus is of a form unique amongst royal sarcophagi because it was not closed with a lid but had a T-shaped sliding panel set in its northern end. This still bore traces of the plaster that had sealed it in position and there were organic remains on top of it, possibly of a shrub or similar plant.

nation possible was that the king had been buried elsewhere, possibly even in the labyrinthine passages of which many have yet to be explored.

KHABA AND HUNI

The last two kings of the 3rd Dynasty did not use Saqqara as the royal burial ground. Sekhemkhet's successor Khaba built his pyramid – the so-called Layer Pyramid – at Zawiyet el-Aryan, a mile south of Giza. This seems to have been intended as a step pyramid, with six or seven steps and a rock-cut entrance on the north side. Similar construction techniques and layout to Sekhemkhet's monument place it in a chronological sequence after his (and not in the 2nd Dynasty as had been suggested many years ago, before the parallel evidence at Saqqara was known). Khaba's name was recovered, written in red ink, on several stone vessels from 3rd Dynasty *mastabas* close by. It would appear that the monument was never used.

Huni, the fifth and last king of the 3rd Dynasty, made an even more drastic move for his burial site. He erected his monument at Meydum on the edge of the Faiyum, 50 miles (80 km) south of Cairo. Today the pyramid rises as a gaunt, almost pharos-like structure just beyond the edge of the cultivation. It was the first pyramid to have a square ground plan and was intended to be the first that was geometrically 'true'; loose packing stones were added to the steps before the whole was encased in white Tura limestone. Now it has three (of an original seven) tall steps at a steep angle of 74 degrees, and rises to about 214 ft (65 m). The present shape has resulted from the collapse of the outer 'skins' of the casing in antiquity, due to the lack of bonding between them. Exactly when this collapse occurred has been the subject of some controversy: Kurt Mendelssohn suggested that it took place during the building of the South or Bent pyramid of Snefru (the first king of the 4th Dynasty) at Dahshur and that both pyramids were being built concurrently; others believe that it was during the New Kingdom, since there are 18th Dynasty visitors' graffiti in the small east face mortuary temple.

In the New Kingdom the Meydum pyramid was obviously thought to have been built by Snefru, since the mortuary temple graffiti mention his name, referring to 'the beautiful temple of King Snefru'. This is clearly somewhat exaggerated since it is a small, plain and windowless structure with just the two large, upright and round-topped funerary stele, both uninscribed and unfinished, standing either side of a low altar in the small courtyard between the back of the temple and the pyramid's east face. Snefru also has two other pyramids 28 miles (45 km) north of Meydum at Dahshur (p. 43), and it is highly unlikely that he would have had three: two are unusual enough. It is now generally agreed that the Meydum pyramid was built for Huni, but that it was basically finished by his son-in-law and successor, Snefru.

Meydum presents us with the first occurrence of what was to become the norm for the layout of a pyramid complex. This consists of the pyra-

(*Above*) The curious lighthouse-like shape of the Meydum pyramid dominates both the desert in which it stands and the nearby agricultural land. Debris from its collapse surrounds its base, seen in the closer view of the mortuary temple (*opposite above*).

(*Below*) Detail of the head of the princess Nofret, seated on the left of her husband, Rahotep, in a pair of statues. The floral decoration on her diadem, the original probably of silver, reflects the ancient Egyptian delight in nature. Cairo Museum.

mid itself, with an entrance on the north face which gives access, via a descending passage, to a burial chamber normally located in the bedrock or at ground surface within the mass. There can be more than one chamber, and at different levels, within this group. On the east face of the pyramid is a small pyramid or mortuary temple. From this a causeway runs down to the edge of the cultivation where the valley temple is located. Very fine reliefs are usually a feature of the later examples of these buildings. At Meydum, the valley temple has never been excavated and is presumed to lie in a small cluster of palm trees at the lower end of the now much denuded causeway on the edge of the agricultural land.

Curiously, there is no evidence of there ever having been a stone sarcophagus in the subterranean burial chamber. This has led to speculation that the burial was made in the large, unidentified *mastaba* number 17 on the north-east side of the pyramid, where there is a typical Old Kingdom, uninscribed granite sarcophagus whose heavy lid has been eased to one side by tomb robbers.

In two of the *mastaba* tombs of nobles in the court of Huni to the north and east of the pyramid, the French Egyptologist Auguste Mariette discovered in 1871 some of the great masterpieces of Egyptian art: the Meydum geese and the pair statues of Rahotep and Nofret. The three pairs of realistic and beautifully painted geese on a frieze were found in the tomb of Nefer-Maat and Atet. The solemnity of the faces on the statues of Rahotep and Nofret from their *mastaba* contrasts with the expressions on the faces of lesser mortals – here, confidence in their immortality by virtue of their connections is well expressed. Amongst Rahotep's titles is that of 'king's son' – he may have been a son of Snefru – and his wife Nofret was 'one known to the king'.

The 24 years or so of Huni's reign ended in about 2613 BC, and with it the 3rd Dynasty drew to its close.

DYNASTY 4
2613–2498

Snefru
2613–2589

Khufu (Cheops)
2589–2566

(*Left*) Cartouche of Khufu on a relief originally from Giza.

(*Right*) This tiny, 3-inch (7.6-cm) high ivory sculpture of Khufu found at Abydos shows the king seated on a throne, holding a flail in his right hand against his right shoulder, and wearing the Red Crown of Lower Egypt. The cartouche on the left side of his throne is broken away, but fortunately his Horus name remains on the right side to identify him. Cairo Museum.

SNEFRU	
Birth name	*Wife*
Snefru ('He of Beauty')	Hetep-heres I
Also known as	*Son*
Sneferu, Snofru, Soris (Manetho)	Khufu (Cheops)
Father	*Burial*
Huni	North (Red) pyramid, Dahshur
Mother	
Meresankh I	

KHUFU	
Birth name	Henutsen, unknown queen
Khufu ('Protected by [Khnum]')	*Sons*
Also known as	Djedefre, Kawab, Khafre (Chephren), Djedefhor, Banefre, Khufukaef
Cheops/Kheops (Greek), Suphis I (Manetho)	*Daughters*
Father	Hetep-heres II, Meresankh II, Khamerernebty I
Snefru	
Mother	*Burial*
Hetep-heres I	Great Pyramid, Giza
Wives	
Unknown queen, Meritates,	

SNEFRU

After the founding of the 4th Dynasty by Snefru *c.* 2613 BC, more historical records and portraits of royalty have survived. Snefru married the previous king Huni's daughter, Hetep-heres, who was to find great fame as the mother of Khufu (p. 49). Manetho says (according to Eusebius) that the dynasty consisted of 17 kings of Memphis who reigned for a total of 448 years (the Africanus version gives only 8 kings and 277 years). The kings of the 3rd Dynasty were also Memphite, but it is specifically said of the 4th Dynasty that, although of Memphis, they were of a different royal line. It would appear that Snefru's marriage to Huni's daughter brought the two lines together, but it was a sufficient break in Manetho's eyes to constitute a new dynasty. He identifies the first king as Soris (= Snefru) who reigned for 29 years, although present opinion is more in favour of about 24 years. Snefru was a son of Huni, probably by a minor wife called Meresankh. By marrying Hetep-heres, who presumably carried the royal blood as the daughter of a more senior queen, he consolidated his claim to the throne. Snefru was probably therefore Hetep-heres' half-brother. Huni is the last king of the 3rd Dynasty in both the Royal Canon of Turin and the later Saqqara List.

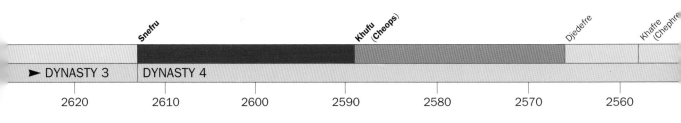

Snefru | Khufu (Cheops) | Djedefre | Khafre (Chephre...

► DYNASTY 3	DYNASTY 4					
2620	2610	2600	2590	2580	2570	2560

(*Right*) On the horizon to the south of Saqqara the pyramids of Dahshur stand out clearly. On the right is the North or Red Pyramid; centre, a mile further on, the Bent Pyramid, both built by Snefru. The low oblong building on the far left is the 'Mastabet el-Fara'un' and next to it the low remains of the pyramid of Pepi II, both located at south Saqqara.

THE LADY OF THE LAKE

The Westcar Papyrus (now in Berlin), written much later during the Hyksos period, mentions Snefru as an amiable pharaoh. A story recounted by Prince Bauefre, a son of Khufu (Cheops), tells how Snefru, wandering one day through the palace in a state of boredom, called for the chief lector priest, Djadja-em-ankh, to provide a solution. The priest suggested that the king should be taken out on the lake, rowed by some of the younger palace ladies, 'all the beauties who are in the palace chamber'. Snefru thought this an excellent idea, and improved on it by commanding, 'Let there be brought to me twenty nets, and let these nets be given to these women when they have taken off their clothes ... and ... the heart of His Majesty was happy at this sight of their rowing.' (This must be the first recorded use of 'fish-net' in an erotic context, later to be taken over by stockings.)

Unfortunately the excursion came to an abrupt halt when one of the strokes lost her fish-shaped turquoise charm from her long tresses and refused to continue. The king offered to replace it, but she wanted her original piece back. There was nothing for it but to summon Djadja-em-ankh to the rescue again, this time in his capacity as a magician. He immediately caused the waters of the lake to part and retrieved the missing bauble, found lying on a potsherd at the bottom, and all was well and the rowing continued.

There are records, principally from the Palermo Stone, of Snefru's expeditions beyond the boundaries of Egypt – to the Lebanon to fetch the great cedar logs needed for temple doors and great ships, and to Sinai for turquoise. Although there is evidence as early as the 1st Dynasty of expeditions to Sinai, Snefru seems to have become particularly associated with the area, and was worshipped there as a god according to a much later inscription left in the Wadi Maghara. Snefru also appears on two contemporary reliefs near each other in the Wadi, here given his full titles and noted as 'Smiter of Barbarians'; he is shown in the already age-old attitude of doing just this.

Snefru moved the royal burial ground yet again, not back to Memphis as might perhaps be expected, but to a new site at Dahshur, 28 miles (45 km) north of Meydum. What governed the choice is not known, but he built two pyramids for himself there, and several kings of the later 12th Dynasty were to follow his choice of site.

The two pyramids of Snefru

Scholars have long debated which of Snefru's two pyramids at Dahshur was the earlier. The current consensus seems to find in favour of the southern pyramid, variously called the Bent, Blunt or Rhomboidal Pyramid because of its curious shape. This pyramid was associated with Snefru in the Old Kingdom, since a 5th Dynasty inscription identifies an official as 'Overseer of the South Pyramid of Snefru'. The explanation for the strange shape of the Bent Pyramid has been much argued. The German Egyptologist Ludwig Borchardt (1863–1938) suggested, in his 'accretion' theory, that the king died suddenly and the pyramid's angle had to be radically reduced from the 54°31' of the lower courses to

(*Above*) The solid construction of the Bent Pyramid and its acute change of angle are very evident at its south-east corner.

(*Below*) Limestone stele from Snefru's Bent Pyramid enclosure. The king is shown, in delicate low relief, seated and wrapped in his *heb-sed* robe, wearing the Double Crown and holding an upright flail. Above and before him are his name and titles, all surmounted by a figure of the Horus falcon. Cairo Museum.

the 43°21' of the upper courses in order to finish the work off rapidly. This reduction, however, actually makes little difference to the volume of the structure (and therefore the amount of work involved), added to which we now know that it was built before the northern pyramid. Kurt Mendelssohn proposed alternatively that the pyramid at Meydum (p. 40) and the southern pyramid at Dahshur were being built concurrently, not consecutively, and that a building disaster occurred at Meydum – possibly after heavy rain when the casing slipped – which caused the architect at Dahshur hurriedly to change the angle of declination when the pyramid was half-built. This theory is only acceptable if the collapse took place at the time of building, and not later during the New Kingdom as some evidence suggests.

The Bent Pyramid is unique amongst Old Kingdom pyramids in not only having an entrance on its north face, as is the norm, but also a second entrance that opens high up on the west face. The north entrance, about 40 ft (12.2 m) above ground level, gives on to a sloping corridor that descends to two high, corbel-roofed chambers cut into the bedrock. From the upper of these two chambers, via a shaft and a passageway, another smaller chamber is reached which also has a corbelled roof. This third chamber, with its unusual access corridor from the west face, was only discovered in 1946–47. The rationale for having entrances on the north face of all the known Old Kingdom pyramids has a religious basis and is connected with the northern stars; why there should be this one instance of a second, western, entrance is a mystery. Like Meydum and the northern pyramid at Dahshur, there was no trace of a sarcophagus ever having been in place in any of the chambers.

Snefru's name has been found in red paint in two places in the Bent Pyramid and his association with the building was substantiated by the discovery of a stele – the remaining one of two – of the king inside a smaller pyramid within the enclosure (see illustration at left). The valley building associated with the pyramid was excavated in 1951–52 and produced evidence of having been decorated with reliefs of superb style and finish, but sadly all had been badly smashed and wrecked in antiquity. There had also been statues of the king, set into recesses, possibly forerunners of the series of freestanding statues that existed in the valley temple of Khafre (Chephren) at Giza.

The northern or 'Red' pyramid at Dahshur is the first true pyramid (although the angle of its sides is slight – only 43°36', as against the later norm of 51°52') and takes its sobriquet from the colour of its stonework in the evening sun. Entrance is via a sloping passageway on the north side which is located several feet above ground level, whence it descends to three consecutive chambers, all now rubble-filled and inaccessible. This pyramid has been attributed to Snefru on the basis of some casing blocks which bear his name in red ink, and an inscription said to have been discovered nearby early this century; the latter is a decree of Pepi I of the 6th Dynasty remitting taxes due from the priests of the 'Two Pyramids of Snefru'. It was probably in this northern pyramid that the king was buried; his wife Hetep-heres had her original tomb nearby (see below, p. 49).

With such an obvious command of resources and manpower to be able to build two pyramids for himself and complete a third for his predecessor, Snefru had clearly consolidated the kingdom to such an extent that he was able to leave a strong inheritance to his son, Khufu (Manetho's Cheops). Khufu was to take his father's achievements even further, to the very apogee of pyramid-building on the Giza plateau.

KHUFU

The ancient authors through whom Manetho's works survive were all agreed that the third king of the 4th Dynasty was 'Suphis, the builder of the Great Pyramid, which Herodotus says was built by Cheops. Suphis conceived a contempt for the gods, but repenting of this, he composed the Sacred Books, which the Egyptians hold in high esteem'. 'Suphis' is better known by the Greek form of Cheops and the Egyptian form of Khufu. It is curious that Khufu should be placed third in line; there do not appear to be any other records of an intervening pharaoh between

(*Below*) The three pyramids of Giza seen from the south-east. From right to left they belong to Khufu, Khafre and Menkaure. The smaller pyramids to the left belong to queens of Menkaure. It is an optical illusion that the middle pyramid, Khafre's, is the largest – it is simply built on slightly higher ground.

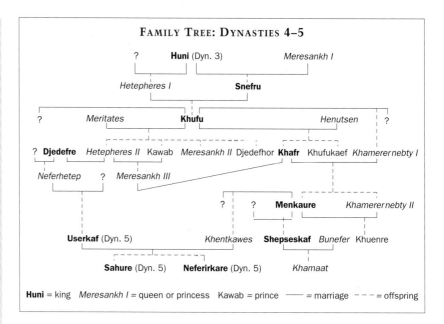

FAMILY TREE: DYNASTIES 4–5

Huni = king   *Meresankh I* = queen or princess   Kawab = prince   —— = marriage   – – – = offspring

him and his father Snefru. The reference to his composing Sacred Books is intriguing – these do not seem to have survived in later literature, although Khufu's character was severely blackened by later chroniclers and strongly contrasted with the lives of his successors Chephren (Khafre) and Mycerinus (Menkaure).

Like his father, Khufu probably reigned for about 23 or 24 years, and he too seems to have initiated military expeditions to the Sinai peninsula. Rock inscriptions in the Wadi Maghara record the presence of his troops in this region, no doubt for the dual purposes of keeping the bedouin in check and exploiting the turquoise deposits there. A now very faint inscription on a large boulder on the island of Elephantine at Aswan also indicates that the king had interests in the far south of the country – quarrying the fine Aswan red granite.

(Right) The west *(left)* and south faces of the Great Pyramid of Khufu at Giza. In front of the south face, and between it and the row of *mastaba* tombs of nobles, is now a boat-shaped building which houses Khufu's ship (p. 48), found there in a sealed pit in 1954.

Statue of Hemon, Khufu's master builder. The eyes have been hacked out by robbers, and restored. Hildesheim Museum.

The Great Pyramid of Khufu

Khufu's greatest achievement was the creation of a monument that was to be recognized as the first of the Seven Wonders of the Ancient World, and the only one now standing: the Great Pyramid on the Giza plateau. Originally 481 ft or 146.6 m high (now only 451 ft or 137.5 m, having lost its top 30 ft) it was until the 19th century AD the tallest man-made building in the world – a proud record held by an ancient Egyptian architect for four and a half thousand years.

It is not known why Khufu should have turned away from the site of his father's burial at Dahshur, or indeed that of his predecessors at Saqqara. Suffice it to say that he did, and that he chose a stretch on the Giza plateau to the south-west of modern Cairo. His work appears to have been the first on the site and it is curious that he did not choose the highest point of the plateau for his pyramid. This area was taken by his successor but one, Khafre (Chephren), and was to produce the optical illusion that his pyramid is therefore taller than Khufu's, which it is not (p. 45).

Khufu channelled all his efforts into the creation of a single monument, rather than several different pyramids. Like its predecessors, the Great Pyramid underwent several changes in its internal arrangements, but its external structure and dimensions appear to have been set from the start. The chief of works is thought to have been Khufu's cousin Hemon, of whom a powerful seated statue was discovered in his *mastaba* tomb close by his masterpiece.

For all its magnificence the Great Pyramid is still a puzzle. Herodotus was quoted some apocryphal figures by the priests: it took 10 years to build the causeway from the valley temple to the mortuary temple, 20 years to build the pyramid itself, and the whole cost was in the region of 1600 silver talents (according to an inscription pointed out to him on the side), or just over £5 million/$7.5 million at present scrap silver prices.

Moreover, we do not know exactly how it was built. Theories about this vary, from the use of a long ramp stretching out into the desert which was continually lengthened and heightened as the pyramid rose higher, to a ramp that rose as it wound round the pyramid face following each course upwards. Neither is very satisfactory and each is rather impractical in one way or another. Herodotus said that the structure had been built as a series of terraces, raising blocks on all four sides simultaneously with the use of 'contrivances made of short timbers'. This approach was tested with some success by the late Peter Hodges, a master builder, using short lengths of timber with a metal-shod foot, and it is certainly more convincing than the other theories.

The internal layout indicates at least two changes in plan during construction. Initially there was to have been a burial chamber deep beneath the surface of the plateau; this plan was then altered to incorporate instead a small chamber, now erroneously known as the Queen's Chamber (and unfinished), within the pyramid bulk and about 50 ft

(Above) Khufu's sarcophagus, cut from a single block of granite, still stands at the west end of his burial chamber in the Great Pyramid.

(Below) View up the Grand Gallery in Khufu's pyramid. It rises to a height of 28 ft (8.5 m), the slightly overlapping blocks forming a corbel that is then closed by a single block.

(15.2 m) above ground level. Exploration in 1993 by a small robot remote-controlled camera up the south 'air' tunnel from the Queen's Chamber has revealed a small door secured by metal bolts. There is no question of access because the door is so tiny, the tunnel being only 8 inches (20.25 cm) square. The results of further investigation are eagerly awaited. The final change was for the construction of the magnificent Grand Gallery, 28 ft (8.5 m) high and closed by a corbelled roof, which led upwards to a horizontal passage that entered the King's Chamber in the heart of the pyramid. Here, at the west end of the chamber, was placed a large granite sarcophagus, cut from a single block of Aswan granite. The sarcophagus must have been put in position before the chamber was roofed by nine flat slabs of granite (each with an average weight of almost 45 tons), because it is about an inch too wide to pass through the entrance to the Ascending Corridor – an early example of 'built-in' furniture.

The exterior of the pyramid was cased with shining white Tura limestone, which was laid, as Herodotus rightly said, from the top downwards. This was largely robbed in the Middle Ages to build medieval Cairo. Of the great limestone mortuary temple (171 x 132 ft, 52 x 40 m) that stood before the pyramid's east face, nothing now remains except its black basalt floor. The valley temple that stood at the foot of the pyramid causeway has disappeared under the Arab village, although parts of it were observed in 1991 when new sewerage was being laid.

Around the Great Pyramid, principally on the west side, were located the tombs of the courtiers, who hoped to serve their king in death just as they had in life. On the east side are three subsidiary pyramids of Khufu's queens. Legend had it, as recounted by Herodotus, that the central pyramid, 150 ft (46 m) square, was a product of the enterprise of one of Khufu's daughters, whom he had placed in a brothel in order to raise more revenue for building the Great Pyramid. In addition to payment, the princess also asked each of her clients for a block of stone, which she used to build her own pyramid. Needless to say, there is no evidence to confirm the story, although the pyramid does appear to be that of a half-sister of Khufu. The first pyramid probably belonged to his full sister-wife, and the third to another half-sister, Queen Henutsen.

Two remarkable discoveries relating to Khufu have been made in the vicinity of his pyramid: the first, found in 1925 on the east side close to the causeway, was the tomb of his mother, Queen Hetep-heres (see box); and the second, uncovered in 1954 close to the south face, was that of an intact wooden ship.

The royal ship of Khufu

During clearance work close to the south side of the Great Pyramid in May 1954, Kamal el-Mallakh found a series of 41 large blocking stones, with an average weight of 18 tons each, which had hermetically sealed a 101-ft (30.8-m) long rock-cut pit. Within it were the remains of a magnificent 141-ft (43-m) long ship of cedar wood. Too long for the pit

The reconstructed cedar-wood ship of Khufu is remarkable for its preservation and slender lines. Boat Museum, Giza.

intended for it, it had been carefully dismantled into 650 parts comprising 1224 pieces. After many years of patient restoration work by Hag Ahmed Youssef Moustafa (who had also been responsible for the restoration of Hetep-heres' furniture), the ship was presented to the world in March 1982 in a specially designed museum which incorporated the pit in which it had lain for 4500 years. Not all the problems posed in conserving the ship have yet been solved by the Egyptian Antiquities Organisation; until they are, the opening of a second sealed pit discovered near the first will be postponed. Recent tests have indicated that it also contains a ship, but not in such good condition.

It is a remarkable quirk of fate that for all the grandeur of Khufu's pyramid, his funeral boat, and the splendid style of his mother's funerary furnishings, there remains only one tiny portrait of the king himself (p. 42), found by Flinders Petrie in the old temple of Osiris at Abydos in 1903. In a curious inverse ratio we find that the smallest statue represents the builder of the greatest pyramid, while some of the finest multiple statues extant from the Old Kingdom represent the builder of the smallest of the Giza pyramids, Menkaure (fifth ruler of the 4th Dynasty).

THE TOMB OF QUEEN HETEP-HERES

The concealed entrance to a 99-ft (30.2-m) deep shaft was found by accident, disguised with plaster, by a photographer in 1925 during survey work in the Giza area. At the bottom of the shaft was a small chamber which, to judge from the blocking that had to be removed to reach it, had remained intact since the day it was sealed during the Old Kingdom. It contained a large alabaster sarcophagus with a canopic chest and a quantity of furniture which included a large dismantled canopy frame, two armchairs, a bed (shown restored, *above right*, Cairo Museum) and a carrying chair. The wood of all these items had suffered over the course of the millennia, but careful recording made their complete reconstruction possible. There were various vessels in gold, copper and alabaster as well as other items of an obviously personal nature, such as a gold manicure set and 20 silver bracelets inlaid with delicate dragonflies. Inscriptions in the gold casing on the wooden furniture identified the owner of the tomb as

Hetep-heres, wife of Snefru and mother of Khufu.

When the sarcophagus was opened it was found to be empty, but the queen had obviously occupied it once since her canopic chest had been used. This chest had four compartments containing the queen's embalmed viscera, and is the earliest known use of evisceration in the mummification process. This strange situation may be explained as follows: at first, the queen had probably been buried close to her husband Snefru's northern pyramid at Dahshur, but the

tomb had been robbed. The robbers were not completely successful, although they had obviously destroyed the queen's body before the guards were able to rescue the remainder of the burial. It was decided, therefore, to move the burial to Giza, to the more secure area close to her son's pyramid (Khufu probably never knew that his mother's body was no longer in the sarcophagus).

One day, perhaps Hetep-heres' original tomb will be found at Dahshur, since little excavation or survey work has been carried out there.

DYNASTY 4
2613–2498

Djedefre
2566–2558

Khafre (Chephren)
2558–2532

(*Above*) Red quartzite head of Djedefre wearing the *nemes* headdress, from Abu Roash. Louvre, Paris.

DJEDEFRE	
Birth name	*Wives*
Djedef-re ('Enduring like Re')	Unknown queen, Hetepheres II
Also known as	*Son*
Djedefra, Redjedef, Radjedef	Setka
Father	*Daughter*
Khufu	Neferhetepes
Mother	*Burial*
Unknown	Pyramid, Abu Roash

KHAFRE	
Birth name	*Wives*
Kha-f-re ('Appearing like Re')	Meresankh III, Khamerernebty I
Also known as	*Sons*
Khafra, Rakhaef, Chephren/ Khephren (Greek), Suphis II (Manetho)	Nekure, Menkaure, etc.
Father	*Daughter*
Khufu	Khamerernebty II
Mother	*Burial*
Henutsen	Second Pyramid, Giza

DJEDEFRE

Khufu's successor was his short-lived son Djedefre, of whom little is known. It was presumably he who completed his father's burial at Giza and was especially responsible for the provision of his funerary boats (pp. 48–49). Djedefre's main significance is that he was the first king to adopt the name 'son of Re'. Moreover, for some unknown reason, he chose not only to construct his funerary monument some 5 miles (8 km) north of Giza on a commanding plateau at Abu Roash, but also to revert to an earlier style of building. Instead of erecting his pyramid and then cutting down into the bedrock to construct a burial chamber, he followed the 3rd Dynasty practice of excavating a huge open trench terminating in a vertical shaft.

It is extremely difficult because of the site's heavily denuded state to make much sense of Djedefre's complex. There was a causeway, but this ran north–south rather than the more usual east–west; no valley temple has been found, and only the rough ground plan of a mudbrick mortuary temple was traceable, with difficulty, in the usual place on the east face of the pyramid. To the south, a deep pit may indicate the provision of a funerary boat. These aspects, together with the fact that

Mottled red and black granite statue of Setka, son of Djedefre, seated in a scribal pose; from Abu Roash. Louvre, Paris.

very little remains of the pyramid's superstructure, imply that – due to the king's relatively short reign – hardly more than a start was made on the overall plan and construction of the pyramid and its attendant buildings.

From the French excavations at Abu Roash in 1907 came a striking dark red quartzite head of the king wearing the *nemes* headdress; a small statuette of his son, Setka, shown as a squatting scribe in the traditional posture; and the lower half of a statuette of the king with his wife. The quality and style of these three pieces (all now in the Louvre, Paris) show that the tradition of 4th Dynasty art was firmly established by this reign.

About a mile to the south of Giza, at Zawiyet el-Aryan, is an unascribed structure that is very similar in construction to Djedefre's pyramid, sharing the plan of a deep open trench. At the bottom of a deep shaft, sunk into the floor, was found an uninscribed oval granite sarcophagus. Two names have been recorded from the site: one, in red paint on some blocks, may be read as Nebka; the other was that of Djedefre, inscribed on a schist plaque. Neither serves as a strong attribution for the pyramid, although its construction technique would place it close in date to that of Djedefre. It presumably belonged to an obscure king of the 4th Dynasty, but the difficulty is to identify one and also where in the known sequence of 4th Dynasty kings he might fall.

KHAFRE

It was another of Khufu's sons, Khafre (Chephren) – builder of the Second Pyramid and Great Sphinx at Giza – who succeeded Djedefre in about 2558 BC. Manetho identifies Khafre as Suphis II and credits him with a reign of 66 years – which cannot be substantiated. Khafre did have quite a long reign, however, probably between the 24 years ascribed to him by the Turin Royal Canon papyrus (and apparently confirmed by an inscription in the nearby *mastaba* tomb of Prince Nekure) and 26 years. At any rate, his reign was long enough to produce a magnificent funerary complex at Giza.

The country was prosperous under Khafre, as is evidenced by the *mastaba* tombs of the nobles of his court. Carved on the wall of one of them – that of Prince Nekure, a 'king's son' – is a will, the only one of its kind known from the period. In it he left 14 towns to his heirs, at least 11 of which (three names are damaged) were named after his father Khafre. Nekure's legacy was divided up amongst his five heirs, but 12 of the towns were earmarked to endow the prince's mortuary cult for his tomb.

The Second Pyramid of Giza

The layout of Khafre's pyramid-complex – valley temple, causeway, mortuary temple and pyramid – was to set the standard for the rest of the Old Kingdom royal tombs. The valley temple, set on the edge of the

The Great Sphinx has been much battered by wind and sand erosion. It did not, contrary to popular belief, lose its nose because of target practice at the time of the French invasion of Egypt in 1798: the nose and its royal ritual beard had vanished long before then. The face had been damaged by religious fanatics in 1380 and part of the beard, a metre-high piece of sandstone carved with criss-crossed plaiting, was found between the paws of the Sphinx by Giovanni Battiste Caviglia in 1818 and is now in the British Museum.

cultivation, is an impressively austere building, the largest Old Kingdom structure to survive other than the actual pyramids. It was built of local limestone, but the walls were then literally veneered with great slabs of red granite brought from the quarries at Aswan, 600 miles (965 km) away to the south. The pillars inside are monoliths of the same stone. Although the temple is no longer roofed, it is thought that light shafts above the pillars lit a series of perhaps as many as 23 diorite, schist and alabaster seated statues, similar in style to the one found by Auguste Mariette in 1860 hidden in a pit just inside the entrance. This larger-than-life-size polished diorite statue of Khafre with the Horus falcon protecting the back of his *nemes* headdress, is one of the finest masterpieces of ancient Egyptian art.

The valley temple played an important role in the funerary ceremonies of the dead king. Indeed, some rituals – particularly the purification ceremonies – seem to have been carried out on the roof beneath a tented pavilion. From the interior of the valley temple an upward-sloping passageway leads out to the beginning of the causeway, which in turn leads to the upper, mortuary temple on the east face of the pyramid. Little now remains of the mortuary temple.

(*Right*) The god-like complacency of the pharaohs as gods on earth is well exemplified in the features on the remarkable diorite statue of Khafre from his valley temple (pp. 54–55). Cairo Museum.

(*Below*) Coloured lithograph published by Giovanni Belzoni in 1820 showing him entering the burial chamber of Khafre's pyramid on 2 March 1818. He was to leave the details and date of the discovery written in lamp black high up on the south wall of the chamber.

Khafre built his pyramid on slightly higher ground than his father, giving the illusion that his was taller than the Great Pyramid of Khufu. In fact, at 447½ ft (136.4 m), it was originally 33½ ft (10.2 m) smaller than its earlier neighbour. Despite the fact that the Great Pyramid has lost its top 30 ft (9 m), the Second Pyramid is still shorter by about 3½ ft (1.1 m). It does have the advantage, however, of retaining some of its original Tura limestone casing on the upper courses leading to the apex.

In classical antiquity it was widely believed that Khafre's pyramid was completely solid with no entrance or rooms within it. This was quite wrong, for it had not one entrance on the northern face of the building (as was the norm for Old Kingdom pyramids) but two on this side – one in the pavement skirting and the second in the outer casing, about 40 ft (13 m) above the surrounding pavement and slightly off

(*Left*) Life-size diorite statue of Khafre, found in his valley temple. The controlled strength of the god on earth, which the king was, and the symbolism of Horus' protection and projection of the king, are brilliantly achieved in the hard stone by yet another unknown and unnamed ancient Egyptian genius craftsman. Cairo Museum.

(*Below*) Detail of Khafre's feet flanked by his cartouche. Cairo Museum.

centre to the west. It was the pioneering Italian-born archaeologist Giovanni Belzoni who realized that the rubbish piled up against the pyramid's north face was higher than the entrance located on the north face of the Great Pyramid. Having obtained a 'firman' (permit), he cleared away the debris and located the steeply sloping upper entrance to the pyramid on 2 March 1818.

The passages descending from the two entrances join up and lead on to the burial chamber, almost centrally placed beneath the pyramidion and cut from the rock at ground level. The chamber's roof consists of large limestone blocks pitched at a gable angle reflecting that of the outer casing of the pyramid (i.e. 52°20', slightly sharper than the Great Pyramid's 52°51'). Belzoni was disappointed to find that medieval Arabs, following on after the ancient tomb robbers, had forestalled him and all that was left in the burial chamber was a plain polished red granite sarcophagus sunk into the floor at the west end, which contained only a few animal bones. Belzoni left his name and the date of the entry writ large in lamp black on the south wall of the chamber, and also inscribed the same message in the granite block above the entrance he had found. It was some years later before the lower passageway was cleared back to its entrance in the outside pavement.

(*Right*) Cross-sections of the principal pyramids of the 3rd and 4th Dynasties, drawn to the same scale.

Step Pyramid, Saqqara (Djoser)

Meydum (Huni/Snefru)

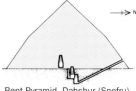

Bent Pyramid, Dahshur (Snefru)

(*Above*) The ancient Egyptians'
complete mastery of working hardstone
is well exemplified in the interior
construction of Khafre's valley temple,
where great blocks of granite may be
seen with most strange, almost tenon-
like joints, often turning corners instead
of being cut to butt ends.

(*Right*) Plan of the Giza plateau pyramid
field.

The Great Sphinx

The Sphinx is an integral part of the funerary complex of Khafre and
was apparently carved from an outcrop of local limestone rock left after
the quarrying of blocks for the nearby Great Pyramid of Khufu. It is a
crouching, human-headed lion that represents Re-Harakhte, the sun god
at his eastern rising at dawn. Some recent nonsensical theories have
suggested that the Sphinx is many thousands of years older than the
pyramids, but there is no foundation for such fantasies. Its face is
believed to represent Khafre and, as such, is the oldest large-scale royal
portrait known.

The Sphinx is about 66 ft (20 m) high and 240 ft (73 m) in length. For
most of the last four and a half millennia it has been enveloped in sand.
A large stele before its chest records that in *c.* 1419 BC the young prince
Tuthmosis (later to be Tuthmosis IV) cleared away the sand that
engulfed it (pp. 113–14). In recent years, since it is no longer protected
by its sand covering, deterioration has been very noticeable, especially
from rising ground water, and a large piece of rock weighing 30 kilos fell
from its right shoulder in February 1988. This was restored and a full
recording and conservation programme begun.

The necropolis at Giza was to be completed by Khafre's son,
Menkaure (Mycerinus), who came to the throne in about 2532 BC.

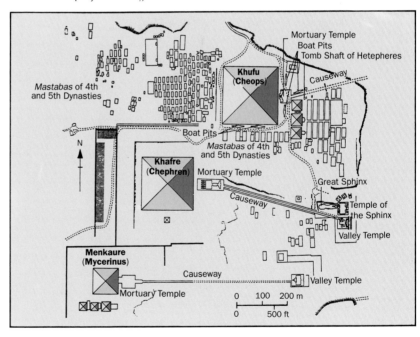

North Pyramid, Dahshur (Snefru)

Great Pyramid, Giza (Khufu)

Second Pyramid, Giza (Khafre)

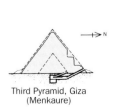

Third Pyramid, Giza
(Menkaure)

DYNASTY 4
2613–2498

Menkaure (Mycerinus)
2532–2504

Shepseskaf
2504–2500

(*Right*) Portrait detail of Menkaure from a slate triad group. Boston Museum.

MENKAURE	
Birth name	*Mother*
Men-kau-re ('Eternal	Khamerernebty I
like the Souls of	*Wives*
Re')	2 unknown queens,
Also known as	Khamerernebty II
Menkaura,	*Sons*
Mycerinus/Mykerin	Khuenre,
us (Greek),	Shepseskaf
Mencheres	*Daughter*
(Manetho)	Khentkawes
Father	*Burial*
Khafre	Third Pyramid, Giza

SHEPSESKAF	
Birth name	*Wives*
Shepses-ka-f ('His	Bunefer
Soul is Noble')	*Daughter*
Father	Khamaat
Menkaure	*Burial*
Mother	Pyramid, South
Unknown	Saqqara

MENKAURE

Menkaure (also known as Mycerinus) succeeded his father in about 2532 BC. According to legend, Menkaure's benevolent rule was an affront to the gods. They had decreed that Egypt would suffer 150 years of hardship, and this had indeed been evident during the reigns of Khufu and Khafre, who were said to have been particularly harsh during the building of their pyramids. Menkaure, by contrast, adopted a much more benign attitude (which does seem to be reflected in his portraits), reopening temples and repealing many of the oppressive measures of his predecessors, and thus flouted the dictate of the gods. The deities therefore decreed, through the oracle of Buto (an ancient capital in the Delta whose patron goddess was Wadjet, the sacred cobra or *uraeus* that protected pharaoh), that Menkaure would only enjoy a reign of six years, after which the oppression would return. Menkaure considered this an unwarranted stricture and determined to overcome it. He ordered that as night fell, candles were to be lit, and he continued to live by day and night, in theory expanding his reign from six to twelve years. The gods, however, were not to be denied: Menkaure, the legend said, died after the six stipulated calendar years.

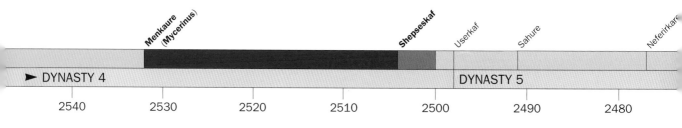

► DYNASTY 4   Menkaure (Mycerinus)   Shepseskaf   Userkaf   Sahure   Neferirkare

DYNASTY 5

2540   2530   2520   2510   2500   2490   2480

(*Above*) The north and east faces of the third pyramid of Giza, built by Menkaure, seen from the south-east corner of Khafre's pyramid.

(*Below*) An early engraving showing the palace-façade-decorated sarcophagus found in the burial chamber of Menkaure's pyramid. It was probably a pious restoration of the Saite Period (6th century BC), and was subsequently lost at sea on its way to England.

Manetho ascribes to Menkaure a reign of 63 years. In fact we now believe he ruled for 28 years – which should have been long enough to build a monument much larger than his small pyramid at the south end of the Giza plateau. With an original height of 228 ft (70 m) – and now a mere 204 ft (62 m) – the so-called Third Pyramid is less than half the height of the Great Pyramid of Khufu. The stunted size has intrigued many commentators, and various explanations have been proposed, the most likely being that its small scale resulted from internal political problems – perhaps the strain on human and other resources caused by the huge building projects of his father and grandfather.

The Third Pyramid of Giza

Although the classical authors were agreed in ascribing the third pyramid at Giza to Menkaure, this was only confirmed early in the 19th century (1837–38) when Colonel Howard Vyse found the king's name written in red ochre on the ceiling of one of the three queens' subsidiary pyramids in Menkaure's complex.

The lower courses of the outer casing of the pyramid were of red granite from Aswan, much of which survives today. The upper casing blocks were of gleaming white Tura limestone: a striking contrast. Although the pyramid was eventually 228 ft (70 m) in height, even this was an expansion because the original plan had been for a structure only about 100 ft (30 m) tall. This plan included an entrance passage on the north face just above ground level, but when the structure was expanded to its present form, the entrance was covered up. A new entrance was thus made on the north face, and what was originally intended as the burial chamber now became simply an antechamber.

(*Above*) Profile of the slate dyad statue of Menkaure and his wife Khamerernebty II. Note the manner in which her right arm enfolds him and her left rests on his left arm. Boston Museum.

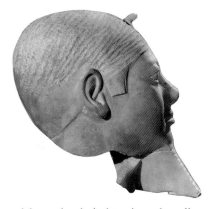

Alabaster head of a king from the valley temple of the third pyramid. Generally identified as being Shepseskaf, it has been suggested that it might be yet another representation of Menkaure. Boston Museum.

When Vyse entered the burial chamber he found against the wall an uninscribed and lidless basalt sarcophagus which was carved with the early Old Kingdom pattern of the articulated palace façade. Inside it was a wooden anthropoid coffin bearing the cartouche of Menkaure. The shape of the coffin was wrong for the period because coffins were rectangular in the Old Kingdom. It would appear, therefore, that the coffin and almost certainly the carved sarcophagus itself were pious restorations carried out during the Saite Period in the later 6th and 5th centuries BC. Both items were shipped to England, destined for the British Museum. Fortunately, they travelled in separate ships: the coffin reached the Museum, but the ship carrying the sarcophagus sank in a storm in 1838 shortly after leaving Leghorn. Efforts made in recent years using highly sophisticated technical equipment have failed to locate the ship.

From 1905 to 1927 the Harvard University/Boston Museum expedition directed by George A. Reisner worked on the pyramid site, clearing the valley and mortuary temples. Reisner found some truly remarkable slate statues in the valley temple that included the splendid triad groups of Menkaure accompanied by the goddess Hathor (given the features of his queen, Khamerernebty II) and a *nome* deity, and also a magnificent dyad statue of the royal pair. Curiously, far more statues survive of Menkaure than of his 4th Dynasty predecessors – in inverse proportion to the size of their pyramids. Although the representations have the typical ethereal god-like look of the Old Kingdom, they are portraits of the king, notable for his snub nose and slightly bulbous eyes. Four complete examples of the king standing with a *nome* deity survived and fragments of others – perhaps all the *nomes* were intended to be represented in a great series of slate triads. The quality of carving of this difficult stone is very high, as is the finish where it occurs – although the majority are in various stages of completion, lending credence to the story preserved in the legends that Menkaure met his death suddenly.

Menkaure's chief queen, Khamerernebty II, was the occupant of the larger of the three subsidiary pyramids associated with his pyramid. Her impressive granite sarcophagus is still in the burial chamber. She was the eldest daughter of Khafre by his wife Khamerernebty I, who was a daughter of Khufu by an unknown queen. Clearly, the royal family was bound by very strong blood ties.

SHEPSESKAF

Menkaure's eldest son by Khamerernebty II, Prince Khuenre, did not succeed him, presumably because he predeceased his father. A small stone statue in the Boston Museum represents the prince in the squatting position of a scribe, kilt stretched between his knees to support his writing board; this was to become the classic pose for scribal statues of nobles in the next dynasty. Instead, the king was followed by

(*Right*) Slate triad representing Menkaure wearing the White Crown flanked on his right by the goddess Hathor, with sun disc and cow's horns headdress, and on his left by the personification of the Hathor name, with her nome sign on her head. Both ladies have the features of Menkaure's queen, Khamerernebty II. Cairo Museum.

Shepseskaf, another son by an unknown queen. His was a short reign of only four years. The fortunes of the kings of the 4th Dynasty were on the wane after Khufu's *magnum opus*, and began to slide rapidly downhill towards the end. This is very evident in Shepseskaf's monument. He moved away from the Giza plateau, returning to the old 3rd Dynasty burial ground at South Saqqara where he erected a most curious tomb. Known as the Mastaba el-Faraoun (Pharaoh's Bench), it originally had the shape of a large rectangular sarcophagus but is now much denuded. His half sister, Khentkawes (daughter of another unknown queen of Menkaure), chose to have a similar style monument, but hers is back at Giza. She married Userkaf who became the first king of the next dynasty.

DYNASTY 5
2498–2345

 Userkaf
2498–2491

 Sahure
2491–2477

 Neferirkare
Kakai
2477–2467

 Shepseskare
2467–2460

 Neferefre
2460–2453

 Niuserre
Ini
2453–2422

 Menkauhor
Kaiu
2422–2414

 Djedkare
Isesi
2414–2375

 Unas
2375–2345

Two portrait heads of Userkaf seen in profile. The smaller of the two wears the Red Crown, the second the *nemes* headdress. Cairo Museum.

The origins of the kings of the 5th Dynasty are recounted in the Westcar Papyrus which is preserved in the Berlin Museum. Probably written down during the Hyksos Period (around 1600 BC), it seems to have been composed in the 12th Dynasty – over 500 years after the events it describes – and endeavours to give a reason for the change of kings that led to the founding of the 5th Dynasty. Essentially the text consists of a series of stories told by one Djedi, a magician or possibly lector priest, at the court of Khufu. As part of one of the stories, Djedi mentions that three children as yet unborn to the lady Reweddjedet (wife of the High Priest of Re at Heliopolis) will become kings. He hastens to assure Khufu, however, that his son and grandson – Khafre and Menkaure – will rule before this happens. Details are given of how the important goddesses Isis, Nephthys, Meskhenet and Heket, with the creator god Khnum acting as their attendant, assist Reweddjedet in her labour. The first born was Userkaf, 'a child one cubit long, whose bones were firm, the covering of whose limbs was of gold, and whose headdress was of real lapis lazuli'. The next two children, Sahure and Neferirkare, were both of similar form. Despite the Heliopolitan origins of the dynasty, Manetho maintained that it stemmed from Elephantine, which is difficult to reconcile with the few known facts.

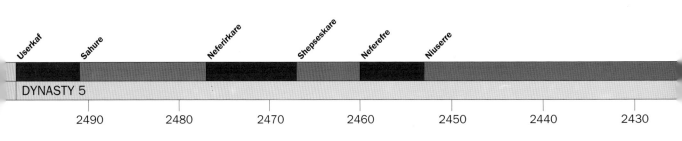

Userkaf   Sahure   Neferirkare   Shepseskare   Neferefre   Niuserre

DYNASTY 5

2490   2480   2470   2460   2450   2440   2430

The sun-temple of Niuserre, based on the sanctuary at Heliopolis and the best preserved of the group at Abu-Gurob.

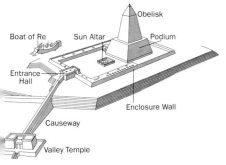

Obelisk
Boat of Re   Sun Altar   Podium
Entrance Hall
Enclosure Wall
Causeway
Valley Temple

USERKAF

Userkaf was in fact the grandson of Djedefre, the short-lived successor of Khufu. His mother was Queen Neferhetep, his father is unknown, and he married Khentkawes, daughter of Menkaure. Thus by that marriage the two lines of descent from Khufu were once more united. It has been suggested that the name Reweddjedet was a pseudonym for Khentkawes, which would mean that there was not so great a change in the ruling royal line as might at first be thought.

Rejecting the tradition established by their 4th Dynasty predecessors of building at Giza, the 5th Dynasty kings moved the site of their funerary monuments south, first to Saqqara, where Userkaf built his pyramid just outside the north-east corner of Djoser's enclosure wall. Uniquely, its mortuary temple is located on the south side of the pyramid instead of the usual east, possibly because the ground was too difficult on the east. Considering, however, the supreme importance accorded to the Sun cult by Userkaf and his 5th Dynasty successors (the 'Sun Kings'), a more likely explanation might be that on the south side of the pyramid the temple would be bathed in the sun's rays throughout the day. Surviving fragments from the reliefs that decorated the temple walls show the high quality of the sculpture, especially in the depiction of birdlife. The impressive and much larger-than-life-size pink granite head of Userkaf (*opposite*) wearing the *nemes* headdress found in the temple courtyard is still the largest surviving Old Kingdom portrait head (if one excludes the Sphinx). The whole complex is terribly ruined and the interior of the pyramid inaccessible.

The solar temple of Abu-Gurob

Further south, at Abu-Gurob, Userkaf built the first of the eventual five sun-temples or sanctuaries that were to become a feature of the architecture of the early 5th Dynasty kings. At this remote spot in the desert, the king constructed a sturdy podium of mudbrick and limestone with a smaller podium upon it at the west end, on which stood a stumpy obelisk (the *benben*) – forerunner of the more lofty obelisks of the New Kingdom. In front of the obelisk podium was a sun altar which was later to become a feature of Akhenaten's apparently innovative temple to the Aten (14th century BC). A causeway led north-west to a valley temple and to the south was a boat of Re constructed of mudbrick. It was from the valley temple that the other fine portrait head of Userkaf was recovered, this time in schist and showing him wearing the Red Crown.

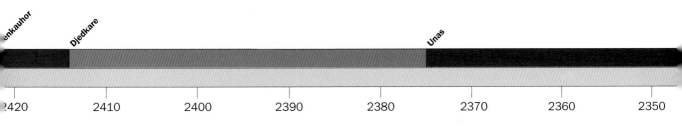

Detail of Sahure from a dyad statue where he is seated beside the standing personification of the Coptos nome. Metropolitan Museum, New York.

THE TOMB OF A NOBLE

A large limestone false door from the mastaba tomb of a noble, Ptahshepses, at Saqqara (now in the British Museum) is of interest in relation to the Westcar Papyrus story. He was born in the reign of Menkaure, educated in the royal palace and married Princess Khamaat, Shepseskaf's daughter. The inscriptions around the great false door, rather unusually, contain a lot of biographical information instead of the more standard religious texts. Ptahshepses records how he served under four consecutive kings of the 5th Dynasty and, in fact, from his birth to his death lived during the reigns of seven kings, the last two of the 4th Dynasty and the first five of the 5th Dynasty, dying in the reign of Niuserre.

Only slightly to the north-west of Userkaf's sun temple his successors proceeded to erect theirs in a row. Little now remains of these, other than mounds with scattered stone blocks on the desert face.

FROM SAHURE TO DJEDKARE-ISESI

Slightly further south lie the pyramid complexes of Neferirkare, Niuserre and Sahure, of which the last is the largest and the best preserved. Like the other 5th Dynasty pyramids, the pyramid of Sahure – the second ruler of the dynasty – is itself a rough rubble mound, but its mortuary temple on the east face is still discernible and preserves stairs that led to the roof or a second storey. A feature of the temple architecture is the splendidly carved red granite date-palm columns and the bold and deeply incised hieroglyphs of the king's name and titulary on huge granite blocks. The walls were highly decorated with finely carved scenes of conquest, hunting and expeditions, all now sadly wrecked and largely disappeared except for odd fragments preserved in museums. Reconstructions of the pyramids produced by the German team who excavated here under Ludwig Borchardt give a good impression of the area's former grandeur, with long causeways stretching down to the valley temples at the edge of the cultivation.

The reliefs in the Abusir mortuary temples offer some of the earliest pictorial evidence of trade beyond the Nile Valley. In Sahure's complex, great ships are illustrated with Egyptians and Asiatics on board. These are thought to be part of a trading fleet returning from the port of Byblos in the Lebanon with the great cedar trees that were to become a major feature in later temple building. There is certainly evidence from the Lebanon of the presence there of 5th Dynasty kings, including fragments of stone vessels bearing their cartouches and the name of Sahure on a piece of thin gold furniture fitting from the 'Dorak Treasure' in Turkey. Widespread trading and expeditions to the south and further into the Near East appear to increase during the next dynasty, but this may simply reflect the better-preserved records and accounts of the later period.

An innovation in this dynasty under the third king, Neferirkare, was the use of a second cartouche. This contained his name Kakai, which may have been his birth name. Thereafter most kings seem to have had a second cartouche, but not all are known. It is from the mortuary temple of Neferirkare at Abusir that the earliest extant hieratic script written on papyrus survives – a series of temple accounts, daily work rosters and equipment lists.

The return to Saqqara

The last kings of the dynasty moved back to Saqqara for their burial place. A small 80-ft (24-m) heap of rubble marks the pyramid of the penultimate ruler, Djedkare-Isesi, on the edge of the plateau; his mortuary temple, largely destroyed in the Second Intermediate Period and then used as a burial ground in the 18th Dynasty, lies nearby. It was only during excavations at the temple in 1946 that it became possible to identify the owner of the associated pyramid as Djedkare-Isesi; hitherto there had been no indication of his name within the pyramid since all the blocks lining the walls of the antechamber and burial chamber had been removed and the black basalt sarcophagus smashed. Fragments of fine reliefs were found in the mortuary temple, and also pieces of statues of foreign prisoners and various animals. The queen's pyramid and attached mortuary temple were found to have similar fine decoration when they were discovered in the early 1950s.

UNAS

The last king of the 5th Dynasty was Unas, whose rubble-core pyramid lies just to the south of Djoser's temenos wall at Saqqara. Although largely ruined, it still preserves the basic pyramid complex with a valley temple at the desert edge from which a long causeway (with a curious kink in it) leads up to the east face of the mortuary temple and the north entrance to the pyramid. The pyramid was first entered in modern times by Gaston Maspero in 1881 when he found that, for the first time, the interior of a pyramid was decorated. The antechamber and most of the walls of the burial chamber were covered by long columns of texts, the so-called 'Pyramid Texts'.

A small section of the causeway leading up to Unas' pyramid has been restored to its full height with its roof closed save for a narrow light slit. The walls were covered with carved reliefs more reminiscent of the *mastaba* tombs of the nobles, showing markets and bargaining in progress, ships in full sail, hunting in the desert, small vignettes of desert life and, most interestingly, scenes of famine which presumably occurred during the reign. On the south side of the causeway are two huge stone-lined boat pits, but whether they actually held wooden boats like that of Khufu or were just symbolic is debatable. The causeway was built over a number of earlier tombs and thus served to preserve them and their decoration; unfortunately, little of their contents remains, since the majority were robbed when the causeway was built, if not before.

On the outer casing of the south side of Unas' pyramid is an inscription recording the restoration of the pyramid, which had fallen into decay, and the restitution of the king's name. This was done in the 19th Dynasty by Khaemwaset, High Priest of Memphis and one of the many sons of Ramesses II who predeceased him: he might be described as the first conservation archaeologist. Found scattered on the desert face, the inscription was restored and replaced high up on the pyramid in the late 1940s.

It appears that Unas left no heir, leading to a short period of political instability. This was apparently resolved, however, when Teti rose to the throne as the first ruler of the 6th Dynasty.

THE PYRAMID TEXTS

When Gaston Maspero entered the pyramid of King Unas in 1881, he found long columns of hieroglyphic inscription covering the walls. Known as the Pyramid Texts, these comprise 228 spells designed to help the soul of the deceased on its journey in the next world, some of which may have been recited during the burial ceremony. Unas' pyramid was the first to feature such texts, but the tradition was quickly established to become the norm in the next dynasty.

Detail of a section of the Pyramid Texts inscribed in the pyramid of Unas. The king's cartouche appears in the left and right hand columns.

No complete series exists in any of the pyramids, but a total of 400 spells have been collated from the pyramids of Unas and his 6th Dynasty successors. The texts were replaced in the Middle Kingdom by the Coffin Texts, which subsequently became the papyrus 'Book of the Dead' in the New Kingdom.

DYNASTY 6
2345–2181

Teti
2345–2333

Pepi I
Meryre
2332–2283

Merenre
Nemtyemsaf
2283–2278

Pepi II
Neferkare
2278–2184

ROYAL NAMES AND BURIALS

TETI
Birth name
  Teti
Wives
  Iput, Kawit,
  Weret-Imtes
Son
  Pepi I
Daughter
  Seshseshet
Burial
  Pyramid, North
  Saqqara

PEPI I
Birth name
  Pepi
Also known as
  Pepy I, Piopi I,
  Phiops I (Greek)
Throne name
  Mery-re ('Beloved
  of Re')
Wives
  Ankhnesmerire I, II,
  Weret-Imtes
Sons
  Merenre, Pepi II
Daughter
  Neith

Burial
  Pyramid, South
  Saqqara
MERENRE
Throne name
  Mer-en-re ('Beloved
  of Re')
Also known as
  Merenra
Birth name
  Nemty-em-sa-f
  ('Nemty is his
  Protection')
Daughter
  Ipwet
Burial
  Pyramid, South
  Saqqara

PEPI II
Birth name
  Pepi
Throne name
  Nefer-ka-re
  ('Beautiful is the
  Soul of Re')
Wives
  Neith, Ipwet
Burial
  Pyramid, South
  Saqqara

TETI

According to Manetho, the 6th Dynasty kings came from Memphis, a statement which seems to be borne out by the location of their funeral monuments at Saqqara, overlooking the capital of Memphis. Teti's accession to the throne as the first king of the new dynasty seems to have resolved the monarchical and political instability in Egypt which followed the death of Unas. By marrying one of Unas' daughters, Iput, he legitimized his right to rule; and by adopting the Horus name Seheteptawy ('He who pacifies the Two Lands'), he symbolized renewed political unity in the country. He also sought the good will of the increasingly powerful nobility and provincial élites by marrying his daughter Seshseshet to the vizier Mereruka (whose *mastaba* tomb close by Teti's pyramid is the best-known monument of the reign).

The surviving manuscripts of Manetho's work all record that Teti (sometimes known as Othoes) was murdered by his bodyguard. There is no direct evidence, although a violent death may help to explain references to another king, Userkare, who may have reigned briefly between Teti and his son Pepi I. At any rate, Teti seems to have reigned for about 12 years, during which he continued to trade with Byblos and Nubia.

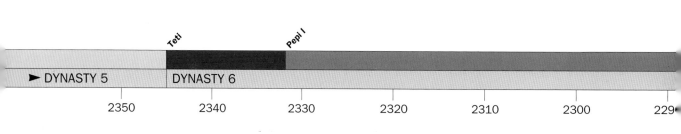

► DYNASTY 5 | DYNASTY 6

2350 2340 2330 2320 2310 2300 229

(*Left*) Small alabaster statuette of Pepi I. Like Khafre, Pepi has the Horus falcon associated with him, but instead of enfolding the king's head in protective wings, the bird stands aloof on the back of the high-backed throne, wings furled and looking obliquely away from the king. Brooklyn Museum.

(*Below*) Green slate kneeling statue of Pepi I. In his two extended hands, resting on the folded kilt over his thighs, he proffers a pair of small globular vases. He is offering wine or water to a god and, as such, this is the earliest example of the genre of statuary that was to become extremely popular with royalty, and more so with the laity, down into the Late Period. Brooklyn Museum.

(*Left*) An almost three-dimensional *ka*-statue of Teti's vizier and son-in-law Mereruka strides from the false door in the main offering hall of his 32-room *mastaba* tomb – the largest at Saqqara because it was a family tomb, with a separate section for his wife Seshseshet and son Meri-Teti. The wall reliefs (*above*) are an incredible record of daily life in ancient Egypt, such as the hippopotamus hunt.

There is relatively little to show for Teti's reign nowadays except for the once finely cased but now rubble mound of his pyramid towards the northern edge of the Saqqara plateau. As usual, the entrance is on the north side and leads to a much damaged burial chamber inscribed with excerpts from the Pyramid Texts and still with its lidless basalt sarcophagus. A wooden coffin found in 1881 is in the Cairo Museum. Although there are the remains of a mortuary temple on the east face, the causeway leading to it from the valley temple has vanished and the valley temple itself has never been found. To the north of the pyramid lie the sand-covered smaller pyramids of two of Teti's queens, Iput and Kawit. Iput was the mother of the next king, Pepi I, and her skeleton was found in a wooden coffin in her pyramid (although many of the other items therein had been robbed).

FROM PEPI I TO PEPI II

Teti's son Pepi I probably acceded to the throne very young, for he appears to have had a long reign of about 50 years. A number of inscriptions from the period record the rising influence and wealth under Pepi I of nobles outside the royal court; these nobles began to build fine tombs for themselves in the provincial areas of Upper Egypt and boasted of privileges resulting from friendship with the king. The king also faced other problems, not least a conspiracy plotted against him by one of his queens, Weret-Imtes; but the plan was thwarted and the wife punished. Despite such difficulties, the king evidently mounted various trading expeditions, often to fetch fine stone for the many building projects he initiated. An inscription found in the alabaster quarries at Hatnub in Middle Egypt has been dated to Year 50 of his reign since it refers to the 25th cattle-count, which was a biennial event.

It is from Pepi's funerary monument that the modern name of Memphis derives. His pyramid was called *Mn-nfr*, '[Pepi is] established and good', and it was the corruption of this title by classical writers that gave the present name. The pyramid itself, at South Saqqara, is badly smashed although surviving fragments of texts from the collapsed burial chamber are of very high quality.

From the temple of Hierakonpolis (Nekhen) in upper Egypt come two remarkable copper statues, the earliest known life-size sculptures in that metal. The larger is a standing, striding figure of Pepi I, holding a long staff in his left hand, while the smaller is his son, Merenre, beside his right leg. A better idea of Pepi's features is given by a small green slate statue of the king wearing the royal *nemes* headdress, while another small alabaster statuette of the king shows him holding the royal emblems of crossed flail and sceptre (crook), and wearing the tall White Crown of Upper Egypt (pp. 64, 65).

Pepi I married the two daughters of a provincial prince of Abydos named Khui; confusingly, the ladies both had the same name, Ankhnesmerire. One became the mother of Merenre and the other bore Pepi II.

Merenre succeeded his father for only a short reign of some five years, after which his brother Neferkare Pepi II came to the throne. Although only six years old when he succeeded his brother, Pepi II, as with any royal child, was acknowledged as ruler from birth. Indeed, an attractive alabaster seated statuette of his mother, Ankhnesmerire, shows him on her lap as a small adult male wearing the royal *nemes* headdress; another represents the king as a young naked child, squatting with his hands on his knees and wearing the *uraeus* on his headdress.

Pepi II married several times, principally to Neith – daughter of his father Pepi I and Ankhnesmerire I (i.e. his half-sister and cousin) – and to his niece Ipwet, daughter of his brother Merenre; there were at least two other senior queens too. His reign was the longest in Egyptian history (if we accept that the scribe recording details of his rule did not

Large copper statue of Pepi I from the temple of Hierakonpolis. The king lacks a crown and a midriff where his kilt would have been; presumably both missing items would have been supplied separately in a material such as gilded plaster. Beside him is his son by Queen Ankhnesmerire I, Merenre. Cairo Museum.

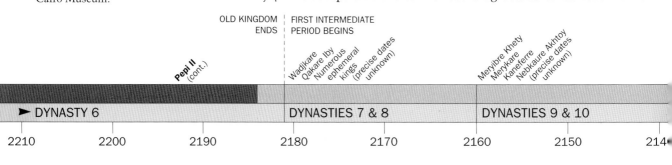

OLD KINGDOM ENDS | FIRST INTERMEDIATE PERIOD BEGINS

Pepi II (cont.)

Wadjkare Iby
Qakare Iby
Numerous ephemeral kings (precise dates unknown)

Meryibre Khety
Merykare
Kaneferre
Nebkaure Akhtoy (precise dates unknown)

► DYNASTY 6 | DYNASTIES 7 & 8 | DYNASTIES 9 & 10

2210 | 2200 | 2190 | 2180 | 2170 | 2160 | 2150 | 214

RAGS TO RICHES: THE STORY OF WENI

The exemplary life of the noble Weni, who served under the first three kings of the dynasty, is inscribed on the walls of his tomb at Abydos. One of the longest narrative inscriptions of the period, the autobiography records how Weni rose from almost obscure origins through the court's hierarchy from an 'inferior custodian' to a 'Friend' of Pepi and a High Court judge at Nekhen (Hierakonpolis) – the important cult centre of the vulture goddess Nekhbet. Eventually he was appointed Governor of the South under Merenre. As a most respected judge ('I was more excellent to the heart of His Majesty than any official of his') he was the sole arbiter in a harem conspiracy case involving the Queen Weret-Imtes: 'Never before had the like of me heard a secret matter of the King's harem, but His Majesty caused me to hear it'. Bearing in mind Manetho's assertion that the previous king, Teti (Pepi's father), had been assassinated, no doubt the sentence on the queen was a capital one.

After that success Weni changed positions to be placed at the head of an army of 'many tens of thousands' that marched against the bedouin in northern Sinai. He boasted that despite the numbers no one suffered on the route thanks to his policy of 'living off the land'. In all he crushed five revolts in the area, culminating in the first recorded Egyptian attack on southern Palestine. Finally, in his capacity as Governor of the South under Merenre, Weni brought stone for the royal pyramid from the First Cataract quarries, and in so doing cut five channels to facilitate passage through the cataract.

THE YOUNG PEPI II

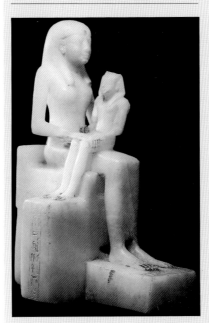

Alabaster statuette of Queen Ankhnes-merire with her young son, Pepi II, on her lap shown as a miniature adult, complete with the royal nemes *headdress. Brooklyn Museum.*

A charming vignette of the young excitable eight-year-old King Pepi II comes from an inscription on the façade of the tomb of the noble and caravan leader Harkhuf at Aswan. Harkhuf made four journeys into the dangerous lands south of Aswan to collect elephant tusks, ebony, incense and other precious commodities. None, however, was more precious than the small pygmy whom he captured on the route to Darfur in Year 2 of Pepi's reign. Returning with his prize, he sent word ahead to the royal court at Memphis and received back explicit instructions in a letter from the young king to 'come northward to the Court immediately ... My Majesty desires to see this dwarf more than the gifts of Sinai and of Punt'. Harkhuf was told to take great care that the dwarf was always accompanied on the deck of the ship so that he should not fall into the Nile and that he should also be inspected ten times a night as he slept to ensure no harm befell him. Harkhuf evidently achieved his mission and presented the dwarf at Court, to the young king's delight.

confuse the numbers 64 and 94, which are very similar in cursive hieratic script), and this longevity was probably partly responsible for the declining power of the Egyptian state.

There is increasing evidence during this period of the decentralization of control away from Memphis. Local governors (nomarchs) cut huge and impressive decorated tombs for themselves in the provinces, and paid only a nodding allegiance to the northern capital. The wealth that the king bestowed on his nobles not only depleted his own treasury but also enhanced their status to the detriment of his. At the same time, the heavy demands of Egypt's foreign interests further accelerated political collapse.

Some sources mention a successor to Pepi II, Merenre II (probably the son of Pepi II and Neith) and his successor Queen Nitocris, thought to be his wife. Manetho, for instance, describes Nitocris as 'braver than all the men of her time, the most beautiful of all the women, fair-skinned with red cheeks'. No archaeological evidence has been found of her reign, nor of Herodotus' story that she avenged the murder of her brother (?Teti I, since he was the murdered king) by tricking the perpetrators of this deed into drowning, before herself committing suicide.

At any rate, with the demise of the 6th Dynasty in about 2181 BC the Old Kingdom as such came to an end.

Mentuhotep I

Mentuhotep III

Senusret I

Amenemhet II

THE FIRST INTERMEDIATE PERIOD
2181–2040 BC

DYNASTIES 7 & 8
2181–2160

Wadjkare

Qakare Iby

DYNASTIES 9 & 10
2160–2040

Meryibre Khety

Merykare

Kaneferre

Nebkaure Akhtoy

THE MIDDLE KINGDOM
2040–1782 BC

DYNASTY 11
2134–1991

Intef I
2134–2117

Intef II
2117–2069

Intef III
2069–2060

Mentuhotep I
2060–2010

Mentuhotep II
2010–1998

Mentuhotep III
1997–1991

DYNASTY 12
1991–1782

Amenemhet I
1991–1962

Senusret I
1971–1926

Amenemhet II
1929–1895

Senusret II
1897–1878

Senusret III
1878–1841

Amenemhet III
1842–1797

Amenemhet IV
1798–1786

Queen Sobeknefru
1785–1782

THE SECOND INTERMEDIATE PERIOD
1782–1570 BC

DYNASTY 13
1782–1650

Wegaf
1782–1778

Ameny Intef IV
(?)–1760

Hor
c.1760

Sobekhotep II
c.1750

Khendjer
c.1747

Sobekhotep III
c.1745

Neferhotep I
1741–1730

Sobekhotep IV
1730–1720

Ay
c.1720

Neferhotep II

DYNASTY 14
Nehesy

DYNASTY 15
(Hyksos)
1663–1555

Sheshi

Yakubher

Khyan

Apepi I

Apepi II

DYNASTY 16
1663–1555

Anather

Yakobaam

DYNASTY 17
1663–1570

Sobekemsaf I

Sobekemsaf II

Intef VII

Tao I
c.1633

Tao II
c.1574

Kamose
1573–1570

OLD KINGDOM ENDS | FIRST INTERMEDIATE PERIOD BEGINS | F.I.P. ENDS | MIDDLE KINGDOM BEGINS

Wadjkare
Qakare Iby
Meryibre Khety
Merykare
Kaneferre
Nebkaure Akhtoy
Intef I
Intef II
Intef III
Mentuhotep I
Mentuhotep II
Mentuhotep III
Amenemhet I
co-regency Senusret I
co-regency Amenemhet II
co-regency Senusret

► DYNASTY 6 | DYNS. 7 & 8 | DYNS. 9 & 10 | DYNASTY 11 | DYNASTY 12

2200   2150   2100   2050   2000   1950   1900

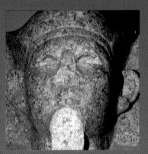

Senusret III   Amenemhet III   Hor   Sobekemsaf I

CHAOS AND REBIRTH
The First Intermediate Period 2181–2040 BC
The Middle Kingdom 2040–1782 BC
The Second Intermediate Period 1782–1570 BC

Fʀᴏᴍ ɪᴛs ɪɴᴄᴇᴘᴛɪᴏɴ at the end of the 4th millennium BC, Egyptian civilization had gone from strength to strength in every sphere of the arts, sciences and technology, reaching its zenith with Khufu's great monument at Giza. Small wonder then that the ancient Egyptians were complacent within the sheltering and protective desert-backed cliffs of the Nile Valley. The shock of the breakdown of that essential concept of stability, *ma'at*, at the end of the Old Kingdom around 2181 BC was therefore even greater because the unimaginable had happened. For 140 years chaos reigned, only to be brought under control, like an unruly horse, by a strong line of princes from Upper Egypt at Thebes. Just 250 years later central government and the concept of *ma'at* broke down once again. The see-saw effect from one extreme to the other was to become an unpleasant aspect of the structure of civilization in the Nile Valley. Out of this period of disruption, now so dark and difficult to interpret, however, emerged the three luminous dynasties that were to comprise the New Kingdom.

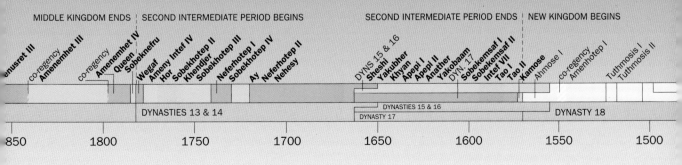

DYNASTIES 7 & 8
2181–2161

 Wadjkare

 Qakare Iby

DYNASTIES 9 & 10
(Herakleopolitan)
2160–2040

 Meryibre Khety

 Nebkaure Akhtoy

 Merykare

 Kaneferre

ROYAL NAMES	
WADJKARE *Throne name* Wadj-ka-re ('Prosperous is the Soul of Re') **QAKARE IBY** *Throne name* Qa-ka-re ('Strong is the Soul of Re') *Birth name* Iby **MERYIBRE KHETY** *Throne name* Mery-ib-re ('Beloved is the Heart of Re') *Birth name* Khety	**MERYKARE** *Birth name* Mery-ka-re ('Beloved is the Soul of Re') **KANEFERRE** *Birth name* Ka-nefer-re ('Beautiful is the Soul of Re') **NEBKAURE AKHTOY** *Throne name* Neb-kau-re ('Golden are the Souls of Re) *Birth name* Akh-toy

With the death of Pepi II, central government broke down completely and the fragile unity that had held Egypt together during the Old Kingdom finally splintered. Papyri from the later Middle Kingdom emphasize the turmoil of the First Intermediate Period, for the country had indeed fallen into political and monarchical disorder.

The later historical sources relating to this period are also confused: Manetho mentions a 7th Dynasty consisting of 70 kings who reigned for 70 days, but rather than being real rulers they were probably dreamt up by the ancient historians to symbolize the demise of central control at the end of the Old Kingdom. More certain, however, seems the existence of an 8th Dynasty. Comprising 17 or so kings, possibly descended from Pepi II, these rulers claimed to govern from Memphis. Their authority was nevertheless mostly limited to the area around this city, for the Delta had been invaded by so-called 'Asiatics' from the east, Thebes (Luxor) had ceased to be the capital of the fourth *nome* in Upper Egypt, and the city of Herakleopolis (near modern Beni Suef) had won control of Middle Egypt. The 8th Dynasty was short-lived, lasting for only 20 years or so, and the kings left little evidence of their rule apart from a royal exemption decree issued by King **Wadjkare** (whose Horus name was Demedjibtawy) and a small pyramid of a king called **Qakare Iby**.

FIRST INTERMEDIATE PERIOD BEGINS

Wadjkare
Qakare Iby
Numerous ephemeral kings

Meryibre Khety
Merykare
Kaneferre
Nebkaure Akhtoy
(precise dates unknown)

DYNASTIES 7 & 8

DYNASTIES 9 & 10 (HERAKLEOPOLITAN)

2180   2170   2160   2150   2140   2130   2120

Following the breakdown of the Memphite government, the provinces began to jockey for power, as nomarchs set themselves up as petty warlords. It was at this time that a ruling family from Herakleopolis emerged, the 9th Dynasty, founded perhaps by one **Meryibre Khety**. This dynasty may have held sway over the whole country for a while, but by the beginning of the second Herakleopolitan dynasty (10th Dynasty) some 30 years later, dual sovereignty had been established, with southern Egypt controlled by a rival family, the 11th Dynasty, at Thebes (p. 72).

The two Herakleopolitan dynasties were somewhat unstable and frequent changes of ruler took place. Manetho mentions the cruelty of a 9th Dynasty king named Achthoes, but goes on to describe how the gods exacted their revenge: the king was apparently driven mad and then eaten by a crocodile. The name of Meryibre Khety has been recorded and maintains the full titulary with the two cartouches; another documented name in a cartouche is that of a king called **Merykare**.

One of the most important of the few monuments from this war-torn period is the tomb of the nobleman Ankhtify, found at el-Moalla 20 miles (32 km) south of Thebes. He was no mean warrior and identifies himself as 'great chieftain' (presumably the nomarch) of the Herakleopolitan *nome* (el-Kab). In such troubled times as these, his power could have been god-like and his word law ('I am the beginning and the end of mankind for my equal has not and will not come into being'), but he could also be humane, as shown by one record of his feeding the famine-struck populace. Nevertheless, he did this at the behest of the king, **Kaneferre**, who was probably the third king of the 9th Dynasty.

The name of another king occurs in the well-known Middle Kingdom 'Tale of the Eloquent Peasant'. This peasant was robbed of his goods on the way to market by a local 'bully boy' landowner, and decided to take his case to the highest in the land. He pleaded his case 'in the reign of his late Majesty King Nebkaure' before the king himself, who was entranced by the humble peasant's eloquence, making him present the case time and again in order to enjoy listening to him. The king concerned was probably **Nebkaure Akhtoy** of the later 9th/10th Dynasty.

As the authority of the Herakleopolitan government grew, so too did that of the Theban dynasty. Increasing hostility between the two powers resulted in frequent clashes along the border (mostly north of Abydos), which only really abated when Egypt was reunified by one of the 11th Dynasty kings.

FIRST INTERMEDIATE
PERIOD ENDS

DYNASTY 11
(Theban)
2134–1991

Intef I
Sehertawy
2134–2117

Intef II
Wahankh
2117–2069

Intef III
Nakjtnebtepnefer
2069–2060

Mentuhotep I
Nebhetepre
2060–2010

Mentuhotep II
Sankhkare
2010–1998

Mentuhotep III
Nebtawyre
1997–1991

ROYAL NAMES AND BURIALS

INTEF I–III
Birth name
  Sa-re Intef ('Son of
  Re Intef')
Also known as
  Inyotef I, II, III
Horus name (I)
  Seher-tawy ('Maker
  of Peace in the Two
  Lands')
Horus name (II)
  Wah-ankh ('Strong
  in Life')
Horus name (III)
  Nakjt-nebtep-nefer
  ('Beautiful and
  Strong Champion')
Burial (I–III)
  Dra Abu el-Naga
  (Thebes)

MENTUHOTEP I
Birth name
  Mentu-hotep ('The
  god Montu is
  Content')
Also known as
  Mentuhotpe

Throne name
  Neb-hetep-re
  ('Pleased is the
  Lord Re')
Burial
  Temple-tomb, Deir
  el-Bahari (Thebes)

MENTUHOTEP II
Birth name
  As Mentuhotep I
Throne name
  Sankh-ka-re ('Giving
  Life to the Soul of
  Re')
Burial
  ?Deir el-Bahari
  (Thebes)

MENTUHOTEP III
Birth name
  As Mentuhotep I
Throne name
  Neb-tawy-re ('Lord
  of the Two Lands is
  Re')
Burial
  Unknown

Strictly speaking, the Middle Kingdom starts with the reunification of Egypt under the fourth king of Dynasty 11, Mentuhotep I. The dynasty itself began with a series of three kings (in fact hardly more than nomarchs), who ruled from Thebes. All known as Intef (or Inyotef), they were each involved in struggles against the northern kings of Herakleopolis. Interestingly, their Horus names indicate more their aspirations than reality: Intef II called himself 'King of Upper and Lower Egypt', whereas his control did not extend beyond the Thebes area; and Intef III gave himself the name Nakhjtnebtepnefer or 'Beautiful and Strong Champion'. Furthermore, they curiously reverted to having their Horus names in a *serekh*, with only their birth names in the cartouche.

The three Intefs were buried in great tombs in the Dra Abu el-Naga, an area to the north of the Theban plain on the west bank, close to where the road starts into the later Valley of the Kings. Because of their row of doorways, or porticoes, these have been called *saff* tombs, *saff* being an Arabic word for row. There is now little indication of their once royal status. One of the so-called 'tomb robbing' papyri dating from the reign of Ramesses IX (*c.* 1115 BC) records that a check on the tomb of Wahankh Intef II found the burial to be intact. It notes furthermore that there was a stele in front of the tomb on which the king was shown with his

---

Intef I   Intef II   Intef III

DYNASTY 11 (THEBAN)

2130   2120   2110   2100   2090   2080   2070

(Above) Deir el-Bahari looking north with the terrace temple of Mentuhotep I in the foreground.

(Below) Detail of the seated statue of Mentuhotep I found in a chamber beneath his temple-tomb. Cairo Museum.

favourite hunting dog, Behka. Auguste Mariette found the broken lower half of the stele in 1860; in fact there was not one dog on it but five. What remains of the inscription indicates that, in the territorial disputes against the Herakleopolitan dynasties, Intef II established his boundary as far north from Thebes as the 10th *nome* (Antaeopolis), taking the 8th *nome* of sacred Abydos on the way. His successor Intef III pushed the border yet further north, almost to Asyut, and it was at this frontier that Mentuhotep I (sometimes known as Mentuhotep II) fought for control of the whole country.

MENTUHOTEP I

The reign of Mentuhotep I reached its pinnacle some years after he came to the throne with the reunification of Egypt. The political progression of his career is eloquently attested by the series of Horus names he adopted: first 'He who gives heart to the Two Lands', then 'Lord of the White Crown' (Upper Egypt), and finally 'Uniter of the Two Lands'.

The king's birth name, Mentuhotep – meaning 'Montu is content', Montu being the Theban god of war – also seems appropriate, since the first part of his reign at least saw a great deal of bitter fighting. Indeed, in

FIRST INTERMEDIATE PERIOD ENDS | Reunification of Egypt
MIDDLE KINGDOM BEGINS

Mentuhotep I

Mentuhotep II

Mentuhotep III

Amenemhet I

50   2050   2040   2030   2020   2010   2000   1990

Two finely detailed wooden models of soldiers were found in the 11th Dynasty tomb of Mesehti at Asyut. Buried c. 2000 BC, they represent 40-strong detachments of Egyptian spearmen and Nubian archers. Cairo Museum.

the 1920s the American archaeologist Herbert Winlock found a mass tomb at Thebes, near Mentuhotep's temple, containing the bodies of 60 soldiers slain in battle. They had almost certainly been killed in Nubia and brought back for burial in Egypt – one of the earliest war cemeteries. The militaristic theme is also evident in two large models of wooden soldiers found in the tomb of a local prince or general, Mesehti, at Asyut in 1894. One represented a troop of 40 marching Egyptian pikemen, each armed with spear and hide shield, and the other a similarly sized group of Nubian archers.

The turning point in the fortunes of the Theban camp came in Year 14 of Mentuhotep's reign, when the Thinite (Abydos) *nome* rose up in revolt. Mentuhotep took immediate steps to crush it, in a series of battles which eventually led to his overall rule of Egypt. By Year 39 of his reign, he was well established as 'Uniter of the Two Lands'. A scratched inscription documents an expedition, mounted in the same year, to Abisko 17 miles (27 km) south of the First Cataract; similar records occur at Shatt er-Rigal, where the king was accompanied by his chancellor Akhtoy, and in the Wadi Hammamat quarries.

The mortuary temple of Mentuhotep I

Mentuhotep I enjoyed an unusually long reign of 50 years (at a time when most kings were short-lived), the latter part of which, following reunification, saw a return to peace and relative prosperity in Egypt. Building works at numerous sites – amongst them el-Kab, Gebelein, Tod, Deir el-Ballas, Dendera and Abydos – all testify to the stability now ruling the land. Mentuhotep's greatest project, however, was the temple-tomb he erected on the west bank at Thebes, in the impressive great bay of cliffs at Deir el-Bahari, south of his predecessors' *saff* tombs. Why he picked that spot and not the prime position nearby (later chosen by the

Part of a jubilee scene of Mentuhotep II from Armant. His throne name, Sankhkare, appears in the cartouches and the king is wearing the Red Crown (left) and a *nemes* headdress (right). The texts wish him Life, Prosperity and Health. Brooklyn Museum.

18th Dynasty Queen Hatshepsut) is a mystery. Nevertheless, the design of the temple-tomb was innovative: a great stepped podium with square-cut pillars around it, and the next terrace with a hypostyle hall at the rear at the base of the cliffs.

In the plain in front of the temple is the entrance to a deep tunnel known as the Bab el-Hosan, the Gate of the Horseman (so-called because Howard Carter's horse stumbled into it and led to its discovery). The tunnel leads to a chamber beneath the temple which held an impressive seated stone statue of the king; he is depicted in the tight white *heb-sed* costume and wearing the Red Crown but with a black face, thereby assimilating him to Osiris as an Underworld deity of fertility (p. 73).

A number of Mentuhotep's high officials – including the chancellor Akhtoy, the viziers Dagi and Ipi, and the chief steward Henenu – chose to be buried close to their master's tomb, some having also served his son. Dagi's splendid limestone sarcophagus had a particularly full version painted on its interior of the Coffin Texts (magic spells introduced in the Middle Kingdom, designed to protect the soul of the deceased on the journey into the Afterworld, similar to the Pyramid Texts).

MENTUHOTEP II

The long reign of Mentuhotep I was used to good advantage, allowing the king to bequeath to his son, Sankhkare Mentuhotep II, the throne of a flourishing country. It also meant that Mentuhotep II was relatively elderly when he came to power in 2010 BC, and indeed he was only to rule for 12 years. Despite the brevity of his reign, the new king continued the policy pursued by his predecessors of maintaining a defensive attitude towards the neighbours on the northern frontiers, as well as looking keenly to the south of the First Cataract to trade goods.

Mentuhotep II carried out a number of building works, including temples and shrines, and he evidently initiated a series of expeditions to gather raw materials. One such excursion in Year 8 of his reign (recorded on a long inscription in the Wadi Hammamat) was led by his steward Henenu, who was sent there to obtain suitable stone for statues to be erected in the temples. The expedition seems to have been the first to the area for some time, since Henenu took 3000 soldiers with him (and that was only after local rebels had been cleared from the road by other troops). Henenu sank a total of 12 wells *en route* and made sure that his force was adequately provided for, everyone having a leather bottle, a carrying pole, two jars of water and 20 loaves a day; furthermore, in that hard terrain, 'the asses were laden with sandals'.

After his death in *c.* 1998 BC, Mentuhotep II was probably buried in a bay in the cliffs to the south of his father's great monument at Deir el-Bahari. Little remains there except for a causeway that apparently ends at a sloping passage going into the rock. Hieratic graffiti scratched on the rocks in the area by priests of the mortuary cult at least indicate that the king found his resting place somewhere close by.

MENTUHOTEP III

Mentuhotep II is given in both the Saqqara and the Abydos king lists as the last king of the 11th Dynasty, immediately preceding Amenemhet I, founder of the 12th Dynasty, but the fragmentary Royal Canon of Turin

---

THE TOMBS OF THE ROYAL LADIES

(Above) Queen Kawit has her hair arranged, from the exterior of her sarcophagus.

In 1920, the shrines and shaft tombs of six young royal ladies – Henhenet, Kemsit, Kawit, Sadeh, Ashayt and Muyet – were found under the pavement at the back of Mentuhotep I's tomb-temple. The youngest, Muyet, was only about five years old and none of the others were more than 20. Henhenet's sarcophagus was made up of six limestone blocks fitted together on a sandstone base, but the lid was inscribed for Kawit and clearly did not belong to it.

Numerous other royal ladies were buried in the area too, including Queen Tem, who was the mother of Mentuhotep II Sankhkare. Another of Mentuhotep I's queens, Neferu (his sister), lay buried in a tomb a little to the north. In later years this obstructed the building of Hatshepsut's temple, but it was carefully conserved and obviously the object of interest for 18th Dynasty tourists. In spite of the earlier visitors, Herbert Winlock's excavations recovered fragments of finely carved wall reliefs and some sad remains of Neferu's funerary provision, including small wax *ushabti* figures.

(Above) Princess Ashayt enjoys the scent of a lotus, from the interior of her sarcophagus. Both Cairo Museum.

THE WOODEN MODELS OF THE CHANCELLOR MEKETRE

The tomb of Meketre, chancellor to Mentuhotep I, was located near his master's, and built according to the contemporary fashion with a steeply sloping approach ramp and a huge entrance with a passage cut deep into the cliff face. Although the tomb had been heavily robbed and damaged in antiquity, investigations conducted by Herbert Winlock in 1919–20 revealed a small concealed chamber containing 25 of the most exquisite wooden models of daily life that have survived. The cache includes the great cattle count model, two female offering bearers, model butchers' and bakers' shops, granaries, weavers' and carpenters' shops, fishing skiffs and the great man's flotilla, including the kitchen tender that obviously must have sailed unobtrusively down wind. There were even two models of Meketre's porticoed house, complete with its garden pool shaded by trees.

The model carpenter's shop from the tomb of the Chancellor Meketre, complete in every detail, even to spare tools being provided in the large chest. Cairo Museum.

papyrus says that there was a period of seven years without a king after Mentuhotep II. Into this lacuna must fit Nebtawyre Mentuhotep III and his short reign of about six years.

Records of this shadowy king are sparse. His name, together with that of Amenemhet I, occurs on a fragment of a slate bowl found at Lisht in the first *nome* and must date to the latter's reign as first king of the 12th Dynasty. Mentuhotep III's vizier and Governor of the South was also called Amenemhet, and it seems highly probable that he and Amenemhet I are one and the same. The vizier Amenemhet is well attested from a long inscription that he left in the Wadi Hammamat. He records that he went with an army of 10,000 men into the Wadi to seek and retrieve a fine block of stone suitable for the lid of the king's sarcophagus. They were led to the block by a pregnant gazelle which, having dropped its young on to the stone to mark it, was immediately sacrificed upon it. A further wonder occurred with a shower of rain. Eventually, the huge block was detached from the rock, and Amenemhet returned with it to Thebes. Unfortunately neither the tomb nor the sarcophagus of Mentuhotep III has ever been found. Perhaps the king was never able to use the stone, since it seems that Amenemhet, with the backing of his 10,000 men, overthrew his master and proclaimed himself king and thus, in what was rapidly becoming the norm, founded a new dynasty.

DYNASTY 12
1991–1782

Amenemhet I
Sehetepibre
1991–1962

Senusret I
Kheperkare
1971–1926

Amenemhet II
Nubkaure
1929–1895

Senusret II
Khakheperre
1897–1878

ROYAL NAMES AND BURIALS	
AMENEMHET I	**AMENEMHET II**
Birth name	*Birth name*
Amen-em-het ('Amun is at the Head')	Amen-em-het ('Amun is at the Head')
Also known as	*Also known as*
Amenemhat I, Ammenemes I (Greek)	Amenemhat II, Ammenemes II (Greek)
Throne name	*Throne name*
Sehetep-ib-re ('Satisfied is the Heart of Re')	Nub-kau-re ('Golden are the Souls of Re')
Burial	*Burial*
Pyramid, el-Lisht	Pyramid, Dahshur
SENUSRET I	**SENUSRET II**
Birth name	*Birth name*
S-en-usret ('Man of goddess Wosret')	S-en-usret ('Man of goddess Wosret')
Also known as	*Also known as*
Senwosret I, Sesostris I (Greek)	Senwosret II, Sesostris II (Greek)
Throne name	*Throne name*
Kheper-ka-re ('The Soul of Re comes into Being')	Kha-kheper-re ('The Soul of Re comes into Being')
Burial	*Burial*
Pyramid, el-Lisht	Pyramid, el-Lahun

AMENEMHET I

According to Manetho, the 12th Dynasty consisted of seven kings from Thebes. Our present lists agree, with the addition of a queen, Sobeknefru, at the close of the dynasty. The first king of the dynasty was Amenemhet I and, assuming that it was he who had been vizier to Mentuhotep III (p. 77), he seems to have risen from humble parents. An inscription from Karnak records a 'god's father' Senusret, a commoner, as the father of Amenemhet; his mother, Nefert, came from the area of Elephantine. Amenemhet was thus of Upper Egyptian origin and his religious allegiance was to the god Amun. It is from this period that Amun begins his rise to prominence, taking over from Montu, god of war, as supreme deity at Thebes; he was to reach his apogee in the 21st Dynasty when Herihor, High Priest of Amun, declared himself pharaoh.

Amenemhet's almost 30-year reign brought a degree of stability to Egypt that it had not seen for 200 years. It also laid the foundations for the strength of the 12th Dynasty, itself to continue for a further two centuries until the breakdown under Queen Sobeknefru and the confusion of the Second Intermediate Period.

Following his enthronement in *c*. 1991 BC, Amenemhet's first move

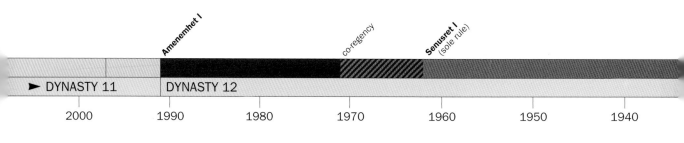

DYNASTY 11 | DYNASTY 12

Amenemhet I

co-regency

Senusret I (sole rule)

2000   1990   1980   1970   1960   1950   1940

(*Left*) Granite bust of Senusret I, from Memphis. British Museum.

(*Above*) Detail of the head of Amenemhet I from a painted and carved lintel block found in his mortuary temple at Lisht. Metropolitan Museum, New York.

(*Below*) Senusret I embraces the creator god Ptah on a pillar from the king's destroyed *heb-sed* temple at Karnak. Cairo Museum.

was to cruise the Nile with his fleet, crushing recalcitrant nomarchs, Asiatics and Nubians on the southern frontiers. He then set up a new power centre, away from both Thebes and Herakleopolis, almost 20 miles (32 km) south of the old capital of Memphis. The king chose the site so that he might keep a watchful eye on both Upper and Lower Egypt, and accordingly called his new city Itj-tawy, 'Seizer-of-the-Two-Lands'. The actual site of this fortified city has yet to be found.

Amenemhet's reign brought many changes, and to emphasize this renaissance, the king took the additional title of Wehem-meswet, 'Repeater-of-Births', implying that he was the first in a new line. Amenemhet's most significant act, however, was the introduction of the practice of co-regency, an institution that was to endure throughout the 12th Dynasty. Thus, in Year 20 of his reign, he associated his son Senusret with him, and they shared the throne for the ten years before Amenemhet's murder. During this period, the younger man was mainly in charge of military matters, such as maintaining the eastern and western borders and continuing to push to the south. An inscription dated in Year 24 of Amenemhet and Year 4 of Senusret, for example, records an expedition against the 'sand-dwellers' – the Asiatics who lurked on Egypt's north-eastern frontier towards the Gaza Strip.

The royal burial ground was moved once again and now located at Lisht, not far from the new capital, at the entrance to the Faiyum. Amenemhet's pyramid was similar to those built during the Old Kingdom, only smaller. The inner core was constructed with small limestone blocks, many of them taken from ruined Old Kingdom monuments at Giza and Abusir, while the exterior was faced with white Tura limestone, long since stolen. Likewise, the once finely relief-decorated mortuary temple on the east face has been largely destroyed. Little is known of the internal arrangements of the pyramid since access is denied by ground water seepage; the burial chamber was probably robbed in antiquity, although this has yet to be confirmed.

SENUSRET I

Judging by the 'The Story of Sinuhe', the young prince Senusret was away on an expedition against the Libyans in the western desert when Amenemhet was murdered. Senusret obviously hurried back to the capital and brought matters swiftly under control: he scotched any further attempts to spread the coup, and made arrangements for his father's burial at Lisht. The old king's astute decision to rule with his son for a

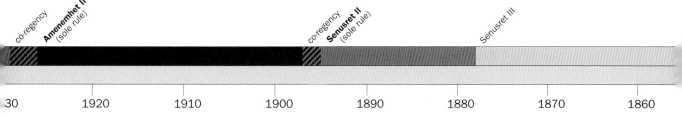

co-regency | Amenemhet II (sole rule) | co-regency | Senusret II (sole rule) | Senusret III

30   1920   1910   1900   1890   1880   1870   1860

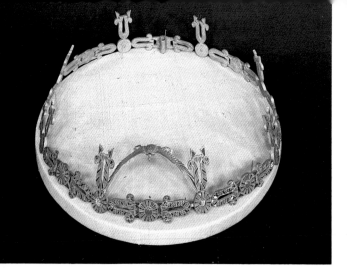

De Morgan's excavations in 1895 west of Amenemhet II's pyramid at Dahshur revealed splendid jewellery of the royal ladies, such as the two circlets of the princess Khnumet – one formal (*above left*), the other a delicate chaplet of golden water-weeds and flowers (*above right*). Her cowrie shell girdle was accompanied by a pectoral with Senusret II's cartouche (*below right*). His cartouche was also on a pectoral of the princess Sit-Hathor-Yunet (*bottom*), found by Petrie at Lahun, and in the king's pyramid there he found a royal *uraeus* (*below*). All in Cairo Museum, except Sit-Hathor-Yunet's pectoral, in Metropolitan Museum, New York.

decade paid dividends, and Senusret entered on a reign that was to last a further 34 years. The period from the 20th to the early 19th century BC in the 12th Dynasty was the zenith of Egyptian literature and craftsmanship, as attested by the remarkable examples of jewellery found in the tombs of the royal ladies at Dahshur and Lahun.

Senusret I consolidated many of the policies established by his father. Egypt looked to the south for gold and agricultural goods, maintaining its control over the region through a series of at least 13 forts which extended as far as the Second Cataract. Quarries and mines were exploited throughout the country, with hardstones coming from the Wadi Hammamat and gold from the mines near Coptos. Senusret also led various expeditions to the south and – for the first time – to the desert oases,

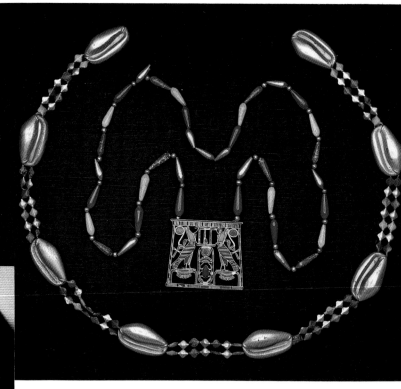

(*Right*) Most of the buildings erected by Senusret I have been wrecked or have disappeared, but this small processional kiosk – a gem of Middle Kingdom architecture – has been reconstructed from blocks rescued from the interior of a later 18th Dynasty pylon at Karnak, where they had been used as filling.

(*Above*) A detail from one of the pillars of the kiosk shows Senusret I offering small pots to the ithyphallic fertility god Amun-Min. The tall plants behind the god, and associated with him, are cos lettuce – still, as in antiquity, regarded as a potent aphrodisiac.

The tomb of the High Priest of Heliopolis, Imhotep, on the east side of Senusret I's pyramid, produced two 23-inch (59-cm) high wooden statues of the king holding a tall crook-topped (*hekat*) staff and respectively wearing the Red and the White Crowns. Cairo Museum (*left*); Metropolitan Museum, New York (*right*).

as recorded on inscriptions and stele at Beni Hassan and Assuit in Middle Egypt. The king's overall control of Egypt is documented at almost three dozen sites, from Alexandria to Aswan, where he carried out building work.

In Year 3 of his reign, Senusret rebuilt the temple to Re-Atum at the ancient centre of the sun cult, Heliopolis, and he actually appears to have performed part of the re-foundation ceremonies there. In Year 30, his Jubilee year, he erected two 66-ft (20-m) red granite obelisks there, each weighing 121 tons. One of the pair still stands and is the oldest standing obelisk in Egypt. Although the temple has entirely disappeared, an exceptionally rare and fragmentary leather scroll records part of the text from the great dedicatory stele of Senusret, probably copied down as a scribal exercise some 500 years afterwards.

Senusret took Amenemhet II, his son by his chief wife Queen Nefru, as co-ruler at least three years before his death, as recorded on a private stele of Simontu now in the British Museum. Senusret died in about 1926 BC, but not before he had built a pyramid at Lisht, a mile south of his father's monument. As in Amenemhet I's pyramid, the burial chamber is inaccessible due to ground water. Nine small satellite pyramids belonging to the royal ladies were also built within the complex. Excavations by the Metropolitan Museum, New York between 1908 and 1934 revealed the names of some of the tomb owners, but others lacked any identifying inscriptions on their sarcophagi or funerary equipment. Queen Nefru's pyramid, slightly larger than the others, stood in the south-east corner and that of Senusret's daughter Itekuyet was to the south of the king's pyramid. Other daughters probably included the princesses Nefru-Sobek, Nefru-Ptah and Nenseddjedet.

AMENEMHET II

Senusret was succeeded after his death *c.* 1926 BC by his son Amenemhet II, who continued the longevity of the family with a reign of 34 years. It was around this time that the Egyptians first began to recognize the opportunities available in the Faiyum area for hunting, fishing and cultivating, and it was thus to render the irrigation system more effective that the great Bahr Yusuf canal that feeds the Faiyum from the Nile was widened and deepened.

The foreign policy of Amenemhet II

Amenemhet II strove mainly to consolidate the work of his predecessors in foreign affairs, although there are records of an expedition to the Red Sea and, in Year 28, of another to the Land of Punt (p. 106). There is ample evidence of the exchange of diplomatic gifts between Egypt and the Levant during this period. Jewellery bearing the king's cartouche has been found in the royal tombs at Byblos in Lebanon (especially in that of the local prince, Ipshemuabi), together with local copies of typical 12th Dynasty jewellery. In Egypt, a great treasure was discovered in the foundations of the temple of Montu at Tod, just south of Luxor (Thebes), consisting of four bronze boxes inscribed on the lid in hieroglyphs with the name of Amenemhet II. The boxes contained a large number of silver cups of Levantine and Aegean origin, as well as Babylonian cylinder seals and lapis lazuli amulets from Mesopotamia. The whole hoard was probably either a diplomatic gift or tribute; the silver cups represented an extremely high intrinsic value at the time, since silver was far more precious than gold in Egypt.

There is also an apparent increase at this time in the number of Levantine names recorded in Egypt, presumably belonging to those brought in as domestic servants. Contacts with Crete to the north-west across the 'Great Green' (*wdj-wr*), as the Egyptians called the Mediterranean, are evident from Egyptian finds in Crete at Knossos (including the lower half of a statue of a man named User) and typical Minoan pottery – Kamares ware – in Egypt, at town sites such as Lahun and in a tomb at Abydos.

Amenemhet II built his pyramid at Dahshur to the east of the earlier 4th Dynasty pyramids of Snefru. Why he should have turned to that site is not known, although the choice may have been connected with the building projects close by in the Faiyum. All that now remains of his pyramid is a great mass of eroded mud brick, originally the core of a pyramid some 263 ft (80 m) square.

SENUSRET II

Continuing the family tradition of alternating names, Senusret II succeeded his father Amenemhet II in about 1895 BC, having been associated with his father as co-regent for at least three years. His reign was a

(*Above*) Seated diorite statue of Senusret II as a young man, found in the excavations of the temple at Nag-el-Medamoud, north of Thebes. Cairo Museum.

(*Above*) Black granite statue of Nofret, chief queen of Senusret II, found at Tanis. The queen wears a pectoral (incorporating her husband's cartouche) of similar workmanship to those of his daughters found at Dahshur and Lahun (p. 80). Cairo Museum.

(*Right*) The mud brick inner structure of Senusret II's pyramid at Lahun was stabilized by stone cross walls. Once the outer limestone casing had been robbed, however, the inner core swiftly deteriorated.

peaceful one, in which he continued the expansion of cultivation in the Faiyum and established a good rapport with the provincial élites. Indeed, inscriptions in the great tombs of the nomarchs at Beni Hassan in Middle Egypt (especially that of Khnumhotep II), bear witness to their cordial relations with the king and the honours he had bestowed upon them.

Senusret II chose to build his pyramid at Lahun, once again essentially of mudbrick that became heavily eroded when the outer limestone casing was gone. An innovation in an attempt to beat the tomb robbers was the location of the pyramid entrance in the surrounding pavement on the south (instead of the usual north) side, rather than in the actual structure. Even this failed to deter the looters, although in 1889 Flinders Petrie did find in the flooded burial chamber a marvellous gold and inlaid royal *uraeus* that must have come from the king's despoiled mummy (p. 80).

Returning to the site in 1913, Petrie excavated four shaft-tombs belonging to members of the royal family in a gulley on the south side of the pyramid. All had been robbed, but one, that of the princess Sit-Hathor-Yunet, produced a vast collection of personal jewellery and cosmetic items which had been placed in three ebony caskets in a side-wall niche. Due to the early flooding of the tomb the niche had filled up with mud and the robbers, who had smashed into the princess's sarcophagus, missed the hoard. Amongst the group were two extremely fine gold inlaid pectorals and a delightful diadem with tall thin gold plumes and inlaid rosettes on the headband (p. 80).

Near the pyramid Petrie found the 'pyramid town' built for the workers employed on the construction. Now known as Kahun, its original name was Hetep-Senusret – 'Senusret is satisfied'. Kahun was like an Egyptian Pompeii since it seems to have been suddenly abandoned, with many possessions left behind. Excavations at the site yielded fascinating new information about the social and economic life of the ancient Egyptians – the differences in prosperity within the community were revealed by the varying sizes and quality of the houses. Dozens of papyri – covering a great range of topics from accounts and legal texts to gynaecological and veterinary treatises – shed new light on the administration and logistics of a multi-racial and disciplined work force.

DYNASTY 12
1991–1782

Senusret III
Khakhaure
1878–1841

Amenemhet III
Nymaatre
1842–1797

Amenemhet IV
Maakherure
1798–1786

Queen Sobeknefru
Sobekkare
1785–1782

ROYAL NAMES AND BURIALS

SENUSRET III
Birth name
  S-en-usret ('Man of goddess Wosret')
Also known as
  Senwosret III, Sesostris III (Greek)
Throne name
  Kha-khau-re ('Appearing like the Souls of Re')
Burial
  Pyramid, Dahshur

AMENEMHET III
Birth name
  Amen-em-het ('Amun is at the Head')
Also known as
  Amenemhat III, Ammenemes III (Greek)
Throne name
  Ny-maat-re ('Belonging to the Justice of Re')
Burial
  Pyramid, Hawara

AMENEMHET IV
Birth name
  As above
Throne name
  Maa-kheru-re ('True of Voice is Re')
Burial
  ?Pyramid, Mazghuna (S. Dahshur)

QUEEN SOBEKNEFRU
Birth name
  Sobek-nefru ('Beautiful of the god Sobek')
Also known as
  Nefrusobk
Throne name
  Sobek-ka-re ('Sobek is the Soul of Re')
Burial
  ?Pyramid, Mazghuna (S. Dahshur)

SENUSRET III

Senusret came to the throne in about 1878 BC, and is thought to have reigned for 37 years. He is probably the best known, visually, of all the Middle Kingdom pharaohs with his brooding, hooded-eyed and careworn portraits, carved mainly in hard black granite. In Middle Kingdom royal portrait sculpture there is a move away from the almost bland, godlike and complacent representations of the Old Kingdom to a more realistic likeness. Part of this stems from the realization that the king, although still a god on earth, is nevertheless concerned with the earthly welfare of his people. The Egyptians no longer placed huge emphasis and resources on erecting great monuments to the king's immortal hereafter, as the rather inferior Middle Kingdom pyramids show. Instead, greater emphasis was placed on agricultural reforms and projects, best exemplified by the great Bahr Yusuf canal (p. 82).

Manetho describes Senusret as a great warrior, and unusually mentions that the king was of great height: '4 cubits 3 palms 2 fingers breadth' – over 6 ft 6 in (2 m). His commanding presence must have helped the success of his internal reforms in Egypt. Most notably he managed to curtail the activities of the local nomarchs, whose influence

Senusret III

co-regency
Amenemhet III
(sole rule)

1880   1870   1860   1850   1840   1830   1820

(*Left*) Seated black granite statue of Senusret III, immediately identifiable by his distinctive world-weary features and confirmed by the cartouche that is carved on his belt. Cairo Museum.

had once again risen to challenge that of the monarchy, by creating a new system of government that subjugated the autonomy of the nomarchs. The king divided the country into three administrative departments – the North, the South and the Head of the South (Elephantine and Lower Nubia) – each administered by a council of senior staff which reported to a vizier.

Senusret III as military leader

With the internal stability of the country assured, Senusret III was able to concentrate on foreign policy. He initiated a series of devastating campaigns in Nubia quite early in his reign, aimed at securing Egypt's southern borders against incursions from her bellicose neighbours and at safeguarding access to trade routes and to the mineral resources of Nubia. To facilitate the rapid and ready access of his fleets he had a bypass canal cut around the First Cataract at Aswan. A canal had existed here in the Old Kingdom, but Senusret III cleared, broadened and deepened it, repairing it again in Year 8 of his reign, according to an inscription. Senusret was forced to bring the Nubians into line on several occasions, in Years 12 and 15 of his reign, and he was clearly proud of his military prowess in subduing the recalcitrant tribes. A great stele at Semna (now in Berlin) records, 'I carried off their women, I carried off their subjects, went forth to their wells, smote their bulls: I reaped their

(*Left*) Red granite head of Senusret III, one of the most powerful portraits of the king. Found at Karnak in 1970. Luxor Museum.

(*Right*) Stele of Senusret III from Elephantine, with his name in both a cartouche and a *serekh,* that records building work on the fortress there during military activities to the south in Kush. British Museum.

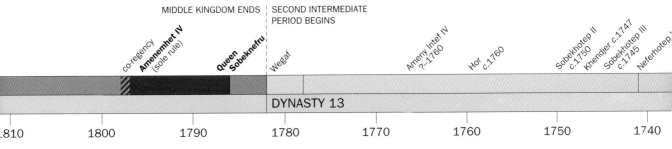

MIDDLE KINGDOM ENDS | SECOND INTERMEDIATE PERIOD BEGINS

co-regency
Amenemhet IV (sole rule)
Queen Sobeknefru
Wegaf
Ameny Intef IV ?–1760
Hor c.1760
Sobekhotep II c.1750
Khendjer c.1747
Sobekhotep III c.1745
Neferhotep

DYNASTY 13

810 1800 1790 1780 1770 1760 1750 1740

Two of Queen Mereret's pectorals deserve special attention for their workmanship. A cartouche on the first (*top*) indicates that this splendid piece was given to her by her husband Senusret III, but the second (*above*), a gift from her son Amenemhet III (evidencing that she outlived her husband), is of inferior workmanship and its design exhibits a *horror vacui* that detracts from the iconography and symbolism of the piece. From Dahshur; Cairo Museum.

A finely detailed relief from the temple of Medamoud, north of Thebes, shows the *heb-sed* festival of Senusret III with the king seated in the special pavilion and wearing respectively the Red Crown of Lower Egypt and the White Crown of Upper Egypt. Cairo Museum.

grain, and set fire thereto'. He pushed Egypt's boundary further south than any of his forebears and left an admonition for future kings: 'Now, as for every son of mine who shall maintain this boundary, which My Majesty has made, he is my son, he is born of My Majesty, the likeness of a son who is the champion of his father, who maintains the boundary of him that begat him. Now, as for him who shall relax it, and shall not fight for it; he is not my son, he is not born to me.' No wonder Senusret was worshipped as a god in Nubia by later generations, or that his sons and grandsons maintained their inheritance.

Although most of Senusret's military energies were directed against Nubia, there is also record of a campaign in Syria – but it seems to have been more one of retribution and to gain plunder than to extend the Egyptian frontiers in that direction.

The king as builder

Much of the wealth acquired in the Nubian campaigns was directed towards the temples in Egypt and their renewal. An inscription from Abydos of the official Ikhernofret tells of the king's commission that he refurbish Osiris's barge, shrine and chapels with gold, electrum, lapis lazuli, malachite and other costly stones. A series of six life-size granite standing figures of the king wearing the *nemes* headdress were commissioned for the temple of Mentuhotep I at Deir el-Bahari, Thebes, where they lined the lower terrace. Local graffiti record the maintenance of a large body of priests associated with the cult of Amun, indicating that although the capital and burial ground of the kings had moved to the north, interest and respect were still maintained for the religious centre of Thebes.

Just to the north of Karnak (Thebes) at Nag-el-Medamoud, Senusret III erected a large temple to the old god of the Theban area, the war god Montu. Remodelled in the New Kingdom, and also later in Ptolemaic and Roman times, the Middle Kingdom structure has disappeared, although the remains of two finely carved granite gateways of the original temple were found in 1920, together with some splendid statues and other inscriptions.

MILITARY ACTIVITY IN NUBIA

The Egyptians focused their military aspirations on Nubia (or Kush as they called it) during much of the 12th Dynasty, and sought to reinforce the border with a series of forts. Some of these were founded by Senusret I and II, but the majority were built by Senusret III. Papyrus dispatches from this period report the slightest movements within the area, and one lists 13 fortresses between Elephantine (Aswan) – the official southern boundary of Egypt – and Semna far to the south at the end of the Second Cataract. Seven of these fortresses were located within the 40-mile (64-km) stretch of the Second Cataract itself, and all were built in strategic positions with thick mud-brick walls.

Due to the imminent destruction of many of these sites during the flooding of Nubia in the 1960s when Lake Nasser was created,

The mudbrick fortification walls of the Middle Kingdom fortress at Buhen predate their later medieval European counterparts with enfilading fire bastions by some 3200 years.

international rescue excavations revealed much information about them. They were evidently big enough to be self-sufficient and to house all the necessary personnel – their like unparalleled until the great fortifications of medieval Europe. Sadly, the huge rounded bastion towers, complete with arrow slits covering angles of fire across a wide ditch, of the great fort at Buhen were excavated only to be lost once more under some 200 ft (61 m) of water of the lake formed by the Great High Dam at Aswan.

Senusret III built his pyramid in the Middle Kingdom cemetery at Dahshur. At 350 ft (107 m) square it is the largest of the 12th Dynasty pyramids, but the disappearance of the limestone casing has caused the mudbrick core to deteriorate severely. Like his father, he also attempted to conceal the entrance, this time under the paving of the surrounding court on the west side. Needless to say, the device was ineffective against tomb robbers. Excavations by Jacques de Morgan in 1894–95 in the northern section of Senusret's pyramid enclosure revealed the tombs of his queen, Mereret, and the princess Sit-Hathor – his sister and possibly wife. Both tombs produced some fine jewellery which survived because it was placed elsewhere in the tomb and not on the subsequently rifled mummies.

FROM AMENEMHET III TO QUEEN SOBEKNEFRU

Senusret's son, Amenemhet III, reigned for 45 years and, like his father, he left a series of portraits remarkable for their individuality and fine work. His reign was the apogee of economic growth in the Middle Kingdom. Interest in the agricultural potential of the Faiyum increased, and a huge temple was erected to the local crocodile god, Sobek, at Kiman Faris where he is associated with the falcon, Horus the Elder. Above all, Amenemhet III exploited the quarries of Egypt and the turquoise mines in Sinai. There are more than 50 rock inscriptions in

(*Above*) The softer features of a limestone statue of Amenemhet III from Hawara – the location of his pyramid – contrast with the strength of his priestly representation found not far away at Medinet el-Fayum (*below right*). Cairo Museum.

Sinai recording almost continual mining expeditions between Years 2 and 45 of his reign.

It is a curious fact that, despite his long reign, there are very few inscriptions of Amenemhet III from Egypt itself: over 90 per cent are from outside the country, e.g. from Sinai. They do, however, give a valuable insight into his reign and provide long lists of officials and works in the quarries.

Amenemhet's pyramids

An unusual feature of Amenemhet's reign, not seen since the Old Kingdom under Snefru, was that he built two pyramids for himself. One at Dahshur was 342 ft (104 m) square, the other at Hawara was 334 ft (102 m) square. The first must have been abandoned since the king was buried at Hawara, where his pyramid and the large associated structure on the south side of the pyramid, his mortuary temple, attracted the attention of several of the classical writers. From Herodotus (mid-fifth century BC) onwards, the great 1000 by 800 ft (305 x 244 m) building was hailed as a wonder, a veritable labyrinth to be compared with the fabled structure at Knossos, Crete. Strabo described its many rooms and corridors in minute detail, but when Petrie excavated the devastated site in 1888–89, he had the greatest difficulty in reconciling the few architectural details he uncovered with Strabo's description, so great was the ancient destruction.

Amenemhet's pyramid, as usual for the period, was built of mudbrick and cased with limestone. Once more the entrance was moved for better concealment and was located off-centre on the pyramid's south face. The internal arrangement of Amenemhet's pyramid was quite extraordinary, with dead-end passages, concealed trapdoors and sliding panels in passage roofs. A complicated series of three quartzite blocks topped by two relieving chambers of limestone blocks and a huge brick arch overall completed the arrangements. The burial chamber was a vast block of quartzite (22 x 8 ft, 7 x 2.5 m), hollowed out like a lidless box, which had

(*Left*) Detail of the cartouches of Amenemhet III on the shoulder of a black granite lion-maned sphinx with the king's face, from Tanis. Cairo Museum.

(*Right*) Amenemhet III is represented in a unique statue as a *setem*-priest with the appropriate regalia of heavy wig and necklace and wearing a leopard-skin cloak. From Medinet el-Fayum. Cairo Museum.

Once the outer limestone casing of the Middle Kingdom pyramids was robbed away, the mudbrick interior core soon became an eroded mass, as here with the pyramid of Amenemhet III at Dahshur.

been sunk into the ground and the pyramid built over it. Within the box/burial chamber were two quartzite sarcophagi, the larger for the king, the smaller for his daughter the princess Neferu-Ptah, together with their quartzite canopic chests. When the burials had been completed, the chamber was sealed by a single roofing slab of some 45 tons and then everything was backfilled to remove all traces. The internal security arrangements (reminiscent of the false doors and trapdoors seen in some curse-of-the-mummy-type films) should have been impenetrable, yet robbers still managed to penetrate the tomb, ravage the bodies and burn the wooden coffins.

The end of the dynasty

Amenemhet III was the last great ruler of the Middle Kingdom, as numerous inscriptions on monuments from Syria to the Third Cataract on the Nile testify. Little is known about his successor, Amenemhet IV. It is even possible that he did not reign independently but only as co-regent with his elderly father. It is presumed that he died prematurely and that a queen, Sobeknefru, acted as regent, apparently ruling later in her own right for a short time. Neither Amenemhet IV nor Queen Sobeknefru feature much in the written records. No pyramid definitely ascribed by inscriptions is known for either ruler, although it has been suggested that two pyramids located about 3 miles (4.8 km) south of Dahshur at Mazghuna might belong to them. This theory is based on the fact that the structures appear to be more sophisticated technically than the Hawara pyramid of Amenemhet III and should therefore be later. Since there are no other known rulers between Amenemhet III and the end of the dynasty, the theory may be correct.

A light blue glazed steatite cylinder seal gives the name of Queen Sobeknefru in a cartouche, followed by her Horus name 'The female Hawk, Beloved of Re', in a *serekh* with, beneath, her titles as 'Mistress of the South and North'. British Museum.

DYNASTY 13
1782–1650

 Wegaf
Khutawyre
1782–1778

 **Ameny Intef IV**
(Amenemhet V)
Sankhibre
(?)–1760

 Hor
Auyibre
c.1760

 **Sobekhotep II**
(Amenemhet VI)
Sekhemre Khutawy
c.1750

 Khendjer
Userkare
c.1747

 Sobekhotep III
Sekhemre Sewadjtawy
c.1745

 Neferhotep I
Khasekhemre
1741–1730

 Sobekhotep IV
Khaneferre
1730–1720

 Ay
Merneferre
c.1720

  Neferhotep II
Sekhemre Sankhtawy

DYNASTY 14

 Nehesy
Aasehre

The transition to the 13th Dynasty seems to have been a smooth one, despite the successional difficulties suggested by the presence of a woman on the throne at the end of the 12th Dynasty. Ten kings are listed for the new dynasty, which lasted for about 70 years, and they appear to have kept a degree of control over both Upper and Lower Egypt, still ruling from Itj-tawy near the Faiyum, until the reign of the penultimate king, **Merneferre Ay** (c. 1720 BC). Indeed, the internal chaos ascribed to the period in earlier literature is not so extreme as was once thought:

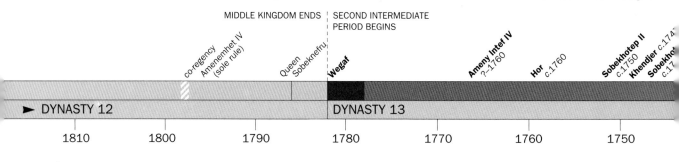

MIDDLE KINGDOM ENDS | SECOND INTERMEDIATE PERIOD BEGINS

co-regency Amenemhet IV (sole rule)

Queen Sobeknefru

Wegaf

Ameny Intef IV ?–1760

Hor c.1760

Sobekhotep II c.1750

Khendjer c.1747

Sobekhot c.17

► DYNASTY 12   DYNASTY 13

1810   1800   1790   1780   1770   1760   1750

ROYAL NAMES AND BURIALS

WEGAF
Birth name
Wegaf
Throne name
Khu-tawy-re ('Re
Protects the Two
Lands')

AMENY INTEF IV
Birth name
Ameny Intef Amen-
em-het ('Ameny
Intef, Amun is at
the Head')
Throne name
Sankh-ib-re ('The
Heart of Re Lives')

HOR
Birth name
Hor
Throne name
Auy-ib-re ('Re
Succours the
Heart')
Burial
Dahshur

SOBEKHOTEP II
Birth name
Amen-em-het
Sobek-hotep ('Amun
is at the Head,
Pleasing to the god
Sobek')
Also known as
Sebekhotpe II
Throne name
Sekh-em-re Khu-
tawy ('Powerful is
Re, Protector of the
Two Lands')
Burial
?Dahshur

KHENDJER
Birth name
Khendjer
Throne name
User-ka-re ('The
Soul of Re is
Powerful')
Burial
Pyramid, South
Saqqara

SOBEKHOTEP III
Birth name
Sobek-hotep

('Pleasing to the
god Sobek')
Throne name
Sekh-em-re Se-wadj-
tawy ('Powerful is
Re, He makes to
Flourish the Two
Lands')

NEFERHOTEP I
Birth name
Nefer-hotep
('Beautiful and
Pleasing')
Also known as
Neferhotpe I
Throne name
Kha-sekh-em-re
('Powerful is the
Soul of Re')

SOBEKHOTEP IV
Birth name
Sobek-hotep
('Pleasing to the
god Sobek')
Throne name
Kha-nefer-re
('Beautiful is the
Soul of Re')

AY
Birth name
Ay
Also known as
Aya
Throne name
Mer-nefer-re
('Beautiful is the
Desire of Re')

NEFERHOTEP II
Birth name
Nefer-hotep
('Beautiful and
Pleasing')
Throne name
Sekh-em-re S-ankh-
tawy ('Powerful is
Re, Giver of Life to
the Two Lands')

NEHESY
Birth name
Nehesy
Throne name
Aa-seh-re ('Great in
Council is Re')

central government was sustained during most of the dynasty and the country remained relatively stable. Evidence in the shape of inscriptions recording the Nile levels during some of the 13th Dynasty reigns indicates that a presence was maintained in the south, which says much for the strength of monarchical authority to the north.

The true chronology of the 13th Dynasty is rather hard to ascertain since there are few monuments dating from the period; many of the kings' names are known only from an odd fragmentary inscription or, a little later in the period, from scarabs. Merneferre Ay was the last king of the dynasty to be mentioned by name on monuments in Upper and Lower Egypt, and it seems that the eastern Delta broke away under its own petty kings about the time of his death. The confusion that followed is evident from the tales of woe in the contemporary papyri.

Our knowledge of the first few monarchs is rather scanty, but the burial of **Hor**, the third king, was found at Dahshur near the pyramid of Amenemhet III. This site was presumably chosen to indicate solidarity and continuity with the previous dynasty. According to the fragmentary Royal Canon of Turin papyrus, Hor's reign lasted only a matter of months, and his burial was relatively poor and low-key. Nevertheless it was intact and yielded a wooden shrine enclosing an impressive life-size wooden *ka*-statue of the king (p. 92).

At Saqqara there are four small, originally limestone-cased, brick pyramids ascribed to kings of the period, one at least to be identified with the fifth ruler **Khendjer Userkare**. Gustave Jéquier, the Swiss excavator, found very well-preserved internal arrangements within this pyramid. Its entrance passage, from the west face, was protected by two great quartzite portcullises, after which a complicated system of small passages eventually led to the burial chamber which had been hollowed out of a monolithic block of quartzite. Despite all these precautions, the robbers succeeded in reaching the chamber and effecting a small entry through the hard stone, although it is unclear whether there had ever been a burial within it. The identity of the builder was only revealed when fragments of palm-shaped columns found in the nearby mortuary temple produced cartouches of Khendjer. Jéquier also found the king's inscribed black granite pyramidion, badly smashed, in the temple ruins. Within a nearby enclosure were three burial shafts leading to underground rooms, each with a roughly finished quartzite sarcophagus, and there was also a small brick-core pyramid. All were, no doubt, intended for royal ladies, but were apparently never used. Graffiti on some blocks indicated a reign of four years for King Khendjer.

...otep I   Sobekhotep IV   Ay c.1720   Neferhotep II (precise dates unknown)   DYNASTY 14 Nehesy (precise dates unknown)

[DYNASTY 14 ? Contemporaneous with late DYNASTY 13]

| 1730 | 1720 | 1710 | 1700 | 1690 | 1680 | 1670 |

Around the middle of the dynasty three brothers – **Neferhotep I**, **Sobekhotep IV** and Sihathor seem to have reigned, although the last may not actually have been a king, but merely a prince. Evidence of overseas connections is furnished by inscriptions and a relief from Byblos of Neferhotep with his vassal, Yantin Prince of Byblos, seated before him; there are also records of an expedition to the mines of the eastern desert. Neferhotep's son, Wahneferhotep, is known from a wooden *ushabti* found at Lisht (now in New York), but he presumably predeceased his father. Several large red granite statues of Sobekhotep survive, three of them found at Tanis in the Delta where they were probably taken either from Memphis or Avaris (Tell el-Daba) later in the 21st or 22nd Dynasty.

Coincidental with the last years of the 13th Dynasty, the obscure 14th Dynasty ruled from the eastern Delta. It lasted for some 57 years, although only two kings are known from contemporary monuments.

(*Right*) The life-size wooden *ka*-statue of King Hor from Dahshur has the upraised arms of the *ka* (soul) sign on its head and is made remarkably lifelike by the use of rock crystal and white quartz in a copper surround to represent the eyes. Cairo Museum.

(*Far right*) Red granite life-size seated statue of Sobekhotep IV, a rare royal statue of the period. Louvre, Paris.

DYNASTY 15
Sheshi
Yakubher
Khyan
Apepi I
Apepi II
DYNASTY 16
Anather
Yakobaam
DYNASTY 17
Sobekemsaf II
Intef VII

Sanakhtenre Tao I
c.1633

DYNASTIES 15/16
DYNASTY 17

1660   1650   1640   1630   1620   1610   1600

DYNASTY 15 (Hyksos)
1663–1555

 Sheshi
Mayebre

 Apepi I
Auserre

 **Yakubher**
Meruserre

 Apepi II
Aqenenre

 **Khyan**
Seuserenre

DYNASTY 16
1663–1555

 **Anather**

 Yakobaam

DYNASTY 17 (Thebes)
1663–1570

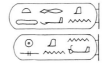 **Sobekemsaf II**
Sekhemre Shedtawy

 Tao II
Seqenenre
*c.*1574

 Intef VII
Nubkheperre

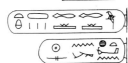 **Kamose**
Wadjkheperre
1573–1570

 **Tao I**
Sanakhtenre
*c.*1633

Scarabs (*left to right*) of Sheshi, Khyan and Apepi I.

The ephemeral kings of the 14th Dynasty were not the only group to set themselves up alongside the main house at the end of the 13th Dynasty: a series of Semitic kings was beginning to assume control in the eastern desert and Delta regions of Egypt. These rulers, the 15th Dynasty, are known as the Hyksos, 'Desert Princes' (*Hikau-khoswet*), often inaccurately referred to as the 'Shepherd Kings'.

Manetho's account of this period is preserved at great length in

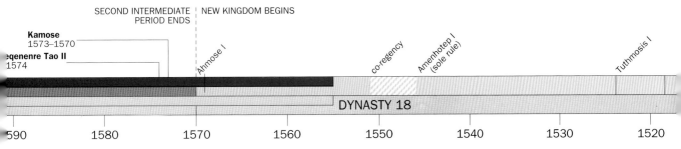

ROYAL NAMES	
SHESHI	**SOBEKEMSAF II**
Birth name	*Birth name*
Sheshi	Sobek-em-sa-f
Throne name	('Sobek is his
Ma-yeb-re ('Seeing	Protection')
is the Heart of Re')	*Also known as*
	Sebekemzaf II
YAKUBHER	*Throne name*
Birth name	Sekh-em-re Shed-
Yakubher	tawy ('Powerful is
Throne name	Re, Rescuer of the
Mer-user-re ('Strong	Two Lands')
is the Love of Re')	
	INTEF VII
KHYAN	*Birth name*
Birth name	Intef
Khyan	*Also known as*
Also known as	Inyotef VII
Khian	*Throne name*
Throne name	Nub-kheper-re
Se-user-en-re	('Golden is the
('Powerful like Re')	Manifestation of
	Re')
APEPI I–II	
Birth name	**TAO I–II**
Apepi	*Birth name*
Also known as	Tao
Apophis I, II (Greek)	*Also known as*
Throne name (I)	Taa I, II
Au-ser-re ('Great	*Throne name (I)*
and Powerful like	Sa-nakht-en-re
Re')	('Perpetuated like
Throne name (II)	Re')
Aqen-en-re ('Spirit	*Throne name (II)*
of Re')	Seqen-en-re ('Who
	strikes like Re')
ANATHER	
Birth name	**KAMOSE**
Heka Khaswt	*Birth name*
Anather ('Ruler of	Kamose
the Desert Lands	*Throne name*
Anather')	Wadj-kheper-re
	('Flourishing is the
YAKOBAAM	Manifestation of
Birth name	Re')
Yakobaam	

Contra Apionem by the Jewish historian Josephus, but it must be remembered that Manetho was writing as a Graeco-Egyptian about the greatest disaster that ever struck ancient Egypt: rule by foreign nationals. While later Egyptian records suggest a great invasion of a desperate horde through the eastern Delta, in reality Semitic immigrants had been steadily entering Egypt for some time. This is evident not only from the names recorded on Middle Kingdom stele and in some lists of servants, but also from the 12th Dynasty paintings of Asiatics in the tomb of the noble Khnumhotep II at Beni Hassan in Middle Egypt. These settlers gradually acquired increasing authority, but it was not until late in the 18th century BC that they began to extend their rule beyond their base at Avaris (the modern Tell el-Daba, currently being excavated by Manfred Bietak of the University of Vienna).

The five (possibly six) main Hyksos rulers identified by Manetho are allocated a span of 108 years in the Turin papyrus, the lengths of their individual reigns being uncertain. Unfortunately, most of the Turin papyrus is damaged, and the figure given for **Sheshi**, the nominal founder, may be 13 or 23 years; likewise his successor, **Yakubher**, may have reigned for either 8 or 18 years. The longest reigning king was the fourth in the sequence, **Auserre Apepi I** (also known as Apophis), who ruled for about 40 years.

The Hyksos sacked the Egyptian capital of Memphis in about 1720 BC, but they still preferred to operate from their eastern Delta strongholds such as Avaris and Tell el-Yahudiyeh. Appropriately for a people associated with the desert, they chose as their pre-eminent deity a god of the desert wastes, Seth. They also introduced other foreign gods and goddesses from their Phoenician homelands, such as the mother-goddess, Astarte, and the storm and war god, Reshep.

Diplomatic relations outside Egypt

At Tell el-Daba (Avaris) in the north-eastern Delta, there is evidence from the recent excavations of terrible destruction wrought upon the palaces there. Incredible Minoan-style wall-painting fragments (which might even predate the Minoan frescoes at Knossos on Crete) have been found scattered in a garden area at the site, testifying not only to the intensity of the onslaught but, more importantly, to connections with the Minoan artistic world. Another Cretan connection is a circular alabaster jar lid found in the palace of Knossos, inscribed with the cartouche of the third Hyksos king, Khyan. His name has also been found in a graffito inscription scratched on the shoulder of a red granite Middle Kingdom couchant sphinx which was, curiously, found in Baghdad. Khyan is better known from inscribed material than his brother kings, most of whom are only known from scarabs (which are the characteristic artifacts of the dynasty).

Records for the period of the Hyksos are sparse, probably due to two main factors. First, their influence was largely confined to the Delta and the northern areas of Egypt, where they had their centre of authority.

Excavations at Tell-el-Daba in the eastern Delta (*right*: late Hyksos period) have produced a remarkable series of painted wall plaster fragments, many of which have close parallels with well-known Minoan frescoes from Knossos, e.g. the bull-leaping sports where an athlete somersaults over the back of a charging bull (*below*).

Secondly, to have foreign rulers was regarded as a terrible thing in ancient Egypt and – once the essential equilibrium had been restored – there was a definite movement of *damnatio memoriae*, and Hyksos monuments would have been obliterated or destroyed.

The ephemeral 16th Dynasty (minor kings who almost certainly operated in the shadow of and by the authority of the Hyksos rulers at Avaris) produces only two names – **Anather** and **Yakobaam** – which do not occur in cartouches and are largely only known from scarabs found in northern Egypt and southern Palestine.

The rise of the 17th Dynasty

While the Hyksos kings assumed control in the north of the country, a new line of rulers, the 17th Dynasty, was evolving in Thebes. The Theban kings ruled an area from Elephantine to Abydos, and in spite of the scant resources at their disposal they largely succeeded in preserving the culture of the Middle Kingdom. The earlier rulers of the dynasty made no apparent attempt to challenge the authority of the Hyksos, and an uneasy truce existed between the two lineages for some time. Evidence of this comes from a fragmentary letter (now in the British Museum) in which the Hyksos king Apepi I complains to his Theban counterpart **Seqenenre Tao** that he was unable to sleep in Avaris because

(*Right*) The terrible wounds on Seqenenre's skull were caused by at least two people attacking him with a dagger, an axe, a spear and possibly a mace. The horizontal nature of four of the five wounds indicate that he was lying on his right side, either asleep or having been felled by a blow. The body was hurriedly embalmed (perhaps on the battlefield) without the usual careful preparation and straightening of limbs. Cairo Museum.

of the roaring of hippopotami 500 miles (800 km) away at Thebes, and suggests that Seqenenre do something about it. Sadly, the end of the tale is not preserved. Later members of the Theban dynasty were more militant, and rose against the Hyksos in a series of battles which were eventually to force the interlopers from Egypt. Seqenenre himself was probably killed in one of the battles since his mummy, discovered in the royal cache at Deir el-Bahari in 1881, shows evidence of terrible wounds about the head. His death was not in vain, for it was one of his sons, Ahmose, who was finally to drive out the Hyksos and found the 18th Dynasty.

Many of the first kings of the 17th Dynasty were known as **Intef**, and their large and heavy coffins with vulture-wing feathered decoration (called *rishi* coffins) have been found at Thebes in the area of the Dra Abu el-Naga on the west bank. The tombs themselves were poor, cut

(*Left*) Several coffins are known for the Intef kings, but they are difficult to distinguish. This example may have belonged to Intef VII (Nubkheperre). British Museum.

(*Right*) A hard green-stone heart scarab set in a gold surround inscribed on its base with Chapter 30B of the Book of the Dead and the cartouche of a king Sobekemsaf, possibly the same whose tomb was robbed by the stone mason Amun–pnufer around 1124 BC. British Museum.

into the Theban hillside and usually marked by steep-sided brick-built pyramids.

The tomb of another 17th Dynasty king, **Sobekemsaf II**, had apparently remained intact until the reign of the 20th Dynasty king Ramesses IX, when a certain Amun-pnufer and a gang of seven accomplices robbed the burial of the king and his queen, Nubkha-es, in about 1124 BC. A green-stone heart scarab set in gold inscribed on the base for a Sobekemsaf may refer to this king. Now in the British Museum, it was acquired in the 19th century with the coffin of his successor, **Nubkheperre Intef**; they were possibly found together, in which case the scarab may have been in a re-used context.

The expulsion of the Hyksos

The simmering hostilities between the Thebans and their northern rivals erupted, as we have seen, during the reign of Seqenenre Tao, and his son **Kamose** was to continue the battle for complete sovereignty of Egypt. The official account of Kamose's campaign is related on two stele from Karnak. The first survives only in a much damaged condition, but fortunately the introductory text is known from another source, a writing board now in the British Museum known as the Carnarvon Tablet. A preamble on the first stele outlines the current situation in Egypt: the country was nominally at peace, with Kamose holding the middle areas, the Hyksos controlling the north and the princes of Kush in command south of Elephantine. Unsurprisingly, the court could not see why Kamose should wish to upset the status quo, but the king was determined to march. According to the stele, Kamose had some success by virtue of the element of surprise – the Hyksos had not apparently expected to be attacked outright. However, the king's reign was short, no more than three regnal years being recorded, and he was buried at Thebes in an unpretentious, *rishi*-type coffin that was found in 1857 buried in rubble near where his tomb was recorded by inspectors under Ramesses IX.

The account of the struggles against the Hyksos is continued in a small private tomb at el-Kab, just to the north of Aswan. Carved in vertical columns of hieroglyphs immediately inside the entrance is the autobiography of a local noble of the city of Nekheb (el-Kab), Ahmose son of Ebana; it is the only contemporary account extant of the final defeat of the Hyksos. Ahmose served in the army under Kamose's successor, Ahmose I. The new king resumed the war with the Hyksos about half way through his 24-year reign, leading a series of attacks against Memphis, Avaris, and other Hyksos strongholds. Ahmose son of Ebana not only took part in the siege of Avaris, the second and third battles of Avaris, and the city's eventual capture, but also pursued the beleaguered Hyksos into Palestine and laid siege to their town of Sharuhen.

At last, after a hard-fought campaign, the Hyksos were expelled from Egypt and the princely line of Thebes, in the person of Ahmose I, inaugurated the 18th Dynasty and the New Kingdom.

THE AUTOBIOGRAPHY OF AHMOSE, SON OF EBANA

The noble Ahmose came from a military family. His father had served under Seqenenre II, and Ahmose himself entered the army as a young man. In his autobiography (inscribed on the walls of his tomb at el-Kab) he wanted the world to know how he had served under three successive kings: Ahmose I, Amenhotep I and Tuthmosis I, their reigns spanning the years 1570 to 1524 BC. His proud opening remarks set the scene:

I will tell you, O all ye people; I will cause you to know the honours which came to me. I was presented with gold [by the king for bravery] seven times in the presence of the whole land; male and female slaves likewise. I was endowed with many fields. The fame of one valiant in his achievements shall not perish in this land forever.

Promoted to officer, Ahmose served in many of the campaigns to expel the Hyksos. He boasts that, 'I took captive there [Avaris] one man and three women, total four heads, and His Majesty gave them to me for slaves'. He also fought in Nubia. In all he took part in ten campaigns – small wonder that he twice received the 'gold of valour'. This was the order of the 'Golden Fly' (the ancient Egyptian equivalent of the British Victoria Cross) of which three examples were found on a gold chain in the coffin of Queen Aahotep (p. 102). Ahmose eventually died an old and honoured warrior, loaded down with decorations and land.

| Tuthmosis I | Queen Hatshepsut | Tuthmosis III | Amenhotep III |

DYNASTY 18
1570–1293

Ahmose I
1570–1546

Amenhotep I
1551–1524

Tuthmosis I
1524–1518

Tuthmosis II
1518–1504

Tuthmosis III
1504–1450

Queen Hatshepsut
1498–1483

Amenhotep II
1453–1419

Tuthmosis IV
1419–1386

Amenhotep III
1386–1349

Amenhotep IV
(Akhenaten)
1350–1334

Smenkhkare
1336–1334

Tutankhamun
1334–1325

Ay
1325–1321

Horemheb
1321–1293

DYNASTY 19
1293–1185

Ramesses I
1293–1291

Seti I
1291–1278

Ramesses II
1279–1212

Merneptah
1212–1202

Amenmesses
1202–1199

Seti II
1199–1193

Siptah
1193–1187

Queen Twosret
1187–1185

DYNASTY 20
1185–1070

Setnakhte
1185–1182

Ramesses III
1182–1151

Ramesses IV
1151–1145

Ramesses V
1145–1141

Ramesses VI
1141–1133

Ramesses VII
1133–1126

Ramesses VIII
1133–1126

Ramesses IX
1126–1108

Ramesses X
1108–1098

Ramesses XI
1098–1070

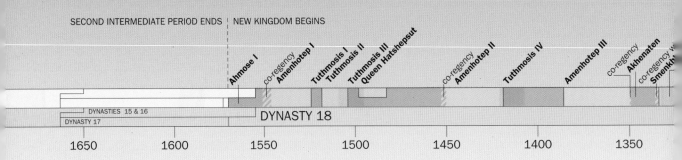

SECOND INTERMEDIATE PERIOD ENDS | NEW KINGDOM BEGINS

Ahmose I   co-regency Amenhotep I   Tuthmosis I   Tuthmosis II   Tuthmosis III   Queen Hatshepsut   co-regency Amenhotep II   Tuthmosis IV   Amenhotep III   co-regency Akhenaten   co-regency Smenkh

DYNASTIES 15 & 16
DYNASTY 17
DYNASTY 18

1650   1600   1550   1500   1450   1400   1350

Akhenaten

Tutankhamun

Ramesses II

Ramesses VI

RULERS OF AN EMPIRE
The New Kingdom 1570–1070 BC

THERE CAN BE little doubt that the pharaohs of the New Kingdom, spanning half a millennium of Egyptian history, were indeed god-like beings on earth. Their immense works, temples and fortresses have left their stamp upon the face of Egypt. We can gaze upon many of their actual faces for, by a strange quirk of fate, the despoiled mummies of the major pharaohs of the period were preserved hidden in two great caches of bodies found in the last century at Deir el-Bahari and in the tomb of Amenhotep II in the Valley of the Kings. Here lay Tuthmosis III, the 'Napoleon' of ancient Egypt; Ramesses II, great soldier, builder and the original of Shelley's 'Ozymandias, King of Kings'; and Ramesses III, who repulsed the Sea Peoples and left graphic representations of his land and sea battles at Medinet Habu.

There are other, perhaps to some people more emotive, names: Akhenaten – was he a heretic, the first monotheist in history, or simply a religious maniac? And, most famously, the pitiful remains of the boy pharaoh Tutankhamun, found in his virtually intact tomb in the Valley of the Kings in 1922, surrounded by gold, his slim teenage body encased in a solid gold coffin.

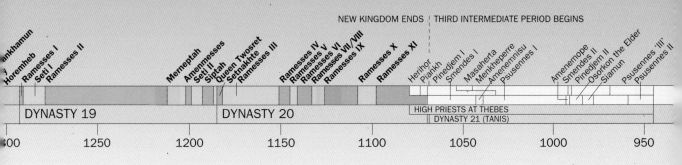

NEW KINGDOM ENDS | THIRD INTERMEDIATE PERIOD BEGINS

Tutankhamun
Horemheb
Ramesses I
Seti I
Ramesses II

Merneptah
Amenmesses
Seti II
Siptah
Queen Twosret
Sethnakhte
Ramesses III

Ramesses IV
Ramesses V
Ramesses VI/VIII
Ramesses VII/IX

Ramesses X
Ramesses XI

Herihor
Piankh
Pinedjem I
Smendes I
Masaherta
Menkheperre
Amenemnisu
Psusennes I

Amenemope
Smendes II
Pinedjem II
Osorkon the Elder
Siamun
Psusennes 'III'
Psusennes II

DYNASTY 19

DYNASTY 20

HIGH PRIESTS AT THEBES
DYNASTY 21 (TANIS)

1300 · 1250 · 1200 · 1150 · 1100 · 1050 · 1000 · 950

DYNASTY 18
1570–1293

Ahmose I
Nebpehtyre
1570–1546

Amenhotep I
Djeserkare
1551–1524

Tuthmosis I
Akheperkare
1524–1518

Tuthmosis II
Akheperenre
1518–1504

ROYAL NAMES AND BURIALS

AHMOSE I
Birth name
  Ah-mose ('The
  Moon is born')
Also known as
  Ahmosis I (Greek)
Throne name
  Neb-pehty-re ('The
  Lord of Strength is
  Re')
Burial
  ?Dra Abu el-Naga
  (Thebes)

AMENHOTEP I
Birth name
  Amen-hotep ('Amun
  is Pleased')
Also known as
  Amenhotpe I,
  Amenophis I
  (Greek)
Throne name
  Djeser-ka-re ('Holy
  is the Soul of Re')
Burial
  ?Dra Abu el-Naga
  (Thebes) or ?Tomb
  KV 39, Valley of the
  Kings (Thebes)

TUTHMOSIS I
Birth name
  Tuthmosis (Greek)
  ('Born of the god
  Thoth')
Also known as
  Thutmose I,
  Thutmosis I
  (Greek),
  Djehutymes I
  (Egyptian)
Throne name
  A-kheper-ka-re
  ('Great is the Soul
  of Re')
Burial
  Tombs KV 20 & KV
  38, Valley of the
  Kings (Thebes)

TUTHMOSIS II
Birth name
  As Tuthmosis I
Throne name
  A-kheper-en-re
  ('Great is the Form
  of Re')
Burial
  ?Tomb KV42, Valley
  of the Kings

AHMOSE I

With the expulsion of the Hyksos, the princes of Thebes now reigned supreme. The war against the Hyksos had not been without cost: Ahmose lost his father Seqenenre II and his brother Kahmose within about three years of each other, leaving him heir to the throne at a very young age. His mother, the redoubtable Queen Aahotep, was a powerful force in the land and may have been co-regent with him in the early years of his reign.

After expelling the Hyksos, Ahmose was faced with the task of consolidating Egypt's borders, which he did with a series of rapid campaigns that sealed the Syrian border and brought Nubia (Kush) to heel. There must also have been much to do domestically and Ahmose seems to have devolved a great deal of the responsibility on to local governors in the *nomes*. He encouraged support for his regime with gifts of land – as recorded by Ahmose son of Ebana in his tomb at el-Kab (p. 97) – and initiated temple building projects, the best evidence of which comes from remains and inscriptions at Abydos.

Manetho gives Ahmose I a reign of 25 to 26 years, which is substantiated by Josephus, who allocates 25 years and 4 months to the king.

NEW KINGDOM
BEGINS

DYNASTY 18

1570   1560   1550   1540   1530   1520   1510   15

(*Left*) Painted seated statue of Amenhotep I. Turin Museum.

Scarab of Tuthmosis I pursuing a foe that well illustrates the king's military prowess. British Museum.

After his death, Ahmose was buried in the Dra Abu el-Naga area of the Theban necropolis, in front of the Theban hills. Curiously, although his well-preserved mummy was found in the great royal cache of 1881, and Wallis Budge bought a unique limestone portrait *ushabti* of the king for the British Museum in the 1890s, the location of his tomb is unknown.

AMENHOTEP I

Amenhotep I, who reigned for a quarter of a century like his father Ahmose I, has left us few records. According to Ahmose son of Ebana, the king led a military expedition to Kush, where 'His Majesty captured that Nubian Troglodyte in the midst of his army.' A contemporary of Ahmose at el-Kab, Ahmose-Pen-Nekhbet, also mentions a Nubian campaign, and possibly a Libyan one. The king initiated building work at the temple of Karnak, too, as is attested in the autobiographical inscription of Ineni the architect, 'Chief of all Works at Karnak' (Theban tomb 81).

Amenhotep appears to have been the first king to take the radical decision to site his mortuary temple away from his burial place. The location of the latter, however, is uncertain, for although an uninscribed tomb at the Dra Abu el-Naga has been assigned to him, some suggest that a small, undecorated and anciently robbed tomb in the Valley of the Kings (KV 39) belonged to him. Wherever the tomb was, the commission of inspection in Year 16 of Ramesses IX reported it to be intact, according to the Abbott Papyrus. Like his father Ahmose, Amenhotep I's mummy was found in excellent condition in the 1881 royal mummy cache.

TUTHMOSIS I

Amenhotep I was succeeded not by his son (a break with tradition that would usually indicate a change in dynasty), but by a military man, Tuthmosis, already in middle-age when he achieved supreme power. He may have partly legitimized his rule by acting as co-regent with Amenhotep in the last years of the old king's reign. His main claim to the throne, however, was through his wife, the princess Ahmose, who was the daughter of Ahmose I and Queen Ahmose Nefertary. Since ancient Egypt was a matrilineal society, he had thus married into the royal blood line.

Although Tuthmosis had a short reign of only about six years, it was marked by a series of brilliant military campaigns that were to set the seal on most of the rest of the 18th Dynasty (the Amarna period apart, pp. 120ff). Presumably some start or preparations must have been made in the last years of Amenhotep I for Tuthmosis to have been able to inaugurate his military movements so rapidly and effectively. Ahmose son of Ebana was still on active service during this period, and he recounts how he was promoted to admiral, was highly successful in the

TWO LADIES OF THE COURT

Ahmose had two strong-willed and influential women in his immediate family. The first was his grandmother, Tetisheri, the founding matriarch of the dynasty. Greatly honoured by her descendants, she was provided not only with a lavish tomb but also with a pyramid and chapel at the sacred site of Abydos, complete with a full staff of mortuary priests. Tetisheri gave birth to Ahmose's father Seqenenre II and his mother, Aahotep, who was herself a formidable character.

Aahotep was extolled in a most unusual way on the great stele of Ahmose at Karnak as 'one who cares for Egypt. She has looked after her [Egypt's] soldiers; she has guarded her; she has brought back her fugitives and collected together her deserters; she has pacified Upper Egypt, and expelled her rebels.' So, as well as probably being co-regent with her son, she was evidently also an active military leader. This is further demonstrated by a superb battleaxe (*below*) and three 'Golden Fly' awards for valour which were found in her intact coffin at Thebes in 1859.

The blade of King Ahmose's ceremonial axe, found in his mother's coffin. Here he is shown killing an Asiatic. Cairo Museum.

Nubian campaign and returned therefrom with 'that wretched Nubian Troglodyte being hanged head downward at the prow of the barge of His Majesty'.

Under Tuthmosis the grip of the priests of Amun at Karnak began to take hold, as the king extensively remodelled and restored the great temple to the chief of the gods under his architect Ineni. On his great Abydos stele, Tuthmosis records not only his vast building work there but also the fact that 'I made the boundaries of Egypt as far as that which the sun encircles . . . I made Egypt the superior of every land.'

TUTHMOSIS II

Tuthmosis I died in about 1518 BC, leaving behind a complicated situation *vis à vis* his successor to the throne. His two elder sons – the princes Wadjmose and Amenmose – predeceased their father, so the young third son became heir. Also called Tuthmosis, the new king was son of a minor royal wife, the princess Mutnefert (sister of Tuthmosis I's queen, Ahmose). In order to strengthen the youngster's position, therefore, he was married to his half-sister Hatshepsut, elder daughter of Tuthmosis I and Queen Ahmose. Together Tuthmosis II and Hatshepsut reigned for about 14 years until he died in his early thirties. Despite his apparent poor health, the king prosecuted successful campaigns in both Syria and Nubia, attested by a short inscription in the temple at Deir el-Bahari and a rock inscription at Aswan. Old retainers such as Ineni the architect were still serving the court: 'I was a favourite of the king in his every place . . . I attained the old age of the revered, I possessed the favour of His Majesty every day. I was supplied from the table of the king with bread.'

Tuthmosis II had one son, likewise Tuthmosis, by Isis, a harem-girl. He may also have had a daughter, Neferure, by Hatshepsut. The king must have realized the overweening ambition of his wife and half-sister and endeavoured to curtail it by declaring his son his successor before he died. In the event, Tuthmosis III was still a young child when he succeeded to the throne and his stepmother and aunt Hatshepsut initially acted as regent for the young king. As Ineni's autobiography succinctly noted, 'His son [Tuthmosis III] stood in his [Tuthmosis II's] place as King of the Two Lands, having become ruler upon the throne of the one who begat him. His sister the Divine Consort, Hatshepsut, settled the affairs of the Two Lands by reason of her plans. Egypt was made to labour with bowed head for her, the excellent seed of the god, which came forth from him.' Ineni, however, remained in the queen's favour: 'Her Majesty praised me, she loved me, she recognized my worth at court, she presented me with things, she magnified me . . . I increased beyond everything.'

By regnal Year 2 of the young Tuthmosis III, Hatshepsut had her propaganda machine in place and working, and usurped her stepson's position.

THE ROYAL MUMMY CACHES

The burials of the New Kingdom pharaohs were continually subject in ancient times to the depradations of tomb robbers. In about 1000 BC, the priests, growing concerned over the rewrapping and burying of the ravaged mummies, decided to gather them together and hide them in two caches, where they lay for almost 2000 years. The first group was found in the 1870s near Deir el-Bahari at Thebes by three brothers who plundered the tomb in secret until Egyptologists were led to the tomb in 1881 (DB 320). The cache consisted of an astonishing 40 mummies belonging to many famous pharaohs. The second group of a further 16 mummies was discovered in the tomb of Amenhotep II (KV 35) in the Valley of the Kings in 1898. Some are now displayed in a special room at the Cairo Museum.

Mummies found in the 1881 royal cache (DB 320)
Ahmose Hentempet (p)
Ahmose Henuttimehu (q)
Ahmose Inhapi (q)
Ahmose Meryetamun (q)
Ahmose Nefertary (q)
Ahmose Sipair (prince)

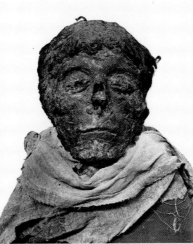

Ahmose I, founder of the New Kingdom.

Ahmose Sitkamose (q)
Amenhotep I (k)
Ahmose I (k)
Bakt (f)
Djedptahaufankh (m)
Henuttawy (q)
Isiemkheb (p)
Maatkare Mutemhet (q)
Masaharta (m)
Neskhons (q)
Nestanebtishru (p)
Nodjmet (q)
Pinedjem I (k)
Pinedjem II (k)

Rai (f)
Ramesses II (k)
Ramesses III (k)
Ramesses IX (k)
Seqenenre Tao (k)
Seti I (k)
Siamun (k)
Sitamun (p)
Taweret (q)
Tuthmosis I (k)
Tuthmosis II (k)
Tuthmosis III (k)
8 anonymous mummies, not all necessarily royal (but the 'unknown woman B' may be Queen Tetisheri)

Mummies found in the 1898 royal cache (KV 35)
Amenhotep II (k)
Amenhotep III (k)
Merneptah (k)
Ramesses IV (k)
Ramesses V (k)
Ramesses VI (k)
Seti II (k)
Siptah (k)
Tiy (?) (q), the 'Elder Woman'
Tuthmosis IV (k)
6 anonymous human remains, not all necessarily royal

KEY   k = *king*   m = *male*
         q = *queen*   f = *female*
         p = *princess*

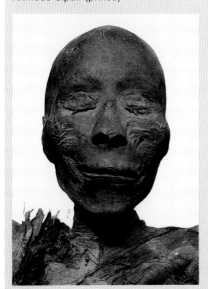

Tuthmosis I

Tuthmosis II

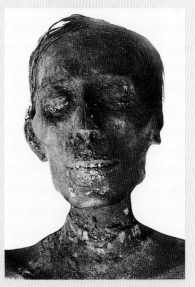

Tuthmosis IV

DYNASTY 18
1570–1293

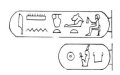

Queen Hatshepsut
Maatkare
1498–1483

Tuthmosis III
Menkheperre
1504–1450

Several fine seated and standing statues of Hatshepsut were found in almost pristine condition in the quarry in front of her temple at Deir el-Bahari, where they had been tumbled under Tuthmosis III. Metropolitan Museum of Art, New York.

QUEEN HATSHEPSUT	
Birth name	*Husband*
Hat-shepsut	Tuthmosis II
('Foremost of Noble	*Daughters*
Ladies')	Neferure
Throne name	*Burial*
Maat-ka-re ('Truth is	Tomb KV 20, Valley
the Soul of Re')	of the Kings
Father	(Thebes)
Tuthmosis I	
Mother	
Ahmose	

TUTHMOSIS III	
Birth name	*Father*
Tuthmosis (Greek)	Tuthmosis II
('Born of the god	*Mother*
Thoth')	Isis
Also known as	*Wives*
Thutmose III,	Neferure,
Thutmosis III	Hatshepsut-
(Greek),	Meryetre, Menhet,
Djehutymes III	Menwi, Merti
(Egyptian)	*Son*
Throne name	Amenhotep II
Men-kheper-re	*Burial*
('Lasting is the	Tomb KV 34, Valley
Manifestation of	of the Kings
Re')	(Thebes)

HATSHEPSUT

As Tuthmosis II had realized early on, Hatshepsut was a strong-willed woman who would not let anyone or anything stand in her way. By Year 2 of her co-regency with the child king Tuthmosis III she had begun her policy to subvert his position. Initially, she had been content to be represented in reliefs standing behind Tuthmosis III and to be identified simply by her titles as queen and 'great king's wife' of Tuthmosis II. This changed as she gathered support from the highly placed officials, and it was not long before she began to build her splendid mortuary temple in the bay of the cliffs at Deir el-Bahari (pp. 73, 106).

Constructed under the supervision of the queen's steward Senenmut – who was to rise to the highest offices during her reign – Hatshepsut's temple took its basic inspiration from the 12th Dynasty temple of Mentuhotep, adjacent to the site on the south. The final plan of the temple made it unique in Egyptian architecture: built largely of limestone, it rose in three broad, colonnade-fronted terraces to a central rock-cut sanctuary on the upper terrace. The primary dedication was to Amun but there were also smaller shrines to Hathor (who earlier had a small cave shrine on the site) and Anubis, respectively located on the

Tuthmosis III (king's minority)   Queen Hatshepsut   Tuthmosis III (sole rule)   co-regency   Amenhotep II (sole rule)

A detail from Hatshepsut´s fallen obelisk in the temple of Amun at Karnak shows her as male, kneeling and supported by Amun´s gesture.

south and north sides of the second terrace. A feature of the temple was its alignment to the east directly with the great temple of Amun across the Nile at Karnak.

The queen legitimizes her rule

Hatshepsut recorded that she had built her mortuary temple as a 'garden for my father Amun'. Certainly, it was a garden, with small trees and shrubs lining the entrance ramps to the temple. Her focus on Amun was strengthened in the temple by a propaganda relief, known as the 'birth relief', on the walls of the northern half of the middle terrace. Here Amun is shown visiting Hatshepsut's mother, Queen Ahmose, while nearby are the appropriate deities of childbirth (the ram-headed Khnum and the frog-headed goddess Heqet) and the seven 'fairy-godmother' Hathors. The thrust of all this was to emphasize that she, Hatshepsut, had been deliberately conceived and chosen by Amun to be king. She was accordingly portrayed with all the regalia of kingship, even down to the official royal false beard.

To symbolize her new position as king of Egypt, Hatshepsut took the titles of the Female Horus Wosretkau, 'King of Upper and Lower Egypt'; Maat-ka-re, 'Truth is the Soul of Re'; and Khnemetamun Hatshepsut, 'She who embraces Amun, the foremost of women'. Her coronation as a child in the presence of the gods is represented in direct continuation of the birth relief at Deir el-Bahari, subsequently confirmed by Atum at Heliopolis. The propaganda also indicated that she had been crowned before the court in the presence of her father Tuthmosis I who, according to the inscription, deliberately chose New Year's Day as an auspi-

Several of Senenmut's statues show him carefully holding his royal charge, the princess Neferure. Cairo Museum.

SENENMUT THE ROYAL STEWARD

Despite his humble origins, Senenmut rose through the ranks of the court to become Queen Hatshepsut's closest advisor, and tutor to her daughter Neferure. It was rumoured that he owed his privileged position to intimate relations with the queen. Whatever the truth of the matter, Senenmut was not only Chief Architect and Overseer of Works, but was also Chief Steward of Amun, Steward of the barque 'Amen-userhet', Overseer of the Granaries of Amun, of the Fields of Amun, of the Cattle of Amun, of the Gardens of Amun, and of the Weavers of Amun. He was unrivalled in the administration of the country, and only the Chief Priest of Amun, Hapuseneb (also vizier and architect of Hatshepsut's tomb) could match him in religious affairs.

Senenmut built two tombs for himself, one, of the normal T-shaped plan of the New Kingdom, was amongst those of the other nobles in Sheik 'Abd el-Qurna (no. 71), but his other one was much more presumptuous. The entrance to it was cut in a quarry to the north of the approach road to the Deir el-Bahari temple and just outside its temenos. This had a deep entrance stair heading north-north-west so that the chamber was located under the outer court of the temple. A sketch of Senenmut appears on the northern wall of the stairway entrance, but he had also represented himself kneeling and worshipping in a relief concealed behind the opened doors of the small shrines in the upper sanctuary of Queen Hatshepsut's temple.

(*Right*) Hatshepsut's mortuary temple, nestling at the foot of the cliffs at Deir el-Bahari, is the masterpiece of the architect Senenmut. It is unique amongst Egyptian temples. Its remarkable situation is best appreciated from the air. Immediately behind it lies the Valley of the Kings and in front of it are the tombs of nobles of the New Kingdom and Late Period in the Assasif.

(*Above*) The famous expedition to Punt is represented on a relief on the southern second colonnade of Hatshepsut's mortuary temple. Here, Eti, the steatopygous Queen of Punt, a very large lady is accompanied by her elderly and much smaller husband Perehu, and followed by a diminutive donkey, labelled in the hieroglyphs as 'the donkey of the queen of Punt'. A later New Kingdom artist, seeing the relief, obviously much amused by the queen's figure, drew a rapid sketch of it on a limestone flake (ostrakon), now in Berlin. Cairo Museum.

(*Right*) An Egyptian ship is loaded with the goods from Punt.

cious day for the event! The whole text is fictitious and, just like her miraculous conception, a political exercise. In pursuing this Hatshepsut makes great play upon the support of her long-dead but still highly revered father, Tuthmosis I.

Temples and trading

The cult of Amun had gradually gained in importance during the Middle Kingdom under the patronage of the princes of Thebes. Now the more powerful New Kingdom kings associated the deity with their own fortunes. Hatshepsut had built her mortuary temple for Amun on the west bank, and further embellished the god's huge temple on the east bank. Her great major-domo, Senenmut, was heavily involved in all her building works and was also responsible for the erection of a pair of red granite obelisks to the god at Karnak. Their removal from the quarries at Aswan is recorded in inscriptions there, while their actual transport, butt-ended on low rafts calculated to be over 300 ft (100 m) long and 100 ft (30 m) wide, is represented in reliefs at the Deir el-Bahari temple. A second pair was cut later at Aswan and erected at Karnak under the

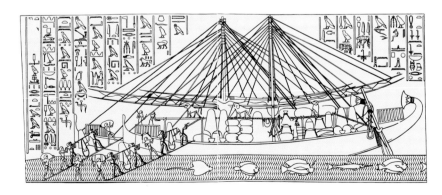

(*Above*) Hathor-headed pillar in the small chapel dedicated to the goddess on the south side of Hatshepsut's mortuary temple (*opposite*).

(*Below*) Hatshepsut represented as a lion-maned sphinx, one of the rare representations in Egyptian art of a sphinx with a female face. Cairo Museum.

direction of Senenmut's colleague, Amunhotep; one of them still stands in the temple.

The queen did not, however, build only to the greater glory of Amun at Thebes: there are many records of her restoring temples in areas of Middle Egypt that had been left devastated under the Hyksos.

While Hatshepsut is not known for her military prowess, her reign is noted for its trading expeditions, particularly to the land of Punt (probably northern Somalia or Djibouti) – a record of which is carved on the walls of her temple. It shows the envoys setting off down the Red Sea (with fish accurately depicted in the water) and later their arrival in Punt, where they exchange goods and acquire the fragrant incense trees. Other trading and explorative excursions were mounted to the turquoise mines of Sinai, especially to the area of Serabit el-Khadim, where Hatshepsut's name has been recorded.

The queen's tomb

Hatshepsut had her tomb dug in the Valley of the Kings (KV 20) by her vizier and High Priest of Amun, Hapuseneb. She had previously had a tomb cut for herself as queen regnant under Tuthmosis II, its entrance 220 ft (72 m) up a 350-ft (91-m) cliff face in a remote valley west of the Valley of the Kings. This was found by local people in 1916 and investigated by Howard Carter in rather dangerous circumstances. The tomb had never been used and still held the sandstone sarcophagus inscribed for the queen. Carter wrote: 'as a king, it was clearly necessary for her to have her tomb in The Valley like all other kings – as a matter of fact I found it there myself in 1903 – and the present tomb was abandoned. She would have been better advised to hold to her original plan. In this secret spot her mummy would have had a reasonable chance of avoiding disturbance: in The Valley it had none. A king she would be, and a king's fate she shared.'

Hatshepsut's second tomb was located at the foot of the cliffs in the eastern corner of the Valley of the Kings. The original intention seems to have been for a passage to be driven through the rock to locate the burial chamber under the sanctuary of the queen's temple on the other side of the cliffs. In the event, bad rock was struck and the tomb's plan takes a great U-turn back on itself to a burial chamber that contained two yellow quartzite sarcophagi, one inscribed for Tuthmosis I and the other for Hatshepsut as king (p. 101). The queen's mummy has never been identified, although it has been suggested that a female mummy rediscovered in 1991 in KV 21 (the tomb of Hatshepsut's nurse) might have been her body.

Hatshepsut died in about 1483 BC. Some suggest that Tuthmosis III, kept so long in waiting, may have had a hand in her death. Certainly he hated her enough to destroy many of the queen's monuments and those of her closest adherents. Perhaps the greatest posthumous humiliation she was to suffer, however, was to be omitted from the carved king lists: her reign was too disgraceful an episode to be recorded.

(*Above)* Tuthmosis III records his successful military campaigns in the age-old icon of pharaoh smiting his enemies on the rear of Pylon 7 at Karnak.

(*Below*) A superb portrait statue of Tuthmosis III, identified as such by the cartouche on his belt. Luxor Museum.

TUTHMOSIS III

With Hatshepsut's death Tuthmosis III came into his rightful inheritance. Senenmut, Hatshepsut's powerful minister and supporter, had died about a year before the queen and could no longer stand in Tuthmosis' way. Hatshepsut had maintained her position with the support of powerful ministers but, above all, by virtue of her impeccable royal lineage. Tuthmosis, too, was to draw on his family credentials, because he had been married to the princess Neferure – daughter of Tuthmosis II by Hatshepsut. Neferure died some time before Year 11, so Tuthmosis III was a widower when he came to the throne; he then took Hatshepsut-Merytre as his principal queen who was to be the mother of his heir, Amenhotep II.

During Hatshepsut's reign Tuthmosis had been kept well in the background. From the prowess he later demonstrated on the battlefield it appears that he probably spent a lot of this time with the army. Egyptian control in Syria and the Lebanon had slipped under Hatshepsut, and a number of the local princes had transferred their allegiance from Egypt to the closer and powerful kingdom of Mitanni. This was to change radically with the new king.

Once Tuthmosis III had a clear field, he set about expunging the memory of his stepmother Hatshepsut from the monuments. He exacted retribution at her temple at Deir el-Bahari, destroying many of the reliefs and smashing numerous of her statues into a quarry just in front of the temple. The tombs of her courtiers were also attacked. Moreover, the obelisks which Senenmut had proudly brought from the granite quarries at Aswan to Karnak were walled up and their inscriptions hidden. This actually helped to preserve the lower inscriptions in pristine condition, and they have now been revealed again.

At Deir el-Bahari, tucked on to a ledge between the southern half of the queen's temple and Mentuhotep's Middle Kingdom temple, Tuthmosis built a small temple of his own. Excavated in recent years by

(*Above*) Tuthmosis III kneels in humble posture to offer two small jars of water or wine to the gods. This genre of statue became very popular in stone and the first, hollow cast-bronze example occurs with Tuthmosis IV. Cairo Museum.

(*Left*) An unusual outline drawing on one of the pillars in the burial hall of Tuthmosis III shows the king being suckled by his mother Queen Iset as the goddess of the sycamore tree, normally an allusion to the goddess Hathor.

the Polish mission, the incredibly fresh condition of the shattered reliefs seems to indicate that the temple was destroyed by a rock fall from the high cliffs above it very shortly after its completion.

Nearby, Tuthmosis had a rock-cut sanctuary dedicated to the cow-goddess Hathor. The shrine was found by accident in the last century during clearance work by the Swiss Egyptologist Edouard Naville. A sudden rock fall exposed the opening to a painted shrine which, local graffiti indicated, had been a place of worship until Ramesside times, when it was destroyed by an earthquake. The shrine was dedicated by Tuthmosis III, accompanied in the wall paintings by his wife Merytre. Within the shrine was a large statue of Hathor as a cow walking forward with a standing figure of the king under her dewlap and a kneeling figure of Tuthmosis' son and successor, Amenhotep II, painted in profile suckling at her udder.

The Napoleon of ancient Egypt

In Year 2 of his independent reign (nominally his Year 23), Tuthmosis III opened up his Near Eastern campaign. A reasonably trustworthy account of the battles was inscribed on the inside walls surrounding the granite sanctuary at Karnak. The author of these so-called *Annals* was the archivist, royal scribe and army commander, Thanuny; he left an inscription in his tomb on the west bank at Thebes (TT 74) saying 'I recorded the victories he [the king] won in every land, putting them into writing according to the facts.' Thanuny must be one of the earliest official war correspondents. By recording details of the war in the great temple of Karnak, Tuthmosis III was not only glorifying his own name, but also promoting the god Amun – under whose banner he literally marched and whose estates were to reap such rich rewards from the spoils of war.

The whole campaign was a masterpiece of planning and nerve. He marched to Gaza in ten days, took the city, and pressed on to Yehem, aiming for Megiddo which was held by the rebellious prince of Kadesh. Here a problem arose as the troops approached Megiddo. There were three possible routes into the town: two were straightforward and would bring the troops out to the north of the town; the third was through a narrow pass, which the officers were quick to point out would be dangerous and open to ambush, since it was really only wide enough for single file. 'Will not', they asked, 'horse come behind horse and man behind man likewise? Shall our advance guard be fighting while our rearguard is yet standing yonder in Aruna not having fought?' The king, however, took the view that the god Amun-Re was on his side and the officers were nominally given the choice of following him through the narrow pass or going the easy way round. Needless to say, they all submitted to the king's plan.

Tuthmosis marched at the head of the column with almost total disregard for his own personal safety, but the gamble paid off. Emerging from the mouth of the wadi he saw that his enemies had wrongly antic-

The tent-pole shaped columns in Tuthmosis III's festival hall at Karnak.

THE CAPTURE OF JOPPA

One of the most interesting events of the Syrian campaigns, and one which entered into folklore, was the capture of the city of Joppa (modern Jaffa, near Tel Aviv) by Tuthmosis III's general, Djehuty. Narrated on a papyrus in the British Museum, the story goes that when direct assault of the city had failed, Djehuty resorted to a ruse that has overtones of the later Ali Baba and the Forty Thieves. He smuggled 200 armed men into the city in baskets, purporting to contain booty captured by the Prince of Joppa. At nightfall, the soldiers emerged and opened the city gates. In the Louvre is a magnificent gold bowl inscribed for Djehuty from his now lost tomb.

Djehuty's gold bowl. Louvre, Paris.

ipated that he would take one of the easier routes – and he had in fact come out between the north and south wings of their army. The next day battle was joined and the enemy decisively routed; the latter fled in panic back to Megiddo where those who were too slow to get in through the gates were hauled up by their clothes over the walls. Unfortunately, the scribe relates, the Egyptian troops stopped in their headlong pursuit to gather loot. The enemy was thus able to escape and fortify its position inside Megiddo, which held out against the Egyptians until the end of a seven-month siege.

In less than five months Tuthmosis III had travelled from Thebes right up the Syrian coast, fought decisive battles, captured three cities and returned to his capital to celebrate his victories. A campaign was launched against Syria every summer for the next 18 years, the Egyptian navy being extensively used for troop movements up the coast. It all culminated in Year 42 when Tuthmosis captured Kadesh, but the lists at Karnak detail over 350 cities that also fell to Egyptian might. Great stele commemorated the victories and there was also a long (but now much damaged) inscription on Pylon 7 at Karnak.

The 17 campaigns into western Asia were the military apotheosis of Tuthmosis' reign and it is not for nothing that he was called the Napoleon of ancient Egypt by the American Egyptologist James Henry Breasted. The king also mounted punitive expeditions into Nubia, where he built temples at Amada and Semna and cleared Senusret III's canal in Year 50 so that his army could easily pass on its return journey (the king was by now in his eighties). For the last dozen or so years of his life he was able to rest content that the empire was now widely spread, and in good order to be handed on to his heir, Amenhotep II.

Many temples were enriched and embellished from the spoils of the campaigns, none more so than the temple of Karnak. Wall reliefs near the sanctuary represent some of the gold jewellery, costly furniture, valuable oils and unguents and other gifts offered by Tuthmosis, as well as the two obelisks that were erected (one of which now stands in the Hippodrome at Istanbul). A great black granite Victory Stele from Karnak records in 25 lines how the king smote all before him, just as he is represented doing on the back of Pylon 7 at Karnak (p. 108).

At the east end of the Karnak complex of temples, Tuthmosis built a new temple that is unique in its design amongst Egyptian temples. Called his Festival Hall, its unusually shaped columns are said to represent the poles of the king's campaign tent. Behind the Hall is a small room with four clustered papyrus columns. This is known as the 'Botanical Garden' because of the representations on its walls of the animals and plants that he brought back from Syria in Year 25.

Queens and burials

Tuthmosis' principal queen was Hatshepsut-Merytre but there were other minor queens, several of whom had been acquired almost as diplomatic exchanges. The court was further expanded for a while by a

(*Right*) Interior of the painted shrine dedicated by Tuthmosis III to Hathor at Deir el-Bahari. The king offers to the god Amun. Cairo Museum.

(*Below*) In July 1916 fellahin discovered a much water-damaged tomb half-way up the cliff face some distance west of Deir el-Bahari. It proved to be the tomb of three young Syrian girls, probably chieftains' daughters, who were part of the harem of Tuthmosis III. Each had been accorded the title of King's Wife and their names were Menhet, Menwi and Merti. Amongst their funerary provision were three headdresses – two long, wig-like examples, almost complete, and a third which had a pair of small three-dimensional gazelle heads attached to the front band. These normally designated minor members of the royal harem, whilst senior queens wore the Mut vulture headdress (p. 148). Metropolitan Museum, New York.

number of foreign princes, who were held hostage while they received strict instruction in Egyptian ways; they would then be returned to their homelands, duly groomed as obedient vassals of Egypt.

The reign of Tuthmosis III was noted for its opulence and this is reflected in the superb quality of the tombs of some of the high nobles that have survived. Principal amongst these is that of the vizier Rekhmire (TT 100), with its teeming scenes of daily life and crafts, and especially the two long inscriptions that provide valuable information on the installation and office of a vizier. The tomb of the High Priest of Amun-Re, Menkheperresoneb (TT 86), Rekhmire's religious 'opposite number', was also nearby.

When Tuthmosis III died in *c.* 1450 BC, his principal queen and mother of his heir, Hatshepsut-Merytre, survived him into the reign of her son as Queen Mother. Tuthmosis was interred in a tomb in the Valley of the Kings (KV 34) with its entrance halfway up the cliff face. Once the burial had been completed, masons hacked away the stone stairway that had led up to the now concealed entrance. Ancient robbers found their way in, nevertheless, and despoiled the tomb, its principal burial hall and the four side chambers. When it was rediscovered in February 1898 by Victor Loret, all he found was the carved sarcophagus and the sorry remnants of smashed furniture and wooden statues. Rather curiously, amongst all this debris there was no trace of even a fragment of a *ushabti* of the king and, indeed, none have ever been recognized. The mummy was missing because it had been discovered 17 years before, in 1881, in the great royal cache at Deir el-Bahari, where it appears to have been reburied after Year 11 of the 22nd Dynasty pharaoh Sheshonq I, *c.* 934 BC. It was identified as the body of Tuthmosis from the scraps of original wrappings still on it and it lay in its once gilded, but now stripped, original outer coffin.

DYNASTY 18
1570–1293

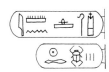

Amenhotep II
(heqaiunu)
Akheperure
1453–1419

Tuthmosis IV
Menkheperure
1419–1386

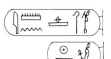

Amenhotep III
(heqawaset)
Nubmaatre
1386–1349

ROYAL NAMES AND BURIALS	
AMENHOTEP II *Birth name +* *(epithet)* Amen-hotep (heqa-iunu) ('Amun is Pleased, Ruler of Heliopolis') *Also known as* Amenhotpe II, Amenophis II (Greek) *Throne name* A-kheperu-re ('Great are the Manifestations of Re') *Burial* Tomb KV 35, Valley of the Kings (Thebes) **TUTHMOSIS IV** *Birth name* Tuthmosis ('Born of the god Thoth') *Also known as* Thuthmose IV, Thutmosis IV (Greek),	Djehutymes IV (Egyptian) *Throne name* Men-kheperu-re ('Everlasting are the Manifestations of Re') *Burial* Tomb KV 43, Valley of the Kings (Thebes) **AMENHOTEP III** *Birth name +* *(epithet)* Amen-hotep (heqa-waset) ('Amun is Pleased, Ruler of Thebes') *Throne name* Nub-maat-re ('Lord of Truth is Re') *Burial* Tomb KV 22, Valley of the Kings (Thebes)

AMENHOTEP II

Amenhotep II seems to have been an athletic youngster. Several representations of the king show him engaged in successful sporting pursuits, and he was keen to establish an equally good reputation in the military field. An opportunity to do just this presented itself early in his reign when, on receiving the news of the death of Tuthmosis III, the Asiatic cities rose up in revolt. Amenhotep II was not slow in showing the rebels that he was not to be toyed with.

In April of Year 2 he moved swiftly overland with the army (presumably because the Mediterranean sea ports were also in revolt), advanced into northern Palestine, fought his way across the Orontes river in Syria, and subdued all before him. One city, Niy, had learnt its lesson under Tuthmosis III and welcomed his son. The area of Tikhsi seems to have been the focal point of the trouble and Amenhotep II captured seven princes there, returning with them in the autumn to the temple of his great god Amun at Karnak. He was also accompanied by much booty, which largely went to swell the coffers of Amun.

Nubia took the king's attention next, in Year 3, when he moved south and completed the temples begun by his father at Aswan on

co-regency with Tuthmosis III

Amenhotep II (sole rule)

Tuthmosis IV

► DYNASTY 18

1460   1450   1440   1430   1420   1410   1400

(*Left*) Schist statue of Amenhotep II. Cairo Museum.

(*Above*) A granite stele from the temple of Amun at Karnak (now in the garden of the Luxor Museum) shows Amenhotep II shooting arrows from a fast-moving chariot with deadly accuracy at an ox-hide ingot of copper. His prowess as a horseman is indicated by the fact that his father, Tuthmosis III, put the best animals in the stable in his care. As an oarsman, too, he could not be beaten, wielding an oar 20 cubits (about 30 ft) in length and rowing six times as fast as the mere mortal crew.

Elephantine Island and at Amada. From stele left by the king at both temples we learn the fate of the seven captive princes: the king sacrificed all seven to Amun in the age-old manner, smiting them with his mace and then hanging them face downwards on the prow of his ship. Six of them were subsequently hung on the enclosure wall of the temple at Thebes, while the seventh was taken south into Nubia and hung from the walls of Napata, 'in order to cause to be seen the victorious might of His Majesty for ever and ever'.

Year 9 saw the king campaigning in Palestine again, but only as far as the Sea of Galilee. Thereafter, for the rest of his 34-year rule, it seems he had made his mark and peace reigned.

Amenhotep II was laid to rest in the Valley of the Kings (KV 35) – but not for long, for his tomb was plundered before the end of the 20th Dynasty. When Victor Loret entered it in March 1898 he found the usual debris, but the king still lay in his sarcophagus where the priests had partly rewrapped the body after its desecration. Impressions preserved in the resin indicated the jewellery that had once lain on the body. Amenhotep was not, however, alone in his tomb. It had been used by the priests in antiquity as a hiding place for other royal mummies (see p. 103).

TUTHMOSIS IV

There may have been some doubt about the legitimacy of Tuthmosis IV's succession, since a long inscription preserved on a tall stele between the paws of the Sphinx at Giza smacks of propaganda in sup-

(*Right*) Until the discovery of Tutankhamun's tomb in 1922, Amenhotep II had the distinction of being the only Egyptian pharaoh discovered in his own sarcophagus in his own tomb, and there he was left until he was moved to the Cairo Museum in 1928. Even after 1898 Amenhotep was not safe: local robbers broke into the tomb during the season of 1900–1, but their ancestors had done the original job too well and there was nothing of great value left to steal, although the modern robbers did search the body. Sadly, the great long bow of Amenhotep II found in his sarcophagus with the mummy, of the type he shoots on his Karnak stele (*above*), was stolen and has never been recovered.

Amenhotep III | 1380 | 1370 | 1360 | 1350 | co-regency Akhenaten (Amenhotep IV) (sole rule) | 1340 | Smenkhkare with (co-regency) Akhenaten) | Tutankhamun | 1330 | Ay | Horemheb | 1320 | 0

(*Right*) Black granite statue of Tuthmosis IV with his mother Queen Tio, curiously set wide apart from each other but still underlining his royal right to the throne. Cairo Museum.

(*Below*) An interesting record of Tuthmosis IV's reign occurs on the sides of the great obelisk that stands outside St John Lateran in Rome, re-erected by Pope Sixtus V in 1588. This, at 105 ft (32 m), is the tallest extant obelisk, despite having lost some 3 ft from its badly damaged base. Originally quarried at Aswan under Tuthmosis III, it was intended most unusually as a single obelisk for the temple at Karnak, and not one of a pair. It lay unfinished for some 35 years on the south side of Karnak until Tuthmosis IV piously had it inscribed with his grandfather's original inscription and added his own record to it.

port of the new king. Known as the Dream Stele, it tells how the young prince Tuthmosis was out hunting in the desert when he fell asleep in the shadow of the Sphinx. Re-Harakhte, the sun god embodied in the Sphinx, appeared to him in a dream and promised that if the sand engulfing the great limestone body was cleared away, the prince would become king. Needless to say, the sand-clearing operation was immediately carried out and the prince became the fourth king of his name.

Little of a military nature appears to have occurred during Tuthmosis IV's reign, although our knowledge may be marred by the lack of texts. A Nubian campaign is recorded in Year 8, which was, of course, highly successful. There also appear to have been some Syrian campaigns, since the king is referred to twice as 'conqueror of Syria' – but these may have been rather low-key policing excursions rather than full-blown military attacks.

It is from the reign of Tuthmosis IV that some of the best known decorated private tombs survive in the Theban necropolis, such as those of Nakht (TT 52) and Menna (TT 69). Tuthmosis's own anciently robbed tomb in the Valley of the Kings (KV 43) was found in 1903 by Howard Carter. A large amount of the damaged and destroyed funerary furniture, *ushabtis*, food provisions and a chariot were found in it. The destruction appears to have taken place before Year 8 of Horemheb (1321–1293), when two graffiti record the restoration of the tomb by the official Maya and his assistant Djehutymose. The king's mummy, however, was not present in the splendidly decorated granite sarcophagus: it had been found five years earlier, as one of those hidden in the tomb of Amenhotep II (p. 103).

Orange alabaster statue of Amenhotep III standing beside the crocodile god Sobek. This remarkable statue was later usurped by Ramesses II, who added his own cartouches. It was found at Dahamsha, at the bottom of a shaft in Sobek's temple. Luxor Museum.

A Marriage Scarab of Amenhotep III, one of his five large commemorative scarabs (p. 116), recording the names of his queen, Tiy, and her parents, Yuya and Tuya. British Museum.

AMENHOTEP III

Amenhotep III's long reign of almost 40 years was one of the most prosperous and stable in Egyptian history. His great-grandfather, Tuthmosis III, had laid the foundations of the Egyptian empire by his campaigns into Syria, Nubia and Libya. Hardly any military activity was called for under Amenhotep, and such little as there was, in Nubia, was directed by his son and viceroy of Kush, Merymose.

Amenhotep III was the son of Tuthmosis IV by one of his chief wives, Queen Mutemwiya. It is possible (though now doubted by some) that she was the daughter of the Mitannian king, Artatama, sent to the Egyptian court as part of a diplomatic arrangement to cement the alliance between the strong militarist state of Mitanni in Syria and Egypt. The king's royal birth is depicted in a series of reliefs in a room on the east side of the temple of Luxor which Amenhotep built for Amun. The creator god, the ram-headed Khnum of Elephantine, is seen fashioning the young king and his *ka* (spirit double) on a potter's wheel, watched by the goddess Isis. The god Amun is then led to his meeting with the queen by ibis-headed Thoth, god of wisdom. Subsequently, Amun is shown standing in the presence of the goddesses Hathor and Mut and nursing the child created by Khnum.

The royal wives

Amenhotep III had a large – and ever-increasing – number of ladies in his harem; several of them were foreign princesses, the result of diplomatic marriages, but his chief wife was a woman of non-royal rank whom he had married before he came to the throne. This was Tiy, the daughter of a noble called Yuya and his wife, Tuya. The family was an important one: not only did it hold land in the Delta but Yuya was a powerful military leader. Tiy's brother, Anen, was also to rise to high office under Amenhotep III, as Chancellor of the King of Lower Egypt, Second Prophet of Amun, *sem*-priest of Heliopolis, and Divine Father. (The undecorated and almost undisturbed tomb [KV 46] of Yuya and Tuya was discovered in a small side wadi of the Valley of the Kings by Theodore Davis in 1905. Their two mummies are amongst the best preserved in the Cairo Museum.)

Tiy gave birth to six or more children, at least two sons and then four daughters. The oldest boy died without reigning, leaving his younger brother (the future Amenhotep IV, later called Akhenaten) heir to the throne. Amenhotep III also married two of his daughters, first Isis and then, in Year 30, Sitamun. Evidence for this comes from a series of kohl eyeliner tubes inscribed for the king together with a cartouche of each royal lady.

The early years

Amenhotep's reign falls essentially into two unequal parts. The first decade reflected a young and vigorous king, promoting the sportsman

The face of the gilded wooden coffin of Tuya, mother of Queen Tiy. Cairo Museum.

image laid down by his predecessors and with some minor military activity. In Year 5 there was an expedition to Nubia, recorded on rock inscriptions near Aswan and at Konosso in Nubia. Although couched in the usual laudatory manner, the event recorded seems to have been rather low key. An undated stele from Semna (now in the British Museum) also records a Nubian campaign, but whether it is the same one or a later one is uncertain. A rebellion at Ibhet is reported as having been heavily crushed by the viceroy of Nubia, 'King's Son of Kush', Merymose. Although the king, 'mighty bull, strong in might . . . the fierce-eyed lion' is noted as having made great slaughter within the space of a single hour, he was probably not present; nevertheless, 150 Nubian men, 250 women, 175 children, 110 archers, and 55 servants – a total of 740 – were said to have been captured, to which was added the 312 right hands of the slain.

The opulent years

The last 25 years of Amenhotep's reign seem to have been a period of great building works and luxury at court and in the arts. The laudatory epithets that accompany the king's name are more grandiose metaphors than records of fact: he took the Horus name 'Great of Strength who Smites the Asiatics', when there is little evidence of such a campaign; similarly, 'Plunderer of Shinar' and 'Crusher of Naharin' seem singularly inappropriate, particularly the latter since one of his wives, Gilukhepa, was a princess of Naharin.

THE COMMEMORATIVE SCARABS OF AMENHOTEP III

The first 12 years of Amenhotep's reign are rather well documented on a series of five large commemorative scarabs, each known in several copies. The earliest one, of Year 2, is known as the Marriage Scarab (illustrated on p. 115) and records the king's marriage to Tiy. The second, also of Year 2, records Amenhotep's sporting prowess. It describes how the king captured 56 out of a total of 170 head of wild cattle in a single day. On the third scarab (known as the Lion Hunt Scarab), he is credited with having slain 102 fierce lions in the first ten years of his reign. This is the most common of the scarabs: many have been found outside the boundaries of Egypt, where they obviously served as an imperial news sheet.

The fourth scarab documents the arrival in Year 10 of the princess

Back of the Lion Hunt Scarab (left), with the text inscribed on its base (right).

Gilukhepa, daughter of King Shuttarna II of Mitanni, to join Amenhotep's harem. The princess was accompanied by an entourage of 317. Interestingly, even on a record such as this, Queen Tiy's name appears closely following the king's. The fifth scarab tells how Amenhotep had a pleasure lake dug in Year 11 for Queen Tiy to sail upon. The lake was huge – just over a mile long

and about a quarter of a mile wide – and probably lay in the area of the king's Malkata palace to the south of Medinet Habu, on the west bank at Thebes. The king and queen celebrated the opening of the lake by sailing on it in the royal barge named 'The Aten Gleams' – an interesting name in relation to his son Akhenaten's later religious beliefs.

(Right) The 60-ft (20-m) high seated statues of Amenhotep III known as the Colossi of Memnon. In antiquity the northern one of the pair (on the right) was heard to make a moaning sound at dawn and dusk, said to be Memnon greeting or bidding farewell to his mother, Eos, the dawn goddess. The phenomenon was probably caused by the effect on the stone of the radical temperature changes at dawn and dusk; whatever the explanation, repairs later carried out by the Roman emperor Septimius Severus (AD 193–211) meant that the sound was heard no more. The lower legs and pedestal of the northern colossus are heavily covered in graffiti from antiquity to 19th-century AD travellers, including even a poem in Greek by the official court poetess to Septimius Severus.

(Below) Head of a fine quartzite statue of Amenhotep III found in the Luxor temple cache in 1989. It was probably a cult statue (p. 118). Luxor Museum.

The wealth of Egypt at this period came not from the spoils of conquest, as it had under Tuthmosis III, but from international trade and an abundant supply of gold (from mines in the Wadi Hammamat and from panning gold dust far south into the land of Kush). It was this great wealth and booming economy that led to such an outpouring of artistic talent in all aspects of the arts.

Since the houses or palaces of the living were regarded as ephemeral, we unfortunately have little evidence of the magnificence of a palace such as Amenhotep's Malkata palace. Fragments of the building, however, indicate that the walls were once plastered and painted with lively scenes from nature. Many of the temples he built have been destroyed too. At Karnak he embellished the already large temple to Amun and at Luxor he built a new one to the same god, of which the still standing colonnaded court is a masterpiece of elegance and design. Particular credit is owed to his master architect: Amenhotep son of Hapu.

On the west bank, his mortuary temple was destroyed in the next (19th) dynasty when it, like many of its predecessors, was used as a quarry. All that now remains of this temple are the two imposing statues of the king known as the Colossi of Memnon. (This is in fact a complete misnomer, arising from the classical recognition of the statues as the Ethiopian prince, Memnon, who fought at Troy.) Of the two, the southern statue is the best preserved. Standing beside the king's legs, dwarfed by his stature, are the two important women in his life: his mother Mutemwiya and his wife, Queen Tiy. A quarter of a mile behind the Colossi stands a great repaired stele that was once in the sanctuary and around are fragments of sculptures, the best of which, lying in a pit and found in recent years, is a crocodile-tailed sphinx.

(*Right*) An aerial view of the Luxor temple, built and added to over the course of 2000 years from Amenhotep III (the colonnaded court, back left), Ramesses II (the pylons) down to the Islamic mosque of Abu Hagag (foreground).

Amenhotep III's master architect, Amenhotep son of Hapu, is one of the few architects to be known to us by name. As a great privilege, he was allowed to place statues of himself – shown sitting cross-legged as a scribe with his scribal palette hanging forward over his left shoulder – outside Pylon X in the temple of Karnak. Like the great 3rd Dynasty architect, Imhotep, Amenhotep son of Hapu was elevated to the status of a god in the later Ptolemaic period. Cairo Museum.

A peak of artistic achievement

Some magnificent statuary dates from the reign of Amenhotep III, such as the two outstanding couchant rose granite lions originally set before the temple at Soleb in Nubia (but subsequently removed to the temple at Gebel Barkal further south in the Sudan). There is also a proliferation of private statues, particularly of the architect Amenhotep son of Hapu, but also of many other nobles and dignitaries.

It is in the great series of royal portraits, however, that the sculptor's art is truly seen. Largest of them all (after the Colossi of Memnon) is the huge limestone statue of the king and queen with three small standing princesses from Medinet Habu. There are many other representations of the king, all of which project the contemplative, almost ethereal, aspect of the king's features. Magnificently worked black granite seated statues of Amenhotep wearing the *nemes* headdress have come from excavations behind the Colossi of Memnon (by Belzoni) and from Tanis in the Delta. A number of statues of the king were reworked by later rulers, often by simply adding their cartouches, or occasionally altering the features or aspects of the body, as with the huge red granite head hitherto identified as being Tuthmosis III from Karnak (also found by Belzoni) and reworked by Ramesses II (now in the British Museum). Several portraits in statues, reliefs and wall paintings show the king wearing the helmet-like *khepresh*, the so-called Blue or War Crown.

One of the most incredible finds of statuary in recent years was made in the courtyard of the Amenhotep III colonnade of the Luxor temple in 1989. It included a superb 6-ft (1.83-m) high pink quartzite statue of the king standing on a sledge and wearing the Double Crown. The only damage the statue had sustained was under Akhenaten when, very carefully, the hated name of Amun was removed from the cartouches where it appeared as part of the king's name. The inscriptions on the statue and its iconography suggest that it is a work from late in the reign, despite the idealized youthful features of the king. It may possibly have been a cult statue (p. 117).

Finely sculpted limestone relief of Amenhotep III wearing the Blue Crown (*khepresh*) from the tomb of the Royal Scribe Khaemhet at Thebes (TT 57). The companion portrait of Queen Tiy is in Brussels. Berlin Museum.

Small greenstone head identified as Queen Tiy by her cartouches and distinctive double *uraei* headdress. Found in the temple of Serabit el-Khadim, Sinai, in 1904 by Flinders Petrie. Cairo Museum.

The two most widely known portraits of Queen Tiy are the small ebony head in Berlin which, in the past, caused many authorities to suggest that she came from south of Aswan, and the petite-faced and crowned head found by Petrie at the temple of Serabit el-Khadim in Sinai which is identified as the queen by her cartouche on the front of her crown. Other fine reliefs of her come from the tombs of some of the courtiers in her service such as Userhet (TT 47) and Kheruef (TT 192).

Death and burial

Inscribed clay dockets from the Malkata palace carry dates into at least Year 38 of Amenhotep's reign, implying that he may have died in his 39th regnal year when he would have been about 45 years old.

His robbed tomb was rediscovered by the French expedition in 1799 in the western Valley of the Kings (KV 22). Amongst the debris, they found a large number of *ushabtis* of the king, some complete but mostly broken, made of black and red granite, alabaster and cedar wood. Some were considerably larger than normal. Excavations and clearance by Howard Carter in 1915 revealed foundation deposits of Tuthmosis IV, showing that the tomb had been originally intended for that king. Despite this, the tomb was eventually used for Amenhotep III, and also for Queen Tiy to judge from the fragments found of several different *ushabtis* of the queen.

Queen Tiy survived her husband by several years – possibly by as many as 12, since she is shown with her youngest daughter, Beket-Aten, in a relief in one of the Amarna tombs that is dated between Years 9 and 12 of her son's reign. (Beket-Aten is shown as a very young child and must have been born shortly before Amenhotep died, or even posthumously.) We know from polite enquiries about Tiy's health in the Amarna Letters (p. 126) that she lived for a while at Akhetaten (modern el-Amarna), the new capital of her son Akhenaten. It has been suggested that there was a period of co-regency between the old king and his successor, but the argument is not proved either way. An interesting painted sandstone stele found in a private household shrine at el-Amarna shows an elderly, rather obese Amenhotep III, seated with Queen Tiy. Whether he actually lived for a time in this city is a matter of conjecture; Tiy certainly did and may well have died there, to be taken back to Thebes for burial.

Amenhotep III's mummy was probably one of those found by Loret in 1898 in the tomb of Amenhotep II (KV 35), although recently it has been suggested that this body was wrongly identified by the ancient priests when it was transferred to the new tomb. On biological grounds, professors Ed Wente and John Harris have proposed it to be the body of Akhenaten, or possibly Ay. A previously unidentified female mummy (the Elder Woman) from the same cache has been tentatively identified as Queen Tiy, based on the examination of her hair and a lock of hair in a small coffin from the tomb of Tutankhamun inscriptionally identified as Tiy's.

DYNASTY 18
1570–1293

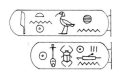

Akhenaten
(Amenhotep IV)
Neferkheperure
1350–1334

Smenkhkare
Ankhkheperure
1336–1334

Yellow steatite seated statue of
Akhenaten, originally paired with
Nefertiti (of whom only her left arm
remains, clasping his waist). The king is
represented in the restrained style of
late in his reign. Louvre, Paris.

AMENHOTEP IV/AKHENATEN	
Birth name Amen-hotep ('Amun is Pleased') *Also known as* Amenhotpe IV, Amenophis IV (Greek) *Adopted name (Year 5)* Akh-en-aten ('Servant of the Aten') *Throne name* Nefer-kheperu-re ('Beautiful are the Manifestations of Re') *Father* Amenhotep III	*Mother* Tiy *Wives* Nefertiti, Merytaten, Kiya, Mekytaten, Ankhesenpaaten *Son* ?Tutankhamun *Daughters* Merytaten, Mekytaten, Ankhesenpaaten, ?Merytaten-tasherit and others *Burial* Akhetaten (el-Amarna); subsequently ?Valley of the Kings (Thebes)

SMENKHKARE	
Birth name + (epithet) Smenkh-ka-re (Djeser-kheperu) ('Vigorous is the Soul of Re, Holy of Manifestations') *Also known as* Smenkhkara *Throne name* Ankh-kheperu-re	('Living are the Manifestations of Re') *Wife* Merytaten *Burial* ?Tomb KV 55, Valley of the Kings (Thebes)

AKHENATEN

Amenhotep IV – better known as Akhenaten, the new name he took early on in his reign – ushered in a revolutionary period in Egyptian history. The Amarna Interlude, as it is often called, saw the removal of the seat of government to a short-lived new capital city, Akhetaten (modern el-Amarna), the introduction of a new art style, and the elevation of the cult of the sun disc, the Aten, to pre-eminent status in Egyptian religion. This last heresy in particular was to bring down on Akhenaten and his immediate successors the opprobrium of later kings.

The young prince was at least the second son of Amenhotep III by his chief wife, Tiy: an elder brother, prince Tuthmosis, had died prematurely (strangely, a whip bearing his name was found in Tutankhamun's tomb). There is some controversy over whether or not the old king took his son into partnership on the throne in a co-regency – there are quite strong arguments both for and against. A point in favour of a co-regency is the appearance during the latter years of Amenhotep III's reign of artistic styles that are subsequently seen as part of the 'revolutionary' Amarna art introduced by Akhenaten; on the other hand, both 'traditional' and 'revolutionary' art styles could easily have coexisted during

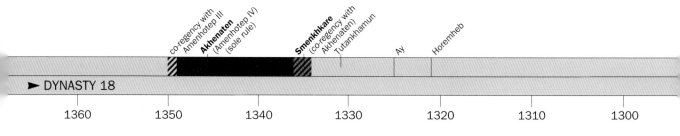

co-regency with
Amenhotep III
Akhenaten
(Amenhotep IV)
(sole rule)

Smenkhkare
(co-regency with
Akhenaten)
Tutankhamun

Ay

Horemheb

► DYNASTY 18

| 1360 | 1350 | 1340 | 1330 | 1320 | 1310 | 1300 |

the early years of Akhenaten's reign. At any rate, if there had been a co-regency, it would not have been for longer than the short period before the new king assumed his preferred name of Akhenaten ('Servant of the Aten') in Year 5.

The beginning of Akhenaten's reign marked no great discontinuity with that of his predecessors. Not only was he crowned at Karnak (temple of the god Amun) but, like his father, he married a lady of non-royal blood, Nefertiti, the daughter of the vizier Ay. Ay seems to have been a brother of Queen Tiy (Anen was another, p. 115) and a son of Yuya and Tuya. Nefertiti's mother is not known; she may have died in childbirth or shortly afterwards, since Nefertiti seems to have been brought up by another wife of Ay named Tey, who would then be her stepmother.

The cult of the Aten

There can be little doubt that the new king was far more of a thinker and philosopher than his forebears. Amenhotep III had recognized the growing power of the priesthood of Amun and had sought to curb it; his son was to take the matter a lot further by introducing a new monotheistic cult of sun-worship that was incarnate in the sun's disc, the Aten.

Painted limestone pair statuette of Akhenaten and Nefertiti which is dated by the form of the Aten's name on the back to after Year 9. There is a rather charming naïvety about the sculpture, but it still follows the laid-down canons that the queen should be shown on a smaller scale. Louvre, Paris.

(*Right*) This detail from two adjacent blocks found at Hermopolis shows a very different aspect of Nefertiti, within a small cabin at the stern of the ship, smiting a captive with upraised mace. Boston Museum.

(*Below*) One of the several colossal sandstone statues of Akhenaten found in a peristyle court east of the temple of Amun at Karnak. The king's curious physiognomy has been the source of much speculation. Cairo Museum.

This was not in itself a new idea: as a relatively minor aspect of the sun god Re-Harakhte, the Aten had been venerated in the Old Kingdom and a large scarab of Akhenaten's grandfather Tuthmosis IV (now in the British Museum) has a text that mentions the Aten. Rather, Akhenaten's innovation was to worship the Aten in its own right. Portrayed as a solar disc whose protective rays terminated in hands holding the *ankh* hieroglyph for life, the Aten was accessible only to Akhenaten, thereby obviating the need for an intermediate priesthood.

At first, the king built a temple to his god Aten immediately outside the east gate of the temple of Amun at Karnak, but clearly the coexistence of the two cults could not last. He therefore proscribed the cult of Amun, closed the god's temples, took over the revenues and, to make a complete break, in Year 6 moved to a new capital in Middle Egypt, half way between Memphis and Thebes. It was a virgin site, not previously dedicated to any other god or goddess, and he named it Akhetaten – The Horizon of the Aten. Today the site is known as el-Amarna.

(*Top*) The painted but unfinished limestone bust of Nefertiti from the workshop of the sculptor Thutmose at Amarna has become an icon of Amarna art. Berlin Museum.

(*Above*) A limestone slab, with traces of the draughtsman's grid still on it, found in the Royal Tomb of Amarna. Its style is characteristic of the early period of Akhenaten's reign. The king is accompanied by Nefertiti and just two of their daughters, but this does not necessarily indicate that these are the eldest, since others of the six may have been omitted. Cairo Museum.

In the tomb of Ay, the chief minister of Akhenaten (and later to become king after Tutankhamun's death, p. 136), occurs the longest and best rendition of a composition known as the 'Hymn to the Aten', said to have been written by Akhenaten himself. Quite moving in itself as a piece of poetry, its similarity to, and possible source of the concept in, Psalm 104 has long been noted. It sums up the whole ethos of the Aten cult and especially the concept that only Akhenaten had access to the god: 'Thou arisest fair in the horizon of Heaven, O Living Aten, Beginner of Life . . . there is none who knows thee save thy son Akhenaten. Thou hast made him wise in thy plans and thy power.' No longer did the dead call upon Osiris to guide them through the afterworld, for only through their adherence to the king and his intercession on their behalf could they hope to live beyond the grave.

According to present evidence, however, it appears that it was only the upper echelons of society which embraced the new religion with any fervour (and perhaps that was only skin deep). Excavations at Amarna have indicated that even here the old way of religion continued among the ordinary people. On a wider scale, throughout Egypt, the new cult does not seem to have had much effect at a common level except, of course, in dismantling the priesthood and closing the temples; but then the ordinary populace had had little to do with the religious establishment anyway, except on the high days and holidays when the god's statue would be carried in procession from the sanctuary outside the great temple walls.

The standard bureaucracy continued its endeavours to run the country while the king courted his god. Cracks in the Egyptian empire may have begun to appear in the later years of the reign of Amenhotep III; at any rate they became more evident as Akhenaten increasingly left government and diplomats to their own devices. Civil and military authority came under two strong characters: Ay, who held the title 'Father of the God' (and was probably Akhenaten's father-in-law), and the general Horemheb (also Ay's son-in-law since he married Ay's daughter Mutnodjme, sister of Nefertiti). Both men were to become pharaoh before the 18th Dynasty ended. This redoubtable pair of closely related high officials no doubt kept everything under control in a discreet manner while Akhenaten pursued his own philosophical and religious interests.

A new artistic style

It is evident from the art of the Amarna period that the court officially emulated the king's unusual physical characteristics. Thus individuals such as the young princesses are endowed with elongated skulls and excessive adiposity, while Bek – the Chief Sculptor and Master of Works – portrays himself in the likeness of his king with pendulous breasts and protruding stomach. On a stele now in Berlin Bek states that he was taught by His Majesty and that the court sculptors were instructed to represent what they saw. The result is a realism that

(*Right*) This sandstone building slab (*talatat*) shows Akhenaten wearing the Red Crown and offering to the Aten's disk, whose descending rays extend the *ankh* sign of life to him. Private collection.

(*Below*) Amongst the distinctly 18th Dynasty jewellery found cached outside the Royal Tomb at Amarna the small gold ring with Nefertiti's cartouche is particularly significant. Royal Scottish Museum, Edinburgh.

(*Below*) An unfinished quartzite head of Nefertiti, showing the draughtsman's guide lines, found in the workshops at Amarna. Cairo Museum.

breaks away from the rigid formality of earlier official depictions, although naturalism is very evident in earlier, unofficial art.

The power behind the throne?

Although the famous bust of Nefertiti in Berlin (p. 123) shows her with an elongated neck, the queen is not subject to quite the same extremes as others in Amarna art, by virtue of being elegantly female. Indeed, there are several curious aspects of Nefertiti's representations. In the early years of Akhenaten's reign, for instance, Nefertiti was an unusually prominent figure in official art, dominating the scenes carved on blocks of the temple to the Aten at Karnak. One such block shows her in the age-old warlike posture of pharaoh grasping captives by the hair and smiting them with a mace (p. 122) – hardly the epitome of the peaceful queen and mother of six daughters. Nefertiti evidently played a far more prominent part in her husband's rule than was the norm.

Tragedy seems to have struck the royal family in about Year 12 with the death in childbirth of Nefertiti's second daughter, Mekytaten; it is probably she who is shown in a relief in the royal tomb with her grief-stricken parents beside her supine body, and a nurse standing nearby holding a baby. The father of the infant was possibly Akhenaten, since he is also known to have married two other daughters, Merytaten (not to be confused with Mekytaten) and Akhesenpaaten (later to become Tutankhamun's wife).

Nefertiti appears to have died soon after Year 12, although some suggest that she was disgraced because her name was replaced in several instances by that of her daughter Merytaten, who succeeded her as 'Great Royal Wife'. The latter bore a daughter called Merytaten-tasherit (Merytaten the Younger), also possibly fathered by Akhenaten. Merytaten was to become the wife of Smenkhkare, Akhenaten's brief successor. Nefertiti was buried in the royal tomb at Amarna, judging by the evidence of a fragment of an alabaster *ushabti* figure bearing her cartouche found there in the early 1930s.

THE SACRED CITY OF AKHETATEN

Akhetaten (or el-Amarna as it is now known) is an important site because it was occupied neither before nor after its short life as capital under Akhenaten. It is ringed by a natural amphitheatre of cliffs on both sides of the Nile and delineated by a series of 15 large stele carved in the rock around its perimeter. On the stele, reliefs show Akhenaten adoring his god in the company of his wife and various of their six daughters, and give instructions that all should be buried within the city's sacred precincts. To this end a royal tomb was cut in a remote wadi situated mid-way between the tombs of the nobles, now referred to as the North and South tombs. None of the tombs was ever finished and probably few of them were actually occupied. If they were, loving relatives almost certainly rapidly removed the bodies immediately after the king's death, because of the backlash unleashed against him and his monuments.

The actual city was a linear development along part of the east bank, stretching back not very far into the desert where a number of small

View of the North Palace at Amarna. It has been suggested that certain rooms at the rear of the palace contained a zoo.

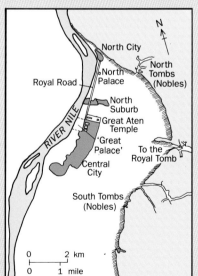

Plan of Akhetaten, essentially a linear development along the King's or Royal Road.

sun kiosks were located on the routes to the tombs. A broad thoroughfare, sometimes called the King's Road or Royal Avenue, linked the two ends of the city and was flanked by a series of official buildings, including the royal palace (Great Palace), the new style open-air temple to the Aten (the Great Temple), and administrative offices. The Great Palace was probably a ceremonial centre rather than a royal residence; the king and his family may have lived in the North Palace (*above*). The houses of the upper classes (mainly young nobles who had accompanied the king in his radical move) were arranged on an open plan, not crowded together as is usually found in the ancient Near East. Most were lavish buildings, with pools and gardens. The overall impression was that of a 'garden city'.

The whole essence of the court and life at Amarna revolved around the king and his god the Aten. Everywhere the royal family appeared they were shown

to be under the protection of the Aten's rays. Reliefs in the tombs of the nobles at the site all focused on the king and through him the Aten. Great scenes covered the walls and continued, unlike earlier and later tomb decoration, from wall to wall. The king, usually accompanied by Nefertiti and a number of their daughters, dominated the walls, normally in scenes showing them proceeding to the temple of the Aten in chariots drawn by spirited and richly caparisoned horses. Small vignettes occur of men drawing water using *shadufs* (the ancient bucket and weighted pole method that until recently was a common sight in Egypt, but is now fast disappearing); fat cattle are fed in their byres; blind musicians, their faces beautifully observed, sing the praises of Akhenaten and the Aten. Everything is alive and thriving under the king's patronage through the beneficence of the Aten.

The king's resting place

Akhenaten died *c.* 1334, probably in his 16th regnal year. Evidence found by Professor Geoffrey Martin during re-excavation of the royal tomb at Amarna showed that blocking had been put in place in the burial chamber, suggesting that Akhenaten was buried there initially. Others do not believe that the tomb was used, however, in view of the heavily smashed fragments of his sarcophagus and canopic jars recovered from it, and also the shattered examples of his *ushabtis* – found not only in the area of the tomb but also by Petrie in the city.

What is almost certain is that his body did not remain at Amarna. A burnt mummy seen outside the royal tomb in the 1880s, and associated with jewellery from the tomb (including a small gold finger ring with Nefertiti's cartouche, p. 124), was probably Coptic, as was other jewellery nearby. Akhenaten's adherents would not have left his body to be despoiled by his enemies once his death and the return to orthodoxy unleashed a backlash of destruction. They would have taken it to a place of safety – and where better to hide it than in the old royal burial ground at Thebes where enemies would never dream of seeking it?

SMENKHKARE

Akhenaten's nominal successor was Smenkhkare, probably a younger brother of the king, but it appears that they may have died within months of each other. Smenkhkare's two-year reign was in reality a co-regency during the last years of Akhenaten's life. A graffito in the tomb of Pairi at Thebes (TT 139) records a third regnal year, and there are indications that Smenkhkare was preparing the ground for a return to the old orthodoxy and had left Akhetaten. He was married to Merytaten, the senior heiress of the royal blood line, but she seems to have predeceased him. Her sister Ankhesenpaaten thus became the senior survivor of the six daughters – having herself borne a small daughter by Akhenaten, named after her – and was married to the young Tutankhaten, the heir apparent (who was later to change his name to Tutankhamun).

The mystery of Tomb 55 in the Valley of the Kings

A great deal of controversy surrounds the question of Smenkhkare's mummy and burial. In January 1907, Edward Ayrton (working for Theodore Davis) discovered the badly water-damaged contents of an unfinished tomb in the Valley of the Kings (KV 55). Arguments have raged ever since over the identity of the occupant of the *rishi*-type coffin, because the cartouches on it had all been hacked out. Initially Davis believed he had found the tomb of Queen Tiy – the damaged body being identified as female – and published it as such. Subsequently, the body changed sex and was identified as Akhenaten, the previously thought female characteristics of the skeleton being paralleled with those of Akhenaten's portrayals, especially the pelvic area. More detailed foren-

Detail of one of the finely carved heads from an alabaster canopic jar found in KV 55. It is now thought to have belonged to Queen Kiya, the possible mother of Tutankhamun (p. 130). Cairo Museum.

sic examination, however, now suggests that the body belonged to Smenkhkare, and serological examination (blood grouping) of tissue, as well as close skull measurement comparisons, indicate that the occupant was a brother, or possibly half-brother, of Tutankhamun – the entrance to whose tomb (KV 62) is a mere 15 yards (13.7 m) away across the Valley floor.

At one time, it appears that there were three bodies in the tomb. One of them was that of Queen Tiy, and parts of her great gold overlaid wooden sarcophagus shrine were found there. Her body was probably taken from here round into the West Valley to join her husband, Amenhotep III, in KV 22 (p. 119). Four alabaster canopic jars with finely carved female heads wearing the characteristic court wig of the period were found in the tomb; they show evidence of having been adapted by the addition of a royal *uraeus* to the brow which was subsequently broken off. Unfortunately they are uninscribed, but were presumably *en suite* with the coffin. It has been suggested that the canopic lids are portraits of Kiya, a hitherto obscure junior queen of Akhenaten (p. 130).

The cartouches on the coffin had all been deliberately hacked out, literally to deny the occupant access to the next world because loss of name was a terrible thing. The texts still in place, however, had feminine endings to the appropriate words, indicating that the coffin had been made for a royal female. This was thought possibly to have been Merytaten, Smenkhkare's wife, or now, Kiya. The cartouches, it was suggested, had been hacked out because the perpetrators believed that the occupant was the hated Akhenaten (his could have been the third body in the tomb at the time). It seems that they hoped to remove the bodies of Queen Tiy and Smenkhkare from the contamination of association with the heretic king Akhenaten, but made a mistake and removed Akhenaten's body instead. On that basis, somewhere in a small undiscovered tomb or cache in or near the Valley of the Kings, Akhenaten's body may still lie undisturbed. It will be accompanied by whatever of Smenkhkare's funerary equipment was removed from Tomb 55, and that should include *ushabti* figures for Smenkhkare because, although examples are known for the rest of the royal family, not even a fragment of one survives bearing his name.

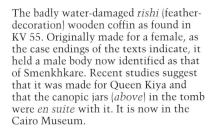

The badly water-damaged *rishi* (feather-decoration) wooden coffin as found in KV 55. Originally made for a female, as the case endings of the texts indicate, it held a male body now identified as that of Smenkhkare. Recent studies suggest that it was made for Queen Kiya and that the canopic jars (*above*) in the tomb were *en suite* with it. It is now in the Cairo Museum.

DYNASTY 18
1570–1293

Tutankhamun
(heqaiunushema)
Nebkheperure
1334–1325

The gold death mask of
Tutankhamun that covered the
mummy's head within the golden
coffin (p. 132). Cairo Museum.

TUTANKHAMUN	
Birth name	Manifestations is
Tut-ankh-aten	Re')
('Living Image of	*Father*
the Aten')	?Akhenaten
Adopted name (Year	*Mother*
2) + epithet	?Kiya
Tut-ankh-amun	*Wife*
(heqa-iunu-shema)	Ankhesenpaaten
('Living Image of	(later
Amun, Ruler of	Ankhesenamun)
Upper Egyptian	*Sons*
Heliopolis')	None
Also known as	*Daughters*
Tutankhamen,	?Two
Tutankhamon etc.	*Burial*
Throne name	Tomb KV 62, Valley
Neb-kheperu-re	of the Kings
('Lord of	(Thebes)

TUTANKHAMUN

Before the spectacular discovery of his almost intact tomb in the Valley
of the Kings (KV 62) in November 1922, Tutankhamun was a shadowy
and little known figure of the late 18th Dynasty. To a certain extent he
still is, despite the prominence he has acquired from the contents of his
tomb.

Tutankhamun's name was known in the early years of this century
from a few references, but his exact place in the sequence of the
'Amarna kings' was uncertain. Like Akhenaten and Ay, his name had
been omitted from the classic king lists of Abydos and Karnak, which
simply jump from Amenhotep III to Horemheb. Indeed, Tutankhamun's
exact identity – and his parentage – is still a matter of some conjecture,
although it is clear that the young prince was brought up at Amarna,
probably in the North Palace. A number of items found in his tomb are
relics of his life at the Aten court, notably the Aten's disc shown protecting him and his young wife, Ankhesenpaaten, on the pictorial back
panel of his gold-inlaid throne (*opposite*).

Towards the end of Akhenaten's reign the senior members of the
court, especially Ay and Horemheb, probably realized that things could

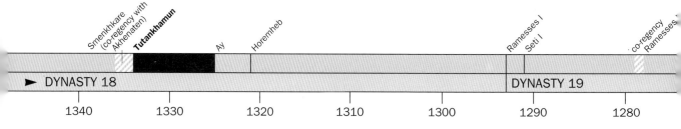

DYNASTY 18

Smenkhkare
(co-regency with
Akhenaten)

Tutankhamun

Ay

Horemheb

DYNASTY 19

Ramesses I

Seti I

co-regency
Ramesses

1340 1330 1320 1310 1300 1290 1280

(*Above*) Gilded wooden statue of Isis, one of the four goddesses that guarded the canopic shrine and chest of Tutankhamun with their outstretched arms. Cairo Museum.

(*Below right*) Detail of the gold-covered and inlaid back panel of Tutankhamun's throne; the king is seated whilst his wife, Ankhesenpaaten (it carries the Amarna form of their names) adjusts his Broad Collar. Cairo Museum.

(*Below*) The king's Aten-style name in a cartouche from the throne's outer arm.

not go on as they were. Smenkhkare, Akhenaten's brother (or son?) and co-regent, must have come to the same conclusion since he had left Akhetaten and moved back to the old secular capital, Memphis, where he may have been in contact with the proscribed members of the priesthood of Amun before his death and burial at Thebes. Soon after Akhenaten's death, Tutankhaten (as he then was) was crowned at Memphis. Aged about nine when he succeeded, the young king would have had no close female relatives left – his probable mother Kiya (p. 130), his stepmother Nefertiti and his elder step-sisters all being dead. He was probably under the direct care and influence of Ay, the senior civil servant, and Horemheb, the military man. Tutankhaten's wife, Ankhesenpaaten, was evidently older than he since she was already of child-bearing age, seemingly having had a daughter by her father, Akhenaten.

As soon as the new king had been installed, a move was made back to the old religion. This was signified radically in Year 2 when both king and queen changed the -aten ending of their names to -amun. Tutankhamun probably had little to do with this or indeed many other decisions – his 'advisors' were the ones who held the reins and manipulated the puppet strings of the boy-king. A great 'Restoration' stele records the reinstallation of the old religion of Amun and the reopening and rebuilding of the temples. The stele is known from two copies, both of which were later usurped by Horemheb, as were many other monuments of Tutankhamun. A large number of reliefs and statues have been identified as originally belonging to Tutankhamun (the majority showing him either in the company of Amun or as the god himself), for

WHO WAS TUTANKHAMUN?

Exactly who Tutankhamun was is still a matter of some conjecture. An inscription on one of the great red granite lions from the temple at Soleb refers to Amenhotep III as his 'father'. Given that Akhenaten reigned for about 16 years, coupled with the fact that Tutankhamun was about nine years old when he became king, it seems highly implausible that Amenhotep could have been his real father (not to mention that Queen Tiy would have been somewhat old for child-bearing). Rather, it is much more likely that the word 'father' was used very loosely to stress the young king's ideological connections with Amenhotep III and the return to orthodoxy. Thus, Amenhotep III was probably his grandfather, and Akhenaten his father.

This raises another question, because Akhenaten's chief wife Nefertiti was always shown accompanied by daughters, never by a son. The assumption is that another queen at the court was his mother. One name is particularly prominent at Amarna: that of a lady named Kiya. She certainly seems to have been married to Akhenaten, as one of her titles testifies, 'Greatly Beloved Wife'. Perhaps she was the Mitannian princess Tadukhepa, the daughter of King Tushratta who was given an Egyptian name. She was clearly high in favour before Year 9, but she disappears about Year 11 – perhaps this was when Tutankhaten was born and Kiya died in childbirth; damaged mourning scenes in the Amarna royal tomb (room alpha, on Wall F) might support this theory. In earlier reliefs Kiya is shown accompanied by a small daughter – possibly Tutankhaten had an elder sister. Many of Kiya's monuments after Year 11 are reinscribed with the name of Akhenaten's eldest daughter, Merytaten, who had succeeded in her mother's role as chief wife after Nefertiti's death (p. 124).

although the inscriptions have been changed, the king's boyish features are clearly recognizable. Extensive building works were carried out at Karnak and Luxor in Tutankhamun's name, especially the great colonnade and the relief scenes of the Festival of Opet at Luxor, but all were subsequently taken over by Horemheb.

Apart from the pivotal return to Thebes and the cult of Amun, few events from Tutankhamun's reign have been documented. Military campaigns were apparently mounted in Nubia and Palestine/Syria, suggested by a brightly painted gesso box from Tutankhamun's tomb which has four spirited scenes featuring the king. One shows him hunting lions in the desert, another gazelles, whilst on the third and fourth he furiously attacks Nubians and then Syrians, who fall to his arrows. Finely carved scenes of prisoners in the Memphite tomb of the military commander-in-chief, Horemheb, lend some veracity to the scenes on the gesso box, as does the painting in the tomb of Huy, Viceroy of Nubia, which shows subservient Nubian princes and piles of tribute. It is doubtful, however, that Tutankhamun actually took part in any of the campaigns.

Tutankhamun's retinue

In addition to the two premier figures of Ay and Horemheb, the names of other high officials who served during Tutankhamun's reign are known to us. Two of them were accorded the privilege of donating objects to the king's burial. One was Nakhtmin, a military officer under Horemheb and a relative of Ay (possibly a son). He presented five large wooden *ushabtis*, each inscribed with his name under the feet. There is a fine portrait head of Nakhtmin in Cairo, broken from a dyad statue with his beautiful but unnamed wife. Another official was Maya, who was Tutankhamun's Treasurer and also Overseer of the Place of Eternity (the royal cemetery), where his name is also known from a graffito in a fine hand on a wall in the tomb of Tuthmosis IV recording restorations being carried out, presumably the checking and rewrapping of the royal mummy (p. 114). To Tutankhamun's tomb Maya contributed a fine large wooden *ushabti* (again with his name recorded under its feet), and a beautifully carved effigy of the mummified king on a lion-headed bier with two delightful *ka* and *ba* birds watching over him. Maya's tomb was located at Saqqara in 1843 by Richard Lepsius when the splendid statues of him and his wife Meryt were removed to Leiden. In 1986 the tomb was rediscovered by Professor Geoffrey Martin through a robbers' tunnel from a nearby tomb.

Another high official to have a tomb at Thebes (TT 40) was Huy, Viceroy of Nubia. A vast wall painting, about 17 ft (c. 6 m) long, shows Huy in the full finery of his office presenting the princes of north and south Nubia, together with their families and retainers, to the king. Not least amongst the representations is the entourage of a Nubian princess, she in her chariot, and the vast piles of tribute. This may all be the result of Horemheb's military foray into Nubia.

The map labels:

Ramesses VII (1)
Road from Qurna and the Nile
Ramesses IV (2)
Yuya and Tuya (46)
Merneptah (8)
Ramesses II (7)
Tutankhamun (62)
? Sons of Ramesses II (5)
Ramesses XI (4)
Ramesses VI (9)
Ramesses IX (6)
Amenhotep II (35)
Smenkhkare (55)
Userhet (45)
Horemheb (57)
Amenmesses (10)
Amenemopet (48)
Maherpra (36)
Ramesses III (11)
Chancellor Bay (13)
Ramesses I (16)
Ramesses X (18)
Seti I (17)
Siptah (47)
Twosret (14)
Hatshepsut (20)
Tuthmosis I (38)
Mentuhirkhopshef (19)
Seti II (15)
Tuthmosis IV (43)
To Deir el-Bahari
0   100 m
0   300 ft
Tuthmosis III (34)
To Deir el-Medina

The death of a king

Tutankhamun died young, probably during his ninth regnal year. Evidence for this is twofold. First, forensic analysis of his mummy has put his age at death at about 17. Secondly, clay seals on wine jars found in his tomb record not only the type of wine, the vineyard and the name of the chief vintner, but also the king's regnal year when each wine was laid down. The highest recorded date is Year 9, suggesting that Tutankhamun died in that year.

There is no positive evidence on Tutankhamun's mummy as to how he met his death: he certainly did not die of consumption as was once thought. However, autopsies and X-rays have located a small sliver of bone within the upper cranial cavity. It may have arrived there as the result of a blow, but whether deliberately struck, to indicate murder, or the result of an accident, such as a fall from a chariot, it is not possible to say.

(*Top*) View of the Valley of the Kings from the cliffs above, in a similar orientation to the plan, *above*. The squared wall in the centre is the entrance to Tutankhamun's tomb (KV 62).

The discovery of Tutankhamun's tomb

Several finds made in the Valley of the Kings over the years led Howard Carter to believe that the king was still somewhere in the Valley: a small faience cup bearing Tutankhamun's name (1905–6 season), the remnants of materials used in the king's embalming and of a funerary feast or wake (1907), followed two years later in 1909 by a cache of gold fragments from chariot and furniture fittings with the king's name and that of Ay as a commoner. The story of Carter's quest and his understanding patron, the Fifth Earl of Carnarvon, is well known.

THE PAINTED BURIAL CHAMBER

The only room to be decorated was the burial chamber, whose four walls are painted with scenes of Tutankhamun's funeral and the Underworld. On the east wall, the king's catafalque is drawn on a sledge to the tomb. The south wall shows him being welcomed into the Afterworld in the company of Hathor, Isis and Anubis. The west wall (upon which the others are focused) has extracts from the 'Book of the Amduat' (That Which Is in the Underworld) and the squatting figures of twelve baboons, representing the hours of the night through which the king will pass.

The north wall is the most interesting, however, for here the decoration falls into three groups. The

first scene, on the right (p. 137), shows Tutankh-amun's successor Ay dressed in a priest's panther skin and wearing the Blue Crown, performing the ceremony of the Opening of the Mouth on the king's standing Osiride-form mummy. This painting is unique amongst royal tomb decoration. Next Tutankhamun is welcomed by the goddess Nut (who is normally found on the underside of the sarcophagus lid or over the whole ceiling of the tomb, arching her body protectively over the king). The final section of the north wall shows Tutankhamun, with his *ka* in close attendance, being embraced by Osiris in welcome to the Underworld.

The entire decoration of the chamber had to be completed in less than 70 days, the period stipulated for the embalming process and burial.

(*Below right*) The solid gold inner coffin of Tutankhamun, weighing 110.4 kg, was found nestled within two other wooden coffins, each overlaid with beaten gold. Inside was the king's mummy, its face covered by the gold funerary mask (p. 128), weighing 10.23 kg, and with over 170 items in all on the body. The second, or middle coffin of the three (*opposite, below*), has a distinctly different face represented on it from those on the first and the gold coffin. It may have been made, like the gold canopic coffinettes found in the tomb which copy it, for Smenkhkare (pp. 126–7). Cairo Museum.

After many years of frustrating and meticulous working through the Valley, clearing down to bedrock, the first of a flight of 16 descending steps was found on 4 November 1922, just in front and to the north side of the entrance to the tomb of Ramesses VI (KV 9). By the next day the stairs had been cleared, revealing the top of a blocked door, sealed with the impression of the necropolis guards (the recumbent jackal over nine captives); behind it was a sloping corridor filled with debris and, at the far end, another blocked doorway. Beyond it and at right angles was a large chamber, dubbed the Antechamber, and off it to the back left was a smaller room, the Annexe. To the right was a blocked doorway in the end wall guarded by two larger-than-lifesize black wood statues of the king. Beyond that was the burial chamber, almost completely filled with the huge catafalque of four gold overlaid wooden shrines enclosing the red quartzite sarcophagus with its cracked granite lid (p. 135).

(*Above*) Three of Tutankhamun's large wooden *ushabtis* wearing (*left to right*) the Red Crown, a wig, and the *nemes* headdress. Two were found in the Treasury (p. 134) but the third (*far right*) was found in the Antechamber, probably thrown down there when the robbers realized it was not solid gold. Its face is very different from its companions, possibly because it had been intended for someone else – perhaps even a woman, judging by its low slim hips. Carter numbers 330C, 326A and 458. Cairo Museum.

Of the nest of three coffins in the sarcophagus, the innermost was of solid gold, the outer two of wood overlaid with gold. The king's mummy lay in the midst of all this splendour with its famous gold mask but, by comparison, the actual remains of the king himself were pitiful, the result of poor embalming. Beyond the painted burial chamber (the only decorated room in the tomb), through an open doorway guarded by a large recumbent wooden figure of the jackal Anubis, lay the Treasury. Here stood the great canopic wooden shrine enclosing the calcite canopic chest. The chest held four jars containing Tutankhamun's viscera, whose human-headed lids were modelled in the likeness of the king.

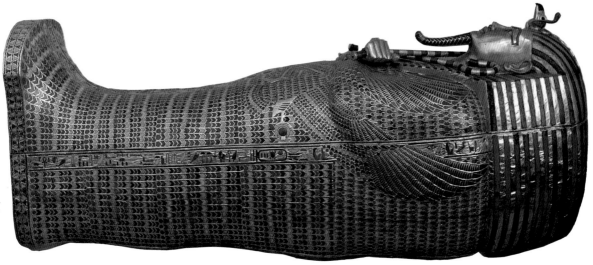

Hopes were high that amongst all the splendour there would be some important literary or historical documentation, but nothing of that nature was found. Apart from the king's own remains, the most moving aspect of the tomb must surely be the two stillborn mummified foetuses of baby girls, aborted at five months and possibly eight or nine months, found in the Treasury. They must have been daughters of Tutankhamun by Ankhesenamun. Had either lived, she would have taken her mother's place in due course as the Great Royal Heiress, carrying on the Amarna blood line – indeed, the whole later history of Egypt's 19th Dynasty could have been changed.

The king's burial

The immediate availability of the gold coffin and mask as well as the large granite sarcophagus box suggests that provision for Tutankhamun's eventual burial had been in hand for some time. However, his actual death was obviously unexpected, for not only were a number of the items provided for the burial 'from stock' and originally intended for previous use, but even the tomb he was laid to rest in was not intended for him. Signs of haste are evident everywhere, since the ritual required that all preparations and the embalming be completed within a period of 70 days.

The tomb is far too small for a royal burial, and had almost certainly been granted as a royal favour to the elderly Ay in recognition of his signal service over the years. (There are other instances of high officials being granted a similar privilege of burial in the Valley of the Kings.) Because of the king's sudden demise, and the fact that this tomb was virtually ready, it was appropriated and steps immediately taken to decorate the burial chamber. Tutankhamun's intended tomb seems to be that found by Giovanni Belzoni in 1816 at the far end of the western Valley of the Kings (KV 23) and later used by Ay. This conforms to the pattern of 18th Dynasty royal tombs and was probably chosen with a propaganda motive in view, that is to bury the king fairly close to his grandfather Amenhotep III, thereby underlining the return to old ways and the old religion.

Amongst Tutankhamun's equipment there were a number of items that had obviously come from a funerary store. At least one of the great wooden shrines had been made for Smenkhkare, as had the four small gold coffinettes that held the king's viscera. It can be seen, sometimes with difficulty, where the earlier name had been excised and Tutankhamun's added over the top. It is also possible that the second (middle) coffin of the three (p. 133) had also been intended for Smenkhkare, since its features are unlike the other two and the miniature canopic coffinettes are copies of it.

Even the sarcophagus box was second-hand. Extensive recutting was undertaken, to the extent of removing all the original texts (thus lowering the surface), and adding new ones; wings were also added to alter the standing figures of the goddesses (possibly because they were originally

(*Above*) A recumbent Anubis jackal guards the open doorway from the burial chamber into the Treasury in Tutankhamun's tomb. In the background is the great gilded wood canopic shrine (p. 129).

(*Below*) One of two life-size figures of Tutankhamun that guarded the seated doorway to the burial chamber, here wearing the *khat* headdress, its companion the *nemes*. Cairo Museum.

THE TOMB ROBBERIES

Contrary to popular belief, Tutankhamun's tomb was not intact when Carter found it: only the burial was undisturbed. The tomb had been robbed twice in antiquity, quite soon after it was sealed. The first robbery was for the gold and precious jewellery, most of which the robbers got away with except for a notable group of seven solid gold rings found still wrapped in the robber's kerchief and stuffed into a box in the Annexe. The jewellery now displayed in the Cairo Museum was mainly recovered from the body of the king, on which there were over 170 items.

After the priests and guards had resealed the tomb, it was broken into again, this time to steal the precious oils and unguents (largely stored in tall rather ungainly alabaster jars) which the thieves had left behind the first time. On this occasion they came equipped with empty goatskins. The tomb was resealed once again, this time for good: the entrance disappeared from view, hidden in the floor of the Valley. Debris from the construction of Ramesses VI's tomb buried the entrance deeper still, and there it lay for over 3000 years, until Carter rediscovered the tomb in 1922.

standing queens, as on Akhenaten's shattered sarcophagus?). The granite lid was made to fit the quartzite box – obviously a different material but, again, time may have been of the essence and a suitable slab of granite was available at Thebes. In the event there was an accident and the lid was split in two.

The succession in question

Tutankhamun's early death left his wife Ankhesenamun a young widow in a very difficult situation. Obviously hemmed in on all sides by ambitious men much older than herself, she took an unprecedented step and wrote to Suppiluliumas I, king of the Hittites, explaining her plight. The evidence comes not from the Egyptian records but from excavations at Hattusas (Boghazköy) in Turkey, the Hittite capital, where a copy was found in the archives. She told him her husband had died and she had no sons while he had many, so would he send one to marry her and continue the royal line. The Hittite king was highly suspicious and made enquiries; messengers were sent to check the details and reported back that such was the case. A Hittite prince, Zannanza, was therefore sent to Egypt to take up the queen's offer. It seems that he got no further than the border before he was murdered, and the deed can easily be laid at the door of Horemheb: he had the means as commander-in-chief of the army, the opportunity and certainly the motive.

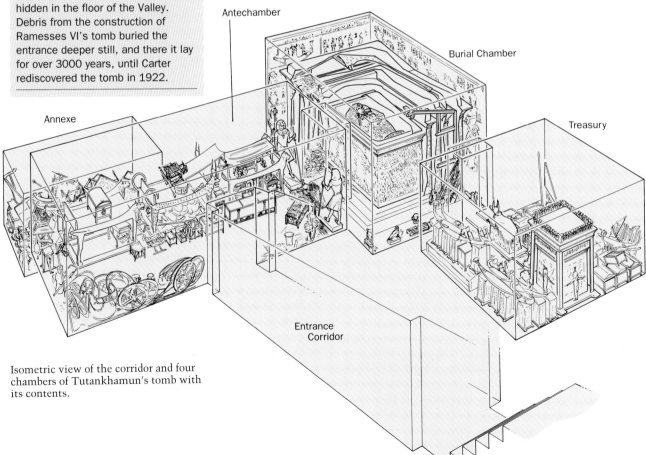

Isometric view of the corridor and four chambers of Tutankhamun's tomb with its contents.

DYNASTY 18
1570–1293

Ay
(itnetjer)
Kheperkheperure
1325–1321

Horemheb
(meryamun)
Djeserkheperure Setepenre
1321–1293

Detail of Horemheb in the *nemes* headdress, flanked by deities, from a wall-painting in his tomb (KV 57).

AY	
Birth name + (epithet)	*Wives*
Ay (it-netjer) ('Ay, Father of the God')	Tiy II, Ankhesenamun
Throne name	*Burial*
Kheper-kheperu-re ('Everlasting are the Manifestations of Re')	Tomb KV 23, Valley of the Kings (Thebes)

HOREMHEB	
Birth name + (epithet)	Re, Chosen of Re')
Hor-em-heb (mery-amun) ('Horus is in Jubilation, Beloved of Amun')	*Father* Unknown
Also known as	*Mother* Unknown
Horemhab, Haremhab	*Wives* Unknown wife,
Throne name	Mutnodjmet (sister of Nefertiti)
Djeser-kheperu-re Setep-en-re ('Holy are the Manifestations of	*Burial* Tomb KV 57, Valley of the Kings (Thebes)

AY

Ay, now an old man, apparently became king by marrying Tutankhamun's widow, Ankhesenamun – probably against her wishes since she was actually marrying her grandfather. Evidence for the marriage came from the bezel of a ring seen by Professor Percy Newberry in Cairo in the 1920s which carried the cartouches of Ankhesenamun and Ay side by side: a normal way of indicating a marriage. The wedding must have taken place rapidly because Ay officiated at Tutankhamun's funeral as a king wearing the Blue Crown. Furthermore, by burying his predecessor he also consolidated his claim to the throne.

In view of his age, it is small wonder that Ay's reign was brief: a mere four years. There are few monuments that can be identified as his – partly, no doubt, because many of them were usurped by Horemheb. At any rate, work continued on Tomb 23 in the Western Valley (probably originally intended for Tutankhamun), and the walls were extensively painted. It is to be noted that the lady accompanying Ay in the paintings is not Ankhesenamun but his older wife, Tiy. A large stone sarcophagus was provided for Ay which, like Tutankhamun's, had goddesses enfolding the corners with their wings. The tomb was

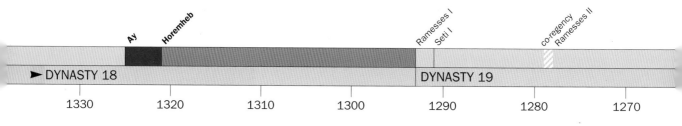

In a painting unique amongst royal tomb decoration Ay, Tutankhamun's successor, performs the ceremony of the Opening of the Mouth on the north wall of Tutankhamun's burial chamber. Shown crowned as king wearing the Blue Crown, he must obviously have married Ankhesenamun, Tutankhamun's widow, and succeeded to the throne all within the 70 days allowed for the embalming and funerary arrangements.

found by Belzoni in 1816, the sarcophagus in fragments. Its complete and domed lid was only rediscovered in the burial chamber debris in 1972. Ay's mummy has not been identified, although Professors Wente and Harris suggested in 1990 that the mummy from the 1881 cache hitherto identified as Amenhotep III might be that of Ay. In fact it is highly unlikely that Ay's mummy survives in view of the destruction wreaked in his tomb. Not only was the sarcophagus smashed, but his figure was hacked out and his name excised in the wall paintings and texts. No *ushabti* figures are known to exist for him either. This *damnatio memoriae* seems to have been carried out on the instructions of Ay's successor, Horemheb, which raises the curious question as to why he did not order Tutankhamun's tomb to be similarly attacked and robbed – after all, he could not have forgotten its location in less than a decade, particularly since he was so involved with the burial.

In his mortuary temple at Thebes near Medinet Habu, Ay inscribed his name on two quartzite colossi of Tutankhamun, taken from the latter's temple nearby (possibly buried below that of Ay). Even these statues were usurped by Horemheb when he took over Ay's temple.

It would appear that Ankhesenamun did not survive Ay and there is no later record of her after the ring bezel mentioned above. With her died the last of the true Amarna royal blood line.

HOREMHEB

Horemheb's background is virtually unknown except that he came from Herakleopolis near the entrance to the Faiyum and was obviously a career officer whose capabilities were early recognized. First serving under Amenhotep III, he became Great Commander of the Army under Akhenaten and was later appointed King's Deputy by Tutankhamun. He was obviously a highly ambitious man, and the death of Ay offered the perfect opportunity to restore to Egypt the strong leadership he felt she needed. Horemheb therefore declared himself king in 1321, consolidating his claim to the throne through his marriage to a lady named Mutnodjme, the sister of Nefertiti. He thus formed a link back to the female royal blood line, albeit a tenuous one. From evidence in his recently rediscovered tomb at Saqqara he appears to have had an earlier wife, but her name is not known.

Horemheb must have been in middle age when he became king and he immediately set about restoring the status quo, reopening the temples, repairing them where necessary, and bringing back the priesthood of Amun. Here he did make a change, however: realizing the stranglehold they had endeavoured to put on Amenhotep III, he reappointed priests from the army, whose loyalties he could rely on. To consolidate his hold over the army, now that he was really no longer primarily a military man, he divided it under two separate commanders, one for the north and one for the south.

(*Above*) Horemheb in his military official capacity represented as a seated scribe in a diorite statue from Memphis. The base inscription invokes four Memphis deities and refers to his law enforcement. Metropolitan Museum, New York.

(*Below*) Relief in Horemheb's Saqqara tomb showing him seated before a table of offerings, represented as a high noble before he became king.

Horemheb usurped the monuments of his immediate predecessors Ay and Tutankhamun. To the two great 'Restoration' stele that detailed the good works of Tutankhamun he simply added his own name. Embellishments were carried out at the great temple of Amun at Karnak where he initiated the great Hypostyle Hall and added a tall pylon, No. 9. Here he achieved two objects: first, he built the pylon to the glory of Amun on the south side of Karnak; and secondly, he destroyed the hated temple to the Aten erected by Akhenaten by simply dismantling it and using its small *talatat* ('two-hands width') blocks as interior filling for the hollow pylon. Archaeologists have recovered thousands of these blocks during the restoration of the pylon and have been able to reconstruct great Amarna scenes. In one sense, therefore, Horemheb's destructive scheme backfired: by hiding the blocks in the pylon he preserved them for posterity.

Horemheb took over Ay's mortuary temple on the west bank at Medinet Habu, together with the two colossal quartzite statues of Tutankhamun that Ay had himself usurped. Thus he set about completely expunging from the record any trace of his four Amarna predecessors. He dated his reign from the death of Amenhotep III, adding the intervening years to his own total; none of the Amarna names appeared in any of the Ramesside king lists at Abydos and Karnak. Furthermore, in the early 19th Dynasty tomb of a certain Amenmosi at Thebes (TT 19), where two rows of seated statues of kings and queens are depicted on the west wall, Horemheb is placed between Amenhotep III and Ramesses I. Kings of the 19th Dynasty were to regard him as the founder of their line, and this probably explains why a number of tombs of officials, as well as that of Ramesses II's sister, the princess Tia, were deliberately placed near his Saqqara tomb.

Although official records of Horemheb's reign go as high as Year 59 (incorporating those of the Amarna pharaohs), his actual reign of almost 30 years was spent in consolidation. There is little evidence of external contact except for a campaign in Kush (possibly simply a royal progress or inspection) and a trading expedition to the south.

The two tombs of Horemheb

Horemheb began his funerary preparations long before he had any inkling that he would become pharaoh, meaning that he already had a private tomb at Saqqara when, as king, he started to build himself a large tomb in the Valley of the Kings. The tomb at Saqqara (like that of Maya, Tutankhamun's Treasurer) had been partly discovered in the early 19th century AD when sculptures and reliefs were removed from both to European collections (principally to Leiden), but it was lost again until the excavations of the Egypt Exploration Society in 1975.

Excavations at the Saqqara tomb revealed that the walls were superbly carved with scenes of Horemheb's military and court career. From these we learn that there were at least two small campaigns

(*Above*) Detail from a relief recovered from Horemheb's Saqqara tomb in the early 19th century AD, showing him adorned with the gold collar of honour bestowed by a grateful pharaoh (?Akhenaten or Tutankhamun). After he became king, workmen added the royal *uraeus* to his brow. Leiden Museum.

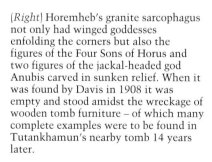

(*Right*) Horemheb's granite sarcophagus not only had winged goddesses enfolding the corners but also the figures of the Four Sons of Horus and two figures of the jackal-headed god Anubis carved in sunken relief. When it was found by Davis in 1908 it was empty and stood amidst the wreckage of wooden tomb furniture – of which many complete examples were to be found in Tutankhamun's nearby tomb 14 years later.

during Tutankhamun's reign against Libyans and Syrians – the faces of the prisoners are especially well represented in the carvings. The tomb was badly wrecked in antiquity, but enough remained of shattered funerary furniture and reliefs and a superb openwork gold earring that the robbers must have dropped to testify that Horemheb's tomb was one of the finest in the area. He himself was not buried in the Saqqara tomb because of his elevation, although it appears that his two wives may have been. After Horemheb became pharaoh, he sent workmen to add the royal *uraeus* to his brow in the sculpted reliefs, even though he himself was not going to make use of the tomb (p. 138).

Horemheb's tomb in the Valley of the Kings (KV 57) was found by Theodore Davis in 1908. As with all the tombs in the royal valley, it was unfinished and had been robbed. Davis found large quantities of shattered furniture and wooden figures of the king, examples of which, some 14 years later, were to be found complete in Tutankhamun's tomb, such as the king standing on the back of a striding panther (already known from the wall paintings in the later 20th Dynasty tomb of Seti II, KV 15). The painting of several rooms in the tomb had been finished to a very high standard. Work in other rooms, however, was still in progress when the king died, and these are particularly interesting because they show the manner of working – the outline grids and the corrections made.

In the burial hall Davis found Horemheb's great red granite sarcophagus. Horemheb's mummy was not discovered, although the remains of four individuals were scattered in the burial hall and a side chamber. These were probably members of Horemheb's family, although it has been suggested that Ay's body may have been brought here from his tomb in the Western Valley after it had been robbed. It is possible that a graffito found in the tomb refers to Horemheb's body being moved to the tomb of Twosret and Setnakhte (KV 14) for restoration, but other than that there is no trace of it – it does not appear to be one of the unidentified bodies from the two mummy caches (p. 103).

DYNASTY 19
1293–1185

Ramesses I
Menpehtyre
1293–1291

Seti I (meryenptah)
Menmaatre
1291–1278

Detail of a wall painting of Ramesses I from his tomb (KV16) at Thebes, showing the king in the hieroglyphic gesture of praise.

RAMESSES I	
Birth name	*Mother*
Ra-messes ('Re has Fashioned Him')	Unknown
Also known as	*Wife*
Ramses	Sitre
Throne name	*Son*
Men-pehty-re ('Eternal is the Strength of Re')	Seti I
	Burial
Father	Tomb KV 16, Valley of the Kings (Thebes)
Troop commander Seti	

SETI I	
Birth name + (epithet)	*Mother*
Seti (mery-en-ptah) ('He of the god Seth, Beloved of Ptah')	Sitre
	Wife
	Tuya
Also known as	*Sons*
Sethos I (Greek)	(Name unknown), Ramesses II
Throne name	*Daughters*
Men-maat-re ('Eternal is the Justice of Re')	Tia, Henutmire
	Burial
Father	Tomb KV 17, Valley of the Kings (Thebes)
Ramesses I	

RAMESSES I

The 19th Dynasty, despite its later luminaries, began on a fairly low note. Ramesses I, from whom the main part of the period takes its name, 'Ramesside', came to be pharaoh almost by default. He was previously the vizier, close friend and confidant of the pharaoh Horemheb, who – having failed to produce an heir – appears to have bestowed the succession on his comrade. Ramesses must have been of advanced years, probably into his fifties, and was not of royal blood. He was a 'career' army officer, the son of the troop commander, Seti. Their family came from the north-eastern Delta area of Avaris, the capital of the Hyksos invaders of 400 years earlier.

The short reign of Ramesses I, probably only about two years, gave him hardly any time to make his mark on history. There are some reliefs on the Second Pylon at Karnak and a stele dated early in his second regnal year found at Wadi Halfa. His small tomb in the Valley of the Kings (KV 16) was found by Belzoni on 10/11 October 1817 and showed all the signs of a hasty interment. The burial chamber was unfinished, in fact it had been intended to be merely an antechamber to a much larger tomb. As so often, the tomb had been robbed in antiquity,

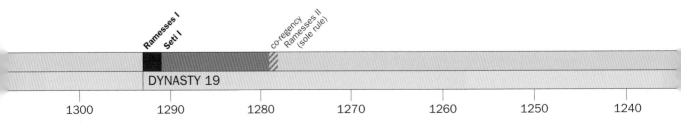

DYNASTY 19

Ramesses I
Seti I

co-regency
Ramesses II (sole rule)

1300   1290   1280   1270   1260   1250   1240

Profiles of the mummies of (*top to bottom*) Seti I, Ramesses II and Merneptah, respectively grandfather, father and son. The first two were found in the 1881 Deir el-Bahari royal cache and the last in the tomb of Amenhotep II in 1898.

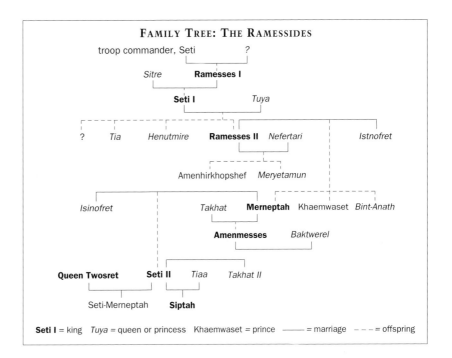

FAMILY TREE: THE RAMESSIDES

troop commander, Seti ⸺ ?

Sitre ⸺ **Ramesses I**

Seti I ⸺ *Tuya*

? ⸺ *Tia* ⸺ *Henutmire* ⸺ **Ramesses II** ⸺ *Nefertari* ⸺ *Istnofret*

Amenhirkhopshef ⸺ *Meryetamun*

Isinofret ⸺ *Takhat* ⸺ **Merneptah** ⸺ Khaemwaset ⸺ *Bint-Anath*

Amenmesses ⸺ *Baktwerel*

Queen Twosret ⸺ **Seti II** ⸺ *Tiaa* ⸺ *Takhat II*

Seti-Merneptah ⸺ **Siptah**

Seti I = king *Tuya* = queen or princess Khaemwaset = prince ⸺ = marriage – – – = offspring

although some of the burial provisions still remained, notably the large granite sarcophagus, a pair of almost 6½-ft (2-m) high wooden statues of the king once covered with thin gold foil, and a number of wooden statuettes of underworld deities with curious animal heads. Robbers had damaged the sarcophagus as they prised the lid off and there is evidence that they actually hurled some of the smaller statuettes against the tomb walls in destructive fury, since tiny slivers of gold foil have been observed attached to the painted plaster. Ramesses' mummy may not have survived (it certainly has not been identified), although it does appear to have been taken from the tomb before 968 BC, around the time when a number of the royal mummies were being moved to safety, eventually to be deposited in the tombs of Amenhotep II (KV 35) and Queen Inhapi (DB 320).

The burial of Ramesses' wife, Queen Sitre, broke with earlier traditions where the queen was apparently buried in her husband's tomb at a later date, if she outlived him. Sitre's tomb set a new precedent: it was placed in what is now known as the Valley of the Queens at Thebes. Like her husband's tomb, Sitre's (QV 38) was unfinished, with only a few paintings on the walls of the first chamber.

SETI I

Seti I had held the same titles of Vizier and Troop Commander as his father, Ramesses I, whom he rapidly succeeded. In order to restore Egyptian fortunes after the instability under the Amarna kings, he inaugurated a policy of major building at home and a committed foreign policy abroad. He took the additional title of 'Repeater of Births', signifying the beginning of a new and legitimate era. It was indeed a period of rebirth for Egypt, and during Seti's 13-year reign Egyptian art and culture achieved a maturity and sophistication that were scarcely equalled in later centuries. Seti married within his own military 'caste', choosing Tuya, the daughter of a lieutenant of chariotry, Raia. Their first child was a boy, who died young, and their second a daughter, Tia. Their third, another boy, took his grandfather's name and later became Egypt's mightiest pharaoh, Ramesses II. A second daughter, born much later, was called Henutmire and she was to become a minor queen of her elder brother in due course.

Seti's military campaigns

Seti led a military expedition into Syria as early as the first year of his reign. The records of this campaign and several subsequent ones over at least the initial six years of Seti's rule are preserved on the outer north and east walls of the great temple of Amun at Karnak. They follow a basic pattern of the army on the march, where Seti followed his predecessor Tuthmosis III's tactic of swift movement up through the Gaza Strip and Palestinian coast, thereby securing his flank and supply lines by sea into Phoenician ports. Fortresses are shown being attacked and Syrians captured, bound and carried off, the whole culminating in a huge representation of prisoners being slain before Amun.

Other campaigns were waged against the Libyans of the western desert, and there was a renewed attack upon Syria and Lebanon where, for the first time, Egyptian met Hittite in battle. One scene at Karnak shows the capture of Kadesh that was to be the focus of the famous battle in later years under Seti's son, Ramesses II (p. 150). All the while Seti was endeavouring to restore the past glories of the earlier 18th Dynasty pharaohs Tuthmosis III and Amenhotep III.

A high point of Egyptian art

During Seti's reign some tremendous building projects were undertaken. The quality of the reliefs that embellished new cult temples and his tomb are virtually unsurpassed in Egyptian art. At Karnak, where his victories were chronicled, Seti began the work of building the great Hypostyle Hall in the Temple of Amun that was to be completed by his son Ramesses. One of the wonders of ancient architecture and planning, the Hall covers an area of 335 x 174 ft (102 x 53 m), and has 134 gigantic columns of which the inner 12, slightly higher than the outer rows at 75 ft (23 m) in height, had clerestory lighting via stone grills through which the only light entered the Hall. Seti's reliefs are on the north side and contrast in their fine style with the later additions.

At Abydos, the ancient cult centre of the god Osiris, Seti built what is undoubtedly the most remarkable decorated temple amongst all those of ancient Egypt. Its construction indicates Seti's determination to demonstrate his devotion to Egypt's most popular deity, and to link himself with the distant origins of Egyptian monarchy. Unusually, the

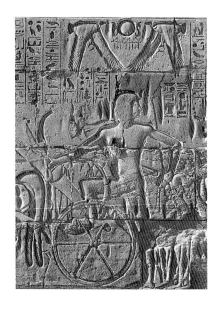

(*Below*) Detail from Seti I's battle reliefs on the outer north wall of the Hypostyle Hall at Karnak – the king mounts his chariot under the protection of two vulture goddesses.

THE MAJOR BUILDINGS OF SETI

Karnak:
Hypostyle Hall in the Temple of Amun

Abydos:
Temple of Seti I
Osireion
Temple to Ramesses I

Thebes, Valley of the Kings:
Tomb KV 17

Gourna, Thebes:
Mortuary Temple

(*Right*) View through the great forest of columns representing the primeval papyrus marsh in the Hypostyle Hall of the temple of Amun at Karnak.

(*Below*) In a series of sculpted and painted niches in the temple of Seti I at Abydos the king is seen making offerings to various gods. Here he offers a bouquet of flowers to the hawk-headed Horus who wears the Double Crown of Upper and Lower Egypt. The iconography is interesting since the king was himself Horus upon earth.

temple has seven sanctuaries, dedicated for the deified Seti himself (who died during its construction), Ptah, Re-Harakhte, Amun-Re, Osiris, Isis and Horus. In the main hall the superb reliefs show the king officiating in the temple as priest, offering to the god in his shrine and carrying out all the necessary daily functions of the priestly office in the service of the god. One part of the Abydos temple of particular interest and importance is the so-called 'Hall of Records' or 'Gallery of Lists'. Here Seti is shown with the young Ramesses before long official lists of the pharaohs from the earliest times to his own reign. It is notable that the names of the Amarna pharaohs are completely omitted, as if they did not exist in Egyptian history. The cartouche sequence jumps from Amenhotep III directly to Horemheb (p. 12).

In the desert at the rear of the great temple at Abydos Seti built a most enigmatic structure known as the Osireion. It is set at a lower level than the main temple (and now subject to almost continual flooding because of the high water table) and was originally entered through

(*Left*) Detail from the eastern section of the unusual astronomical ceiling of the burial chamber in the tomb of Seti I in the Valley of the Kings. It shows the constellations for the northern sky, whilst most royal tombs also have the figure of the sky goddess Nut extending her protection over the sarcophagus of the pharaoh below.

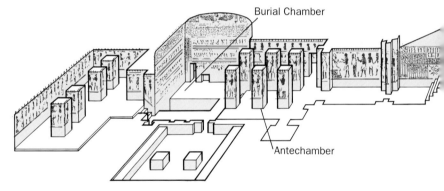

Burial Chamber

Antechamber

(*Below*) Watercolour copy of a scene in the tomb of Seti I by Henry Beechey, *c.* 1818, shortly after Belzoni's discovery of it. The fine and accurate detail by many of the talented early artists has enabled scholars such as Professor Erik Hornung to restore and reconstruct many aspects of the tomb now vanished or badly damaged.

a long tunnel covered with painted scenes from the Book of Gates. The tunnel leads eventually to a huge hall (100 x 65 ft, 30 x 20 m). This hall was the focal point of the building and it was here that the body of Seti, together with his funerary equipment, rested before being taken for burial in the Valley of the Kings. The whole structure, underground with a central mound surrounded by canal water, reflected the origins of life from the primeval waters.

Apart from a small temple at Abydos dedicated to Seti's father, Ramesses I, and his own mortuary temple at Thebes, now largely destroyed, the ultimate building of Seti's reign was his tomb in the Valley of the Kings (KV 17). Discovered by Giovanni Belzoni in October 1817, it is without doubt the finest in the Valley, as well as being the longest and deepest (both measurements being over 300 ft or 100 m). The workmanship in the decorations is superb, with finely delineated low reliefs and vibrant colours. In the burial hall Belzoni found the magnificent translucent alabaster sarcophagus of the king, which, as Belzoni remarked, 'merits the most particular attention, not having its

(*Below*) Isometric cross-section of the tomb of Seti I showing how its corridors dive steeply over 300 ft (100 m) underground to reach the burial hall. Various stratagems were employed in an endeavour to defeat the tomb robbers, such as the deep shaft early on, both to catch any rainwater flooding in and to lead the robbers into thinking that the burial was at its bottom, instead of through the painted false wall on its far side.

(*Below*) Detail of a painted pillar in the burial hall of Seti I's tomb showing the king in the company of the ibis-headed Thoth, god of wisdom, learning and writing.

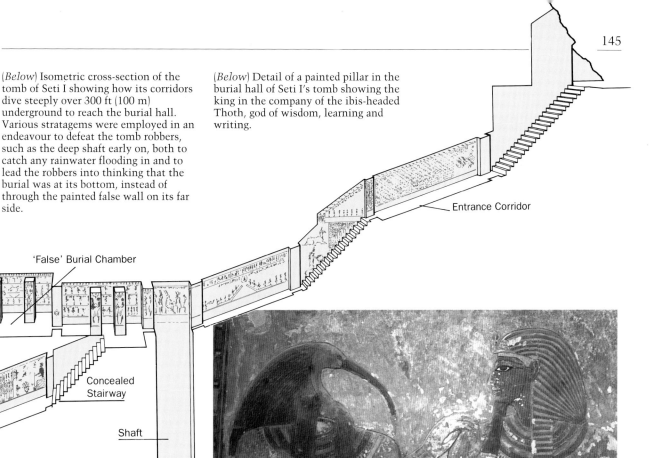

Entrance Corridor

'False' Burial Chamber

Concealed Stairway

Shaft

Queen Tuya

Seti's wife outlived her husband by many years. When Ramesses II became king, she appeared as the queen-mother on the façade at the temple of Abu Simbel. Statues of her were placed in her son's mortuary temple, the Ramesseum, and in his newly founded city, Piramesse in the Delta. She died, a grand old lady, probably in her sixties in Year 22 or early 23 of Ramesses' reign, about 1258 BC, and was buried in a large tomb in the Valley of the Queens (QV 80). Reclearance of the tomb in 1972 produced a canopic jar lid with a delightful portrait of her petite features.

equal in the world'. The lower box or chest was largely intact, but the sculpted lid with the recumbent figure of Seti had been badly smashed by ancient robbers and its pieces lay round about. Inside and out, the sarcophagus is carved with hieroglyphs, once filled with blue-green paint. On the floor of the chest and the outside of the lid are texts from the Book of Coming Forth by Day, and on the inside walls and the exterior, from the Book of Gates.

Seti's mummy, the finest of the surviving royal mummies, shows a noble face. It was not found in his tomb but was amongst the great royal cache of mummies revealed at Deir el-Bahari in 1881. A number of dockets on the mummy record that, before reaching its final resting place, it had been restored during the reign of the High Priest of Amun, Herihor (1080–1074 BC), presumably after the first robbery in the tomb, then again about Year 15 of Smendes (*c.* 1054 BC). After this Seti's mummy was joined in his tomb for a short while by that of his son, Ramesses II, before both were finally hidden in the Deir el-Bahari tomb (DB 320) in Year 10 of Siamun (*c.* 968 BC).

DYNASTY 19
1293–1185

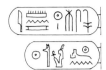

Ramesses II
(meryamun)
Usermaatre
1279–1212

(*Left*) The throne name of Ramesses II, Usermaatre, carved in alabaster hieroglyphs that have been inlaid into a blue faience plaque. Egyptian Art Museum, Madrid.

(*Right*) The upper half of a black granite seated statue of Ramesses II wearing the Blue or War Crown (*khepresh*). Discovered by Drovetti, it is probably the finest existing portrait of the king. Turin Museum.

RAMESSES II	
Birth name + (epithet) Ra-messes (mery-amun) ('Re has Fashioned Him, Beloved of Amun') *Also known as* Ramses *Throne name* User-maat-re Setep-en-re ('The Justice of Re is Powerful, Chosen of Re') *Father* Seti I *Mother* Tuya	*Wives* See list p.148 *Sons* Amenhirkhopshef, Prehirwonmef, Meryatum, Khaemwaset, Merneptah, etc. *Daughters* Meryetamun, Bint-Anath, Nebettawy, etc. *Burial* Tomb KV 7, Valley of the Kings (Thebes)

Ramesses II, who acceded to power at the age of 25, can rightly be said to merit his popular title, 'Ramesses the Great'. During his long reign of 67 years, everything was done on a grand scale. No other pharaoh constructed so many temples or erected so many colossal statues and obelisks. No other pharaoh sired so many children. Ramesses' 'victory' over the Hittites at Kadesh was celebrated in one of the most repeated Egyptian texts ever put on record. By the time he died, aged more than 90, he had set his stamp indelibly on the face of Egypt.

As a young prince, Ramesses was imbued with the military tradition established by his grandfather, after whom he was named. From his earliest years all hopes for the new dynasty were pinned on him. At the age of ten he was recognized as 'Eldest King's Son' by title (despite there being no other, his elder brother having died long before), and by his mid-teens he is found associated with Seti as a diminutive figure in the reliefs of the Libyan campaigns at Karnak. Ramesses was allowed to participate in Seti's subsequent campaigns against the Hittites in Syria.

The young prince rode well in harness alongside his experienced father, learning his trade of statecraft. Ramesses is often found referred to in inscriptions, overseeing the cutting of obelisks from the granite quarries at Aswan, involved in Seti's great building projects, and also inaugurating his own (smaller) temple to Osiris at Abydos. Many inscriptions of up-and-coming young men attest to Seti's keen and acute eye in spotting the high flyers, who were to grow up alongside Ramesses and serve him well in his turn (although he outlived most of them).

The royal wives

The youthful Ramesses took his two principal wives, Nefertari and Istnofret, at least ten years before Seti's death. The old king thus saw his grandchildren around him – at least 5 sons and 2 daughters by them, as well as possibly another 10 to 15 children from other ladies of the harem. No wonder that in later years and after further marriages, Ramesses could boast of over 100 sons and daughters that simply were not numbered.

Virtually nothing is known of the background of either Nefertari or Istnofret except that Nefertari was always the Chief Queen until her death in about Year 24 of the reign. Her recently restored tomb in the Valley of the Queens (QV 66) is one of the wonders of ancient Thebes. Istnofret took Nefertari's place, but only for some ten years as she seems to have died about Year 34. Nefertari bore Ramesses' first son, the Crown Prince Amenhirkhopshef, and at least three other sons and two daughters. Istnofret bore a son named Ramesses, plus two other important sons, Khaemwaset and Merneptah (the king's eventual successor). Khaemwaset later became famous as a 'magician', and is often referred to today as the first archaeologist thanks to his interest in ancient monuments and their restoration. The 5th Dynasty pyramid of Unas at Saqqara, for example, bears his inscription high up on the south face (p. 63).

Following royal custom, Ramesses took many of his other and subsequent wives from his immediate family. They included Henutmire, his younger sister, and three of his daughters: Meryetamun, Bint-Anath (a distinctly Syrian name meaning 'Daughter of Anath', which is curious since her mother was Istnofret) and Nebettawy. After peace had been concluded with the Hittites (see below), Ramesses cemented the new alliance by taking a Hittite princess as his bride, given the Egyptian name Maathorneferure. Seven years later, in 1239 BC, a second Hittite princess joined the court. In his old age, Ramesses' harem was nothing if not cosmopolitan, numbering another Hittite princess together with Syrian and Babylonian royal ladies.

The Hittite wars

Relations with the Hittites on Egypt's Syrian frontier were far from friendly during the first part of Ramesses' reign. In Seti's time, Egypt had kept her influence on the southern Phoenician coastline ports while the Hittites retained the northern city of Kadesh. In Year 4 of Ramesses' reign, however, there was a revolt in the Levant and in the spring of Year 5 (1275 BC) the new king was forced to mobilize his army.

THE QUEENS OF RAMESSES

During his long reign Ramesses took eight principal wives, but Nefertari was his first and favourite among them. Her tomb is the finest in the Valley of the Queens. Everywhere there is superb drawing and colour, recently restored to much of its pristine original condition by a team of international conservationists backed by the J. Paul Getty Museum, Malibu. Details are shown here. (*Right*) The queen, described in the hieroglyphs as 'The Deceased Great Royal Wife Nefertari', being greeted by the goddess Hathor, identified by her name before her rather than by her usual iconography of a woman with cow's ears. (*Below*) Maat, the goddess of truth, kneels with her protective outstretched wings above the entrance to Nefertari's burial chamber. The queen's royal cartouches appear on the lintel and door jambs.

THE GREAT ROYAL WIVES

1 Nefertari

2 Istnofret

3 Bint-Anath
daughter of Istnofret

4 Meryetamun
daughter of Nefertari

5 Nebettawy

6 Henutmire
king's sister

7 Maathorneferure
1st Hittite princess

8 (Name unknown)
2nd Hittite princess

(*Left*) Another detail from Nefertari's tomb is this charming representation of the queen playing the board game *senet*. The word *senet* means 'passing', but its shape as a hieroglyph can also be read as 'to endure', both sentiments appropriate for the queen's role in the afterlife.

(*Above*) This beautiful painted limestone bust of a Ramesside queen found in the Ramesseum has long been unidentified. Recently, an identical but colossal representation was found at Akhmin with the name of Meryetamun on it, a daughter of Ramesses II who became the 'Great Royal Wife' after the death of her mother Nefertari. Cairo Museum.

(*Right*) The diminutive figure of a graceful queen standing between the legs of the colossal granite statue of Ramesses II in the first courtyard of the temple at Karnak may be his daughter Bint-Anath, whose mother was queen Istnofret. Alternatively the figure may represent Nefertari. Some doubt exists because the statue was later usurped by the 21st Dynasty pharaoh Pinedjem I.

Reconstruction painting from a relief of Ramesses II at the siege of Dharpur carved on the inner south wall of the Hypostyle Hall in the Ramesseum. As usual in Egyptian art, the king is shown at huge scale in relation to everyone else. He tirelessly fires his arrows from his charging chariot, guiding the horses by the reins tied around his waist. The Hittite enemy chariotry is thrown into confusion, their citadel attacked with scaling ladders and the defenders plunge from the battlements as they put up a useless resistance. The long hieroglyphic inscription extols, as usual, the great valour of the king, aided by the god Amun.

Ramesses gathered together one of the greatest forces of Egyptian troops ever seen, 20,000 men basically in four divisions of 5000 each, named respectively after the gods Amun, Re, Ptah and Seth.

Following virtually in Tuthmosis III's footsteps of some 200 years earlier, Ramesses moved up through the Gaza Strip and was about 10 miles from Kadesh in early May. With such a large army, plus all the necessary ancillary elements of baggage trains and camp followers, progress was slow and extended over a vast area. Two spies captured and interrogated on the approach to Kadesh indicated that the Hittite army was over 100 miles to the north. Ramesses therefore moved forward confidently with the first division, Amun, crossed the river Orontes and camped to the west of Kadesh, a city that had created strong defences by diverting water through a canal from the river, making the city virtually an island. Ramesses' complacency was soon shaken, however, when a forward patrol captured two more spies who revealed under torture that the previous pair had been a 'plant' – the Hittite army was in fact just the other side of Kadesh, waiting in ambush.

The Hittite king, Muwatallis, had assembled an army even greater than the Egyptian one. In two sections each of about 18,000 and 19,000 men, plus 2500 chariots, it was a formidable force – and it struck almost immediately at the Re division, coming up to join Ramesses. The chariots swept through the Egyptian ranks, scattering the soldiery like chaff, and then plunged into the recently made camp. Confusion reigned and Ramesses found himself isolated, abandoned by all except his personal guard and shield-bearer, Menna. Nevertheless, as a quick-witted commander, he rallied his few forces to resist the attack. He was saved from

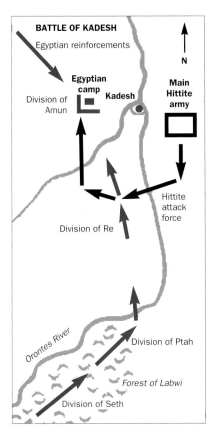

BATTLE OF KADESH

Egyptian reinforcements

N

Egyptian camp

Kadesh

Division of Amun

Main Hittite army

Hittite attack force

Division of Re

Orontes River

Division of Ptah

Forest of Labwi

Division of Seth

Map of troop movements at the battle of Kadesh.

annihilation or, worse, capture by his élite guard which, having taken a different route from the main army, came up rapidly and made a flank attack on the Hittites. Forced to fight on two fronts, Muwatallis retreated and the quiet of night settled over the battlefield, which Ramesses occupied.

The following day the now reunited Egyptian forces attacked, but the outcome was virtually a stalemate. Ramesses, however, did not view it as such. The pharaoh, young and remembering no doubt that his father Seti had not been able to hold Kadesh, reserved his options when Muwatallis proposed a peace. The Egyptian army marched home and the status quo remained.

Bombastic accounts of the battle and Ramesses' personal bravery under the hand of Amun were later inscribed on the walls of the temples at Karnak, Luxor (three versions), the Ramesseum (twice) and Ramesses' temples at Abydos, Abu Simbel and Derr. Many graphic incidents are illustrated in the reliefs: the charging chariotry, the heroic king, mercenaries in distinctive horned helmets cutting off the right hands of the slain for accounting purposes and, ludicrously (on the back of the Second Pylon in the Ramesseum), the fleeing Prince of Aleppo who tumbled into the Orontes, was fished out and suspended upside down by his adherents in an effort to drain him and bring him round. Accounts of the battle were also written in hieratic on papyrus, often as schoolboy exercises, and embellished with drawings of spirited horses.

THE PHARAOHS AND THE EXODUS

The Biblical story of the Exodus chronicles the Hebrews' escape from servitude in Egypt, their 40-year sojourn in the wilderness, and their eventual arrival in the Promised Land. The Hebrews had lived peacefully around the Nile Delta for 400 years. All this changed, however, in the 13th century BC, when Egypt became anxious about their growing numbers. A new pharaoh, now thought to be Seti I, condemned them to hard labour. They were to fare no better under Ramesses II, who set them to work on the construction of his temples and the massive new city of Piramesse.

According to the Bible, God took pity on the Hebrews and appeared to one of their number, Moses, promising to deliver his people from slavery. Ten times Moses petitioned Pharaoh to free the Hebrews. Ten times the king denied them freedom, and after each denial Egypt suffered a terrible catastrophe. The rivers were said to run with blood, until 'the fish that was in the river died, and the river stank, and the Egyptians could not drink of the water'.

Finally, when all the first-born Egyptian children mysteriously died in the night, Ramesses took fright and expelled the Hebrews. But on hearing of their actual flight, he regretted the loss of his work-force, and set out to recapture them. With a vast army, he caught up with the fugitives by the Sea of Reeds (perhaps one of the inland lakes between the Mediterranean and the Gulf of Suez). Heaven-sent help came once more, the waves parting to allow the Hebrews to cross, but closing behind them to engulf their pursuers.

Needless to say, none of these events are corroborated by ancient Egyptian records since the Exodus was a minor affair in Egyptian annals.

Further campaigns were undertaken against the Hittites in subsequent years, but eventually Ramesses realized that he could not hold the northern reaches of Syria, just as his opponents could not control the south. Internal troubles and a growing Assyrian menace to the east made the new Hittite king, Hattusilis III, realize that there was no point in the almost annual cat-and-mouse game with Egypt. He proposed a peace treaty. The outcome was terms agreed in Year 21 (1259), essentially of mutual non-aggression and support.

The treaty survives carved on the walls of Karnak and the Ramesseum and, by one of those coincidences of fate, in the Hittite version on clay tablets from Hattusas, the Hittite capital. (Perhaps not surprisingly, the two accounts do not quite agree. The Hittite sources say, for example, that it was Ramesses who sued for peace.) Letters and gifts were exchanged between the two royal families. An affable situation obtained, so much so that in 1246 Hattusilis III proposed an even closer link by offering one of his younger daughters to Ramesses as wife; her Egyptian name was Maathorneferure. There was a slight contretemps over the size of the dowry to accompany the princess, with Ramesses incongruously pleading poverty and asking for more, but it was resolved and she joined the court. A second princess, Hattusilis's oldest daughter, was offered some seven years later in 1239 and came to Egypt to join her sister. This new liaison was celebrated on marriage stele at Karnak, Elephantine, Abu Simbel and Amara West.

Ramesses the builder

As a monument builder Ramesses II stands pre-eminent amongst the pharaohs of Egypt. Although Khufu had created the Great Pyramid, Ramesses' hand lay over the whole land. True, he thought nothing of adding his name to other kings' monuments and statues right back to the Middle Kingdom, so that nowadays the majority of cartouches seen on almost any monument proclaim his throne name – User-maat-re ('the Justice of Re is strong'). Yet his genuine building achievements are on a Herculean scale. He added to the great temples at Karnak and Luxor, completed his father Seti's mortuary temple at Gourna (Thebes) and also his Abydos temple, and built his own temple nearby at Abydos. On the west bank at Thebes he constructed a giant mortuary temple, the Ramesseum. Inscriptions in the sandstone quarries at Gebel el-Silsila record at least 3000 workmen employed there cutting stone for the Ramesseum alone. Other major mortuary temples rose in Nubia at Beit el-Wali, Gerf Hussein, Wadi es Sebua, Derr and even as far south as Napata.

Ramesses' greatest building feat must be counted not one of these, but the carving out of the mountainside of the two temples at Abu Simbel in Nubia. The grandeur of the larger, the Great Temple, is overwhelming, fronted as it is by four colossal 60-ft (18-m) high seated figures of the king that flank the entrance in two pairs. It is strange to reflect that whilst the smaller temple, dedicated to Hathor and

(*Left*) Without a doubt Ramesses' greatest monument is the huge temple carved from the natural sandstone rock at Abu Simbel, far to the south in Nubia. Four great seated figures of the king flank the entrance in two pairs. So high was the overburden of sand around the entrance that for several years after its rediscovery by Burckhardt in 1813 it was not known whether the figures were in fact seated or standing. Giovanni Belzoni was the first European to enter the temple on 1 August 1817.

(*Below*) The magnificent black granite head of Ramesses II that stands in the Ramesseum is considered to be the second finest extant portrait of the king, after the Turin seated statue (p. 146). Lying nearby is the colossal fallen statue of over 1000 tons that inspired Shelley's immortal sonnet with its lines:
'My name is Ozymandias, King of Kings: Look on my works, ye mighty, and despair!'

(*Above*) The four seated colossi fronting the Great Temple at Abu Simbel.

Ramesses' favourite queen Nefertari, has lain open for centuries, the Great Temple was only rediscovered in 1813 by the Swiss explorer Jean Louis Burckhardt and first entered by Giovanni Belzoni on 1 August 1817. A miracle of ancient engineering, its orientation was so exact that the rising sun at the equinox on 22 February and 22 October flooded directly through the great entrance to illuminate three of the four gods carved seated in the sanctuary over 200 ft (60 m) inside the mountain (the fourth of the seated gods, Ptah, does not become illuminated as, appropriately, he is a god associated with the underworld).

Nefertari was probably present at the dedication of the two Abu Simbel temples in Year 24 (1256/55) and apparently died the following year, so at least she saw herself associated with her husband

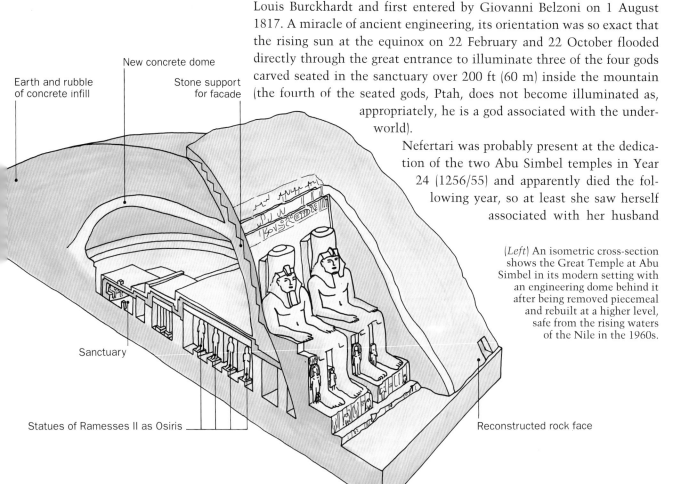

New concrete dome

Earth and rubble of concrete infill

Stone support for facade

Sanctuary

Statues of Ramesses II as Osiris

Reconstructed rock face

(*Left*) An isometric cross-section shows the Great Temple at Abu Simbel in its modern setting with an engineering dome behind it after being removed piecemeal and rebuilt at a higher level, safe from the rising waters of the Nile in the 1960s.

in his greatest work and lived to see the dedication of her temple.

One of Ramesses' preoccupations in all this building work was obviously the payment for it, and that meant gold. The precious metal is represented as being brought as 'tribute' in many Theban nobles' tombs of the 18th and 19th Dynasties, and a papyrus in the Turin Museum from the reign of Seti I actually shows a map of goldmines in the eastern desert.

A lot of the wealth was also diverted into the costs of building a fine new city in the Delta, Piramesse ('Domain of Ramesses'), near modern Qantir. Embellished with great obelisks, Piramesse became the wonder of the age – though little alas remains today – and it was probably on such building works that the Hebrews were employed in the 'land of Goshen'. The Exodus apparently took place from this area in about 1263–62, Year 17: 'And it came to pass at the end of four hundred and thirty years . . . that all the hosts of the Lord went out from the Land of Egypt' (Exodus 12:41). Although a traumatic experience for the Jews and a major element in Judaism, it was not recognized as such in Egypt and the only known reference to Israel in the Egyptian record occurs under Merneptah (p. 157).

Death and burial

In Year 67 (1212 BC) Ramesses II, perhaps 92 years of age, was called to the west to join the gods. His tomb had long been prepared in the Valley of the Kings (KV 7), and was as large, if not larger in area, than that of his father Seti I, although not so well decorated. Now it is much damaged and virtually inaccessible. The splendour of the contents of the tomb must have been incredible, if only by comparison with that of the tomb of the short-lived Tutankhamun. Few items, however, survive that can be associated with the burial: a wooden statuette of the king (British Museum), four pseudo-canopic jars (Louvre), the upper half of a hollow-cast, flattened bronze *ushabti* (Berlin), and two large wooden *ushabtis* (Brooklyn and British Museum).

The mummy of Ramesses was found in the great cache of royal mummies at Deir el-Bahari in 1881 (DB 320). A docket written in hieratic on the coffin in which it lay recorded that the body was moved in Year 15 (*c.* 1054 BC) of Smendes from its previous resting place to the tomb of his father, Seti I, whence it was taken to its last secret hiding place. In 1976 the mummy was flown to Paris where a great Ramesses II exhibition was staged. Deterioration had been noticed on the body and the journey was also for Ramesses to receive the best conservation treatment available. The mummy was examined by xero-radiography which revealed that Ramesses' distinctly aquiline nose had retained its shape because the ancient embalmers had packed it full of peppercorns (other noses on mummies tend to be flattened by the bandaging around them). As befitted visiting royalty, although he had been dead for nearly 3200 years, Ramesses was greeted at the Paris airport by a full Presidential Guard of Honour.

DYNASTY 19
1293–1185

Merneptah
(hetephermaat)
Baenre-merynetjeru
1212–1202

Amenmesses
(heqawaset)
Menmire-setepenre
1202–1199

Seti II
(merenptah)
Userkheperure-setepenre
1199–1193

Siptah
(merenptah)
Akhenre-setepenre
1193–1187

Queen Twosret
(setepenmut)
Sitre-meryamun
1187–1185

Upper half of a granite statue of Merneptah, Ramesses II's 13th son who eventually succeeded him, from his mortuary temple at Thebes. Cairo Museum.

MERNEPTAH	
Birth name + (epithet) Mer-ne-ptah (hetep-her-maat) ('Beloved of Ptah, Joyous is Truth') *Also known as* Merneptah *Throne name* Ba-en-re Mery-netjeru ('The Soul of Re, Beloved of the Gods') *Father* Ramesses II	*Mother* Istnofret *Wives* Isisnofret, Takhat *Sons* Seti-Merneptah/ (?Seti II) Amenmesses *Burial* Tomb KV 8, Valley of the Kings (Thebes)

MERNEPTAH

By the time that Merneptah, Ramesses' 13th son, succeeded his long-lived father he must have been into his sixties. Merneptah's ten-year reign is documented by three great inscriptions: some 80 lines on a wall in the temple of Amun at Karnak; a large stele with 35 lines remaining from Athribis in the Delta; and the great Victory Stele found by Flinders Petrie in 1896 in Merneptah's ruined mortuary temple at Thebes, consisting of 28 lines. All three relate to Merneptah's military campaigns and complement each other. For the last years of Ramesses II peace had

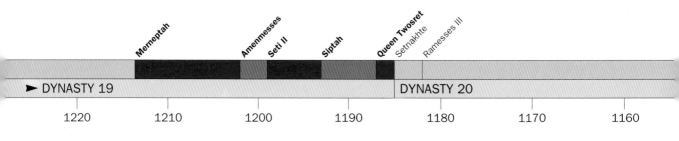

DYNASTY 19 ▶   DYNASTY 20

Merneptah   Amenmesses   Seti II   Siptah   Queen Twosret   Setnakhte   Ramesses III

1220   1210   1200   1190   1180   1170   1160

reigned on the Egyptian frontiers and amongst the vassals, but times were changing. A 'flash' revolt in southern Syria was quickly crushed. The Hittite king, now facing attacks on his northern territories and also famine through crop failure, invoked the old treaty of support to which Merneptah responded by sending grain – once more, as in the Biblical story, Egypt was a granary for the starving Near East.

There was unrest on the western borders with the Libyans who had been quietly infiltrating the Delta and in Year 5 (1207 BC) attempted an invasion, fermenting revolt in Nubia and in the western oases. Rapid mobilization and a heavy pre-emptive strike left the Libyans totally vanquished: the Karnak inscription records Merneptah's valour and the slaughter, 'Libyans, slain, whose uncircumcised phalli were carried off 6359' (the Athribis stele records only 6200!). Nubia had risen to support the Libyans, but so swift was the destruction of the latter that Merneptah could immediately turn south and inflict a crushing blow on the rebels. Merneptah, although elderly, had made the point that insurgents could not tamper with Egypt's security.

Merneptah realized that his time on the throne might be short. He rapidly commenced building his mortuary temple on the edge of the

(*Above*) The red granite lid of Merneptah's sarcophagus in his tomb in the Valley of the Kings, carved with the figure of the king in Osiride form wearing the *nemes* headdress and holding the royal crook and flail.

(*Right*) Merneptah's great Victory stele, which he usurped and stole from the mortuary temple of Amenhotep III at Thebes. It is precisely dated to the third day of the third month of the third season, i.e. summer 1207 BC. Apart from a long list of conquests, its particular interest lies in the second from last line where the only reference in the whole of Egyptian literature to Israel (*below*) occurs: 'Israel is devastated, her seed is no more, Palestine has become a widow for Egypt.' It was this reference that led many scholars to identify Merneptah as the pharaoh of the Exodus, whereas modern opinion now leans towards Ramesses II being the pharaoh 'who knew not Moses'. Cairo Museum.

ROYAL NAMES AND BURIALS

AMENMESSES
Birth name + (epithet)
Amen mcsses (heqa-waset) ('Fashioned by Amun, Ruler of Thebes')
Throne name
Men-mi-re Setep-en-re ('Eternal like Re, Chosen by Re')
Father
Merneptah
Mother
Iakhat
Wife
Baktwerel
Burial
Tomb KV 10, Valley of the Kings (Thebes)

SETI II
Birth name + (epithet)
Seti (mer-en-ptah) ('He of the god Seti, Beloved of Ptah')
Also known as
Sethos II
Throne name
User-kheperu-re Setep-en-re ('Powerful are the Manifestations of Re, Chosen by Re')
Father
Merneptah
Mother
Unknown
Wives
Takhat II, Twosret, Tiaa

Sons
Seti-Merenptah,

Ramesses-Siptah
Burial
Tomb KV 15, Valley of the Kings (Thebes)

SIPTAH
Birth name + (epithet)
Si-ptah (mer-en-ptah) ('Son of Ptah, Beloved of Ptah')
Throne name
Akh-en-re Setep-en-re ('Beautiful for Re, Chosen by Re')
Father
?Seti II
Mother
Tiaa
Burial
Tomb KV 47, Valley of the Kings (Thebes)

QUEEN TWOSRET
Birth name + (epithet)
Two-sret (setep-en-mut) ('Mighty Lady, Chosen of Mut')
Also known as
Twore, Tausert
Throne names
Sit-re Mery-amun ('Daughter of Re, Beloved of Amun')
1st Husband
Seti II
Son
Seti-Merenptah
Burial
Tomb KV 14, Valley of the Kings (Thebes)

desert at Thebes and his tomb in the Valley of the Kings. Like many of his predecessors, he was not averse to using earlier buildings as a quarry. His masons turned to the nearby mortuary temple of Amenhotep III, now largely disused, and removed much of it, including the large stele that was turned round to take Merneptah's Victory Hymn. Merneptah's tomb in the Valley of the Kings (KV 8) lies close to that of his father, but at a slightly higher level, so it has not suffered the effects of flooding that assailed Ramesses' tomb. Fragmentary remains of funerary equipment, including alabaster *ushabtis*, have been recovered from the tomb, but the curious fact is that Merneptah apparently had several sarcophagi, each carved in various stones that included alabaster, rose and black granite. One of Merneptah's granite sarcophagi was found reused in the intact tomb of the pharaoh Psusennes (c. 1033 BC), discovered at Tanis in the Delta (pp. 180–81).

Merneptah's mummy was not found in the tomb, parts of which may have been open from antiquity, neither was it in the great cache of royal mummies discovered in 1881. His absence led many Biblical scholars to underline the fact that he must have been the pharaoh of the Exodus and had perished in the Red Sea; his tomb was merely a cenotaph since the body was not recovered. These arguments were confounded in 1898 when the mummy of Merneptah appeared amongst the 16 bodies found in the royal mummy cache concealed in the tomb of Amenhotep II (KV 35). There is some evidence that Merneptah's queen, Isisnofret, was also buried in his tomb rather than in the Valley of the Queens, and that she predeceased him, but her body has not been identified.

FROM AMENMESSES TO QUEEN TWOSRET

When Merneptah died in 1202 BC a hiatus occurred in the succession. Instead of the Crown Prince Seti-Merneptah – who had been associated with his father as ruler – ascending the throne, an unknown, Amenmesses, became king. The explanation for this is a mystery but it has been suggested that, in the unfortunate absence of the Crown Prince at the time Merneptah died, a lesser prince, the son of a lesser queen (Takhat), seized the initiative. Little is known of Amenmesses apart from a few minor inscriptions and the fact that during his short four-year reign he began cutting a tomb in the Valley of the Kings (KV 10). The decoration in the tomb was, as usual, unfinished. Possibly the king's mother, Takhat, and his wife, Baktwerel, were also buried in the tomb (although it has been suggested that they were the mother and wife respectively of Ramesses IX). None of the three bodies has been identified.

The successor to Amenmesses in c. 1199 BC was Seti II, who may have been the previously ousted Crown Prince. Certainly he seems to have exercised a *damnatio memoriae* on his predecessor's monuments and added his own name to earlier ones. Three of his queens are known: Takhat II; Twosret, who was the mother of the eldest son and heir

apparent, Seti-Merenptah; and Tiaa, who was the mother of Ramesses-Siptah. It seems that the heir apparent died before his father Seti II, and the younger son inherited the throne as a minor, taking the name of Siptah. The older queen, Twosret, in effect ruled in her stepson's name together with the Chancellor, the so-called 'kingmaker' Bay, who was granted the privilege of a small private tomb in the Valley of the Kings (KV 13).

Siptah died in his Year 6 and was buried in the upper part of the Valley of the Kings (KV 47) in a tomb that was apparently intended for himself and his mother Queen Tiaa. His large red granite sarcophagus still remains in the unfinished burial hall but his body, notable for its deformity of a club foot (possibly the result of poliomyelitis when young) was found in the cache in the tomb of Amenhotep II (KV 35) in 1898. Curiously, shortly after the burial the tomb was disturbed and his cartouches erased in the inscriptions, to be subsequently restored in paint. Possibly the restoration was done under the Chancellor Bay.

With Siptah's death his stepmother Twosret declared herself queen, using the full pharaonic titles as Hatshepsut had done some 300 years earlier. Her tomb in the Valley (KV 14) had a chequered history; begun under Siptah in Year 2, it was extended by Twosret, possibly to receive the burials of herself and her first husband Seti II, but later usurped by Setnakhte, first king of the 20th Dynasty. A small cache of rather second-rate gold jewellery found in 1908 in a small pit tomb (KV 56) may have belonged to an infant daughter of Twosret and Seti II.

(*Above*) Detail of the head of a life-size quartzite seated statue of Seti II found at Karnak by Belzoni. British Museum.

A group of jewellery found in a pit tomb in the Valley of the Kings (KV 56), comprising a gold circlet with petals (*right*), five of which are inscribed with the names of Seti II and Queen Twosret; a necklace of gold filigree buds (*left*); and two pairs of earrings (*left* and *right*), the pair at the left with cartouches of Seti II. The quality of the goldwork is poor, which suggests that this parure was probably provided for an infant daughter of the king and queen. Cairo Museum.

DYNASTY 20
1185–1070

Setnakhte
(mereramunre)
Userkhaure Setepenre
1185–1182

Ramesses III
(heqaiunu)
Usermaatre Meryamun
1182–1151

A detail from the Great Harris Papyrus shows Ramesses III in full court dress and regalia wearing the White Crown. British Museum.

SETNAKHTE	
Birth name + (epithet) Set-nakhte (merer-amun-re) ('Victorious is Set, Beloved of Amun-Re')	the Manifestations of Re, Chosen by Re')
	Wife Tiy-merenese
Also known as Setnakht, Sethnakht	*Son* Ramesses III
Throne name User-khau-re Setep-en-re ('Powerful are	*Burial* Tomb KV 14, Valley of the Kings (Thebes)

RAMESSES III	
Birth name + (epithet) Ra-messes (heqa-iunu) ('Re has Fashioned Him, Ruler of Heliopolis')	*Wives* Isis, Titi, Tiy etc.
	Sons Khaemwaset, Parahirenemef, Sethirkhopshef, Amenhirkhopshef, Ramesses IV, V, & VI
Also known as Ramses	
Throne name User-maat-re Mery-amun ('Powerful is the Justice of Re, Beloved of Amun')	*Daughter* Titi
Father Setnakhte	*Burial* Tomb KV 11, Valley of the Kings (Thebes)

SETNAKHTE

The 19th Dynasty had ended with a degree of confusion, not least with the presence of Twosret as queen regnant, only the fourth in Egypt's history to that date. Whether there was a short period of anarchy, perhaps of only a few months, between the end of Twosret's sole reign and the accession of her successor Setnakhte is debatable. How Setnakhte came to the throne, or indeed who he was, is uncertain. The best source for the beginning of the 20th Dynasty comes from about 65 years later, in the account in the Great Harris Papyrus (see box opposite). The last four 'pages' describe how Setnakhte arose and put down the rebellions fermented by Asiatics: he relieved besieged cities, brought back those who had gone into hiding, and reopened the temples and restored their revenues.

Setnakhte reigned for only about three years. His son – the future Ramesses III – by his wife Queen Tiy-merenese was apparently associated with him in a short co-regency. Setnakhte was buried with full royal honours, described in the papyrus: 'he was rowed in his king's barge upon the river [i.e. crossed the Nile to the west bank], and rested in his eternal house west of Thebes'. Setnakhte actually usurped and enlarged

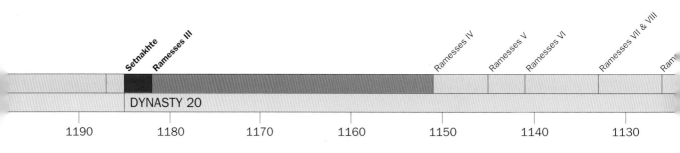

Setnakhte Ramesses III   Ramesses IV   Ramesses V   Ramesses VI   Ramesses VII & VIII   Ram

DYNASTY 20

1190   1180   1170   1160   1150   1140   1130

Queen Twosret's tomb (KV 14), which had already been taken over from Seti II. He had begun to excavate another tomb (KV 11), but this had intruded upon the tomb of Amenmesses (KV 10) and been abandoned; subsequently it was to be realigned and used by his son, Ramesses III. Setnakhte's coffin was found in the royal cache in Amenhotep II's tomb (KV 35, p. 103) in 1898, and it is possible that his may be the unwrapped and unidentified body found on a wooden boat in the tomb.

RAMESSES III

Ramesses III was the last of the great pharaohs on the throne of Egypt. He ruled at a time when the outside world of the Mediterranean was in turmoil – it saw the Trojan War, the fall of Mycenae and a great surge of displaced people seeking new homes, a tidal wave that was to break upon the shores of Egypt during his reign.

The first four years of Ramesses' reign seem to have been quiet ones. He no doubt sought to consolidate his position and continued his father Setnakhte's efforts to stabilize the country. There were no problems in the south, in Nubia, since that had now more or less achieved the status of a subdued colony. The first sign of trouble came in Year 5 with an attack from the west. The Libyans, coupled with two other tribes, the Meshwesh and the Seped, endeavoured to force their way out of their deserts into the fertile lands of the western Delta. The Egyptian army was more than a match for them and they were annihilated, those not slain becoming slaves in Egypt. For a while the states bordering Egypt had learnt their lesson, not to meddle with pharaoh.

In Year 8 the bubbling cauldron of the Middle East boiled over, no doubt exacerbated by several bad harvest years as well as the general upset of nomads trying to settle. As the Great Harris Papyrus records: 'The foreign countries plotted on their islands, and the people were dislodged and scattered by battle all at one time and no land could stand before their arms.' This was not a small skirmish but a major folk movement by people sufficiently desperate and well armed to be able to destroy Egypt's age-old enemy, the Hittite empire. This mass of people was in fact a confederation of which the names are listed, the Peleset (i.e. Philistines), Tjeker (possibly connected with the Teucri of the Troad), Shekelesh (possibly Sikels from Sicily), Weshesh (of uncertain origin), and the Denyen or Dardany (who could be the Danaoi of Homer's *Iliad*). Together, the confederation made up the 'Sea Peoples'.

Ramesses III and the Sea Peoples

The written and graphically illustrated account of Ramesses' fight against the Sea Peoples is recorded on the walls of his great and remarkably well-preserved mortuary temple at Medinet Habu. The written account occurs on the outer wall of the Second Pylon, north side; it is the longest hieroglyphic inscription known. The graphic representations are carved on the outer north wall of the temple.

(*Above*) The mortuary temple of Ramesses III at Medinet Habu, the 'Mansion of Millions of Years of King Ramesses III, "United with Eternity in the Estate of Amon"', is the best preserved of the series of such temples on the west bank at Thebes.

(*Below*) The entrance gateway to Ramesses III's mortuary temple copies a Syrian *migdol* or fortified gateway.

Having halted for a while in Syria, the Sea Peoples resumed their march overland to attack Egypt. This was not simply an act of war, it was with intent to force their way into Egypt and settle – they were a nation on the move, complete with women and children and family possessions piled high on ox-carts. At sea, their fleet of no mean proportions kept station with the march. Ramesses realized that rapid movement was called for; despatches were sent to the eastern frontier posts to stand firm at all costs until the main Egyptian army could be brought up. The clash came at the border and the slaughter of the invaders was great, as the reliefs depict. Pharaoh was everywhere in his chariot and, according to the canon of Egyptian art, represented at far greater size than any of the other participants.

Although the land invasion had been scattered, there was still the threat from the sea. The Sea Peoples' fleet made for the mouth of one of the eastern arms of the Nile, to be met there by the Egyptian fleet. What transpired is rather interesting because the Egyptians had never prided themselves on being great sailors. They hated the sea, *wdj wr*, the 'Great Green', as they called the Mediterranean, but here they were fighting what was virtually a landlocked battle. Ramesses had ranks of archers lining the shore who poured volley after volley into the enemy ships as soon as they were within range. Egyptian 'marine' archers are shown calmly standing on the decks firing in unison, the enemy ships being hauled alongside with grappling hooks. The enemy dead fall before the onslaught in contorted postures and Ramesses returns victorious, by the grace of Amun, the god of Thebes. This was really the beginning of the build up of the fabulous wealth of the priesthood of Amun that was to have such disastrous consequences in the next dynasty.

(*Top and above*) Details of foreign prisoners in the reliefs at Medinet Habu. The Philistine, *above*, is easily recognizable by his very distinct headdress.

Although no follow-up campaign to pursue the Sea Peoples back into the Levant is recorded in the Great Harris Papyrus, or on the walls of Medinet Habu, such a move would have been reasonable. It is interesting to note that the great entrance gateway to the temple is actually modelled on a Syrian fortified tower, a *migdol*, such as are clearly seen on the reliefs of Seti I and Ramesses II at Karnak. Ramesses III's building was merely an ornament, an ancient Egyptian 'folly' in a way, but he did have a use for it because on the walls of some of the upper rooms are scenes of him dallying with the ladies of his harem.

The further campaigns of Ramesses III

For three years Egypt was quiet. Then came trouble on the western borders, again with the Libyans, allied with the Meshwesh and five other tribes. There had been a slight infiltration by immigrants into the area west of the Canopic arm of the Nile for some years, but in Year 11 it came to a head with an invasion. The frontier forts took the brunt of it as the invaders attempted to overrun the Delta. Once more Ramesses crushed all opposition. The attackers left over 2000 dead, and their cattle and possessions were rich booty for the treasury of Amun. The campaign details occur on the inner wall, north side, of the First Pylon at Medinet Habu. At one point army scribes come before pharaoh with a tally of the enemy dead, represented by a pile of severed right hands, and the number above them, 175. Ramesses seems to have questioned the figure. The scribes had to recheck. The next register explains how they did it – by cutting off the phalluses of the uncircumcised enemy, shown piled on the ground with the number above them, 175. The numbers tallied, the accountants are always right!

Other campaigns are mentioned in the inscriptions in the mortuary temple at Medinet Habu. Some of the scenes, however, are suspect.

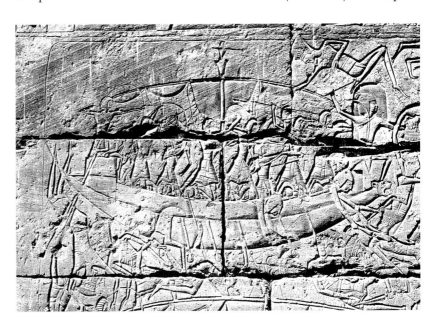

(*Right*) On the outer north wall of Medinet Habu, Ramesses III's battle with the Sea Peoples is carved in graphic detail. Here, an Egyptian warship cuts through the Philistine enemy.

(*Above*) Ramesses III introduces his young son, Amenhirkhopshef, to the gods in the boy's tomb (QV 55).

(*Below*) Belzoni retrieved the great granite lid of Ramesses III's sarcophagus from the king's tomb in 1815, which he presented to the Fitzwilliam Museum, Cambridge, in 1823 (Henry Salt collected the sarcophagus box and sold it to the Louvre, Paris, in 1826).

Ramesses is depicted in a Nubian campaign which finds no other mention and would be highly unlikely in view of the subordination of that area. Other scenes show the king invading territories to the north, going into the country of the Amurru, Khatti and Syrians, none of whom existed any longer as political entities. These reliefs seem in fact to be copies of earlier ones from a building of Ramesses II. Ramesses III is merely modelling himself on his illustrious predecessor who, despite their proximity in numerical sequence, was unrelated to him.

The royal family

Despite the length of Ramesses' reign (31 years and 41 days according to the Great Harris Papyrus), little is known about the ladies of the court and the royal children. Ramesses' chief queen seems to have been named Isis, but for some curious reason the cartouches in the Medinet Habu temple where the queen's name would normally appear have been left blank. Possibly Isis was of Asiatic extraction since her mother's name was Habadjilat, a distinctly un-Egyptian name. Queen Isis had her tomb in the Valley of the Queens (QV 51) and was the mother of Ramesses VI. Ramesses III not only had several wives but also a number of sons (probably at least ten), many of whom predeceased him – as is revealed by the number of their tombs in the Valley of the Queens. Notable amongst the tombs for their preservation and brightly coloured wall paintings are those of Amenhirkhopshef (QV 55) and Khaemwaset (QV 44). Also laid to rest in the Valley are the princes Parahirenemef (QV 42) and Sethirkhopshef (QV 43). All four sons held offices under their father concerned with the royal horses or chariotry.

There are several other unnamed tombs of princes and princesses in the area, a number of which appear to date from Ramesses III's reign and may belong to some of his other children. One of the larger tombs, that of a Queen Titi (QV 52), lacks any proper indication of her royal status, but an analysis of her titles suggests that she was possibly a daughter and, subsequently, wife of Ramesses III who outlived him. No less than 43 times does her title as 'Mistress of the Two Lands' appear; she is called 'Chief Royal Wife' 33 times, 'King's Daughter', 'King's Beloved Daughter of his Body' and 'His Beloved Daughter' 20 times; 'King's Sister' 4 times but, more importantly, 'King's Mother' 8 times – her son could possibly be Ramesses IV. The majority of the tombs in the Valley of the Queens, including the finest, that of Ramesses II's queen Nefertari (p. 148), were found by the Italian Egyptologist Ernesto Schiaparelli in 1903–4.

The conspiracy to kill the king

Another remarkable papyrus from the reign of Ramesses III has a great deal of information on the structure and workings of the court, but from an unusual angle. Known as the Harem Conspiracy Papyrus, it exists in three portions (of which the largest section, the Judicial Papyrus, is in Turin) and concerns the trial of a group who plotted to murder the king.

THE HAREM CONSPIRACY: PRINCIPAL DEFENDANTS

The chief defendants in the conspiracy trial were all personally close to the king. The list of their names and former positions reads: Pekkamen, Chief of the Chamber; Mesedsure, Weren, Peluka and Yenini (a Libyan), all butlers; Pendua, scribe of the harem; Peynok, Petewnteamen, Kerpes, Khamopet, Khammale, Setimperthoth and Setimperamon, all inspectors of the harem; Pere, overseer of the White House (the palace); Binemwese, captain of archers in Nubia, and six wives of the people at the harem gate.

(*Below*) The mummy of Ramesses III was found in the Deir el-Bahari cache of royal mummies in 1881. It was in quite excellent condition: this and the body of Amenhotep II are the only mummies amongst the royal males that do not show any evidence of 'post-mortem trauma', i.e. damage inflicted by the tomb robbers, or further deterioration under later hands. The hiatus that existed in antiquity when the royal bodies were moved can be deduced from the fact that the damaged lower half of Ramesses III's wooden coffin was found in the other cache of royal mummies in 1898 in Amenhotep II's tomb (KV 35). Cairo Museum.

The chief defendant was one of Ramesses' minor queens, Tiy, who hoped to see her son, Pentewere, succeed to the throne. Her name seems to be correct but that of the prince is a circumlocution, as are the names of a number of the other defendants, i.e. they have been given fictitious names such as Mesedsure, 'Re hates him', to indicate how great was their crime.

Fortunately for the king the plot was discovered and the guilty arrested. Ramesses III himself commissioned the prosecution; however, since he is spoken of later in the papyrus as 'the great god', i.e. dead, he must have died during the course of the trial, although not necessarily from any effects of the plot. Fourteen officials were called to sit in judgment, including seven royal butlers (a high office, cf. Joseph), two treasury overseers, two army standard bearers, two scribes and a herald. Interestingly, several of their names betray foreign origins. The commission was given full powers to call whatever evidence was necessary and, most unusually, power to deliver and carry out the verdict – even the death penalty, which was normally reserved to the king.

The majority of the conspirators were all personally close to the king, especially officials in the harem, which indicates how dangerous the situation was. Evidence also emerged of a plot to incite a revolt outside the palace to coincide with the intended coup within. Over 40 people were implicated and were tried in groups. The record of Queen Tiy's trial has not survived, but she would not have been allowed to live. Twenty-eight people, including the major ringleaders, were condemned in the first prosecution, almost certainly to death. The second prosecution condemned six people, who were forced to commit suicide within the court itself. In the third prosecution, the four people involved, who included the misguided prince Pentewere, were likewise condemned to suicide, although not immediately within the court, but presumably in their cells.

The fourth prosecution throws a curious light on the whole case. The defendants were not conspirators but three of the judges and two officers, who were charged that, after their appointment to the commission, they knowingly entertained several of the women conspirators and a general named Peyes. One of the judges was found to be innocent, the others were condemned to have their ears and nose amputated. Pebes, a butler who was one of the convicted judges, committed suicide before the sentence could be carried out.

Ramesses, as mentioned, seems to have died before the verdicts were reached. He was buried in a large tomb in the Valley of the Kings (KV 11) which has an unusual plan by virtue of its having been taken over from an earlier excavation. It is also unusual among the royal tombs in having some secular scenes, of which the paintings of the two blind male harpists are well known, although now sadly much damaged when compared to the early copies made by Sir John Gardner Wilkinson. The tomb is often referred to in the literature as 'The Tomb of the Harpers', or as 'Bruce's Tomb', after its discoverer, James Bruce, in 1769.

DYNASTY 20
1185–1070

Ramesses IV
Heqamaatre
1151–1145

Ramesses V
Usermaatre
1145–1141

Ramesses VI
Nebmaatre
Meryamun
1141–1133

Ramesses VII
Usermaatre
Meryamun
Setepenre
1133–1126

Ramesses VIII
Usermaatre
Akhenamun
1133–1126

Ramesses IX
Neferkhare
Setepenre
1126–1108

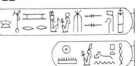

Ramesses X
Khepermaatre
1108–1098

Ramesses XI
Menmaatre
Setepenptah
1098–1070

Detail of a dark green schist kneeling statue of Ramesses IV, with the king's cartouche on his right shoulder. British Museum.

As Ramesses III's long reign of 31 years came to an end, so did the greatness of the Egyptian pharaohs. The exact relationships of the subsequent kings bearing the name Ramesses is at times obscure; certainly Ramesses IV, V, VI and VIII appear to have been sons of Ramesses III (although, as noted, many of his sons had died young), while Ramesses VII seems to have been a son of Ramesses VI.

RAMESSES IV

Ramesses IV succeeded to the throne in about 1151 BC. The identity of his mother – probably either Queen Isis or Queen Titi – is still uncertain, but we do know that he made Tentopet his chief wife (she lies buried in Tomb 74 in the Valley of the Queens). The new king's first task was to bury his father in the Valley of the Kings. Within four days of the ceremony – as ostraka from the workmen's village of Deir el-Medina record – the customary gifts had arrived there and the workmen could look forward to a new commission to cut Ramesses IV's tomb.

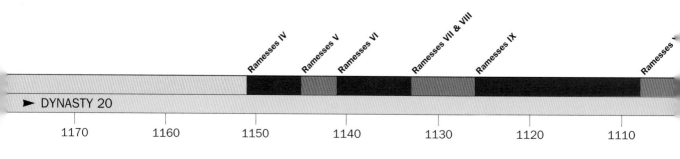

Ramesses IV | Ramesses V | Ramesses VI | Ramesses VII & VIII | Ramesses IX | Ramesses

► DYNASTY 20

1170   1160   1150   1140   1130   1120   1110

ROYAL NAMES AND BURIALS

RAMESSES IV
Birth name
  Ra-messes ('Re has
  Fashioned Him')
Throne name
  Heqa-maat-re
  ('Ruler of Justice
  like Re')
Father
  Ramesses III
Mother
  Titi or Isis
Wife
  Tentopet
Burial
  Tomb KV 2, Valley
  of the Kings

RAMESSES V
Throne name
  User-maat-re
  ('Powerful is the
  Justice of Re')
Father
  Ramesses III
Wife
  Nubkhesed
Burial
  KV 9, V. of Kings

RAMESSES VI
Epithet
  Amun-hir-khopsh-ef
  Netjer-heqa-iunu
  ('Amun is his
  Strength, God,
  Ruler of Heliopolis')
Throne name
  Neb-maat-re Mery-
  amun ('Lord of
  Justice is Re,
  Beloved of Amun')
Father
  Ramesses III
Mother
  Isis
Son
  Ramesses VII
Burial
  KV 9, V. of Kings

RAMESSES VII
Epithet
  It-amun-netjer-heqa-
  iunu ('Father of
  Amun, God, Ruler of
  Heliopolis')
Throne name
  User-maat-re Mery-
  amun Setep-en-re
  ('Powerful is the
  Justice of Re,
  Beloved of Amun,
  Chosen of Re')
Father
  Ramesses VI

Burial
  KV 1, V. of Kings

RAMESSES VIII
Epithet
  Set-hir-khopsh-ef
  Mery-amun ('Set is
  his Strength,
  Beloved of Amun')
Throne name
  User-maat-re Akh-
  en-amun ('Powerful
  is the Justice of Re,
  Helpful to Amun')
Father
  Ramesses III
Burial
  Unknown

RAMESSES IX
Epithet
  Kha-em-waset
  Merer-amun
  ('Appearing in
  Thebes, Beloved of
  Amun')
Throne name
  Nefer-kha-re Setep-
  en-re ('Beautiful is
  the Soul of Re,
  Chosen of Re')
Burial
  KV 6, V. of Kings

RAMESSES X
Epithet
  Amon-hir-khopsh-ef
  ('Amun is his
  Strength')
Throne name
  Kheper-maat-re
  ('The Justice of Re
  abides')
Burial
  KV 18, V. of Kings

RAMESSES XI
Epithet
  Kha-em-waset
  Merer-amun Netjer-
  heqa-iunu
  ('Appearing in
  Thebes, Beloved of
  Amun, God, Ruler of
  Heliopolis')
Throne name
  Men-maat-re Setep-
  en-ptah ('The
  Justice of Re
  Remains, Chosen
  of Ptah')
Daughter
  Henuttawy
Burial
  KV 4, V. of Kings

Several inscribed stele in the Wadi Hammamat record the activities of large expeditions sent by Ramesses IV to obtain good stone for statues. One group, of 8368 men, included 2000 soldiers, indicative of the amount of policing of the workforce required rather than any defence against attack. Expeditions to the turquoise mines at Serabit el-Khadim in Sinai were also recorded and as far south in Nubia as the fort at Buhen, almost to the Second Cataract. Despite all his endeavours and good works for the gods, and his prayer to Osiris – recorded on a stele of Year 4 at Abydos – that 'thou shalt give me the great age with a long reign [as my predecessor]', Ramesses IV reigned for only six years.

The tomb of Ramesses IV lies just outside the earlier main group in the Eastern Valley of the Kings. It has brightly coloured and detailed wall paintings. The large sarcophagus box and its lid, largely intact, still stand in the burial hall. As indicated by its low number, KV 2, the tomb has been open since antiquity; Coptic graffiti cover the walls near the entrance. Like its companion Ramesside tombs it is unfinished, but an interesting papyrus preserved in Turin gives its plan. A puzzling feature was the series of four narrow box-like lines the architect had drawn around the sarcophagus in the burial chamber, the 'house of gold'. Their meaning became abundantly clear when Tutankhamun's burial chamber was opened in 1923 and the four great gold-covered wooden shrines enclosing his sarcophagus were revealed. The mummy of Ramesses IV was found in the royal cache in Amenhotep II's tomb (KV 35) in 1898.

RAMESSES V AND VI

On the evidence of a fragmentary hieratic papyrus in Turin, there appears to have been a civil war raging during Ramesses V's short four-year reign. Workmen stopped digging his tomb (KV 9) in the Valley as they were 'idle from fear of the enemy'. An ostrakon records that the king was buried in Year 2 of Ramesses VI, which is curious since he should normally have been buried no more than 70 days into the new reign. Possibly Ramesses V died during the reign of his brother Ramesses VI, but does this therefore indicate that they ruled jointly or, more probably in light of the civil war, that Ramesses V was usurped by his brother and held captive until his death? Ramesses V's mummy was found in the tomb of Amenhotep II (KV 35). It has a much larger than usual embalmer's incision on its left side for extracting the viscera. Lesions on the face suggest that the king suffered from smallpox.

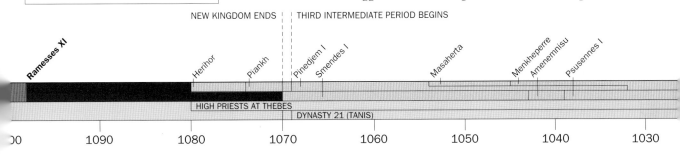

NEW KINGDOM ENDS | THIRD INTERMEDIATE PERIOD BEGINS

Ramesses XI Herihor Piankh Pinedjem I Smendes I Masaherta Menkheperre Amenemnisu Psusennes I

HIGH PRIESTS AT THEBES

DYNASTY 21 (TANIS)

1090   1080   1070   1060   1050   1040   1030

(*Right*) The shattered black granite sarcophagus of Ramesses VI still lies in his burial hall, its huge base tipped on one side. This, it has been suggested, could not have been done by tomb robbers and might therefore be the result of official investigations to retrieve treasure, possibly during the Libyan incursions. The carved granite face from the lid was taken to the British Museum in the last century.

(*Below*) A granite statue of Ramesses VI from Karnak shows him, the last really victorious pharaoh, grasping a diminutive Libyan foe. Cairo Museum.

Ramesses VI enjoyed an eight-year reign, longer than either of his two brothers. It seems that during this time Egypt's long-distance contacts and suzerainty over much of the Near East were drastically reduced. The turquoise mines in Sinai were abandoned and the eastern frontier pulled back from Palestine to the edge of the eastern Delta.

Having usurped his predecessor's tomb in the Valley (KV 9), Ramesses VI extended it considerably. It culminated in a large painted and vaulted burial hall. The grievously battered mummy of Ramesses VI was found in KV 35 (Amenhotep II) in 1898. Of all the royal mummies, it was the one most savagely attacked by the tomb robbers, the head and torso having been hacked to pieces with an axe. The priests had piously rewrapped the pieces on a board in an effort to make it resemble human form. When Elliot Smith examined it in 1905 he found portions of at least two other bodies included within the wrappings: a woman's right hand and the mutilated right hand and forearm of another man. Where the king's neck should have been were his separate left hip bone and part of his pelvis.

The end of the 20th Dynasty, with the last of the pharaohs bearing the name Ramesses, is very obscure. These kings fall mainly into two groups, those related to Ramesses III and those to Ramesses VI. Despite the grandeur of the name, none of them had any ancestral connection with their great predecessor, Ramesses II.

RAMESSES VII AND VIII

Ramesses VII succeeded his father, Ramesses VI, in 1133 BC. Little is known of the seven or so years of his reign. Egypt was economically

(*Above*) Although much damaged, the tomb of Ramesses IX still retains occasional fine details representing the king, here raising his hands in adoration.

(*Below*) One of a pair of massive gold ear-plugs found at Abydos. They are inscribed on the back with the name of Ramesses XI, but came from the body of an unknown lady of the court.

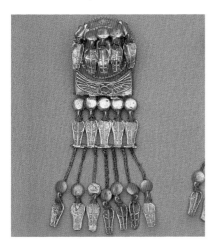

unstable and prices soared, as evidenced in the records on papyri and ostraka from the workmen's village at Deir el-Medina. Everywhere there was unrest. The sites of administration and the capital lay probably in the Delta where almost 100 years earlier Ramesses II had founded several cities. Although Ramesses VII had a tomb in the Valley of the Kings (KV 1), it actually lies well away from the main nucleus in the Eastern Valley, beyond the tomb of Ramesses IV. It has apparently been open since antiquity and the king's body has not been discovered.

Ramesses VIII, who probably reigned only for a year, was a son of Ramesses III. That he should have succeeded a son of Ramesses VI is perhaps indicative of a continuing problem of the rightful succession. He has no known tomb or identifiable mummy.

RAMESSES IX AND X

With Ramesses IX Egypt returned to a degree of stability in as much as the king enjoyed a reign of some 18 years. There is not much to show for it in terms of monuments or records, however. Building work in Ramesses' name at the ancient sun centre of Heliopolis in the Delta indicates the greater emphasis being placed on Lower Egypt. This was probably one of the reasons why the High Priests of Amun at Thebes

(*Left*) Green schist statue of Ramesses IX presenting a shrine with the sacred scarab beetle on top of it. Royal Scottish Museum, Edinburgh.

were increasingly able to assert their own power in Upper Egypt and to sow the seeds of the final insurrection to come during the 21st Dynasty.

Ramesses IX's tomb (KV 6) is a long one in the tradition of the 'syringe' tunnels of the later 19th and 20th Dynasties. It lies almost directly opposite that of Ramesses II in the Valley and it may be wondered if the choice of location was influenced by the proximity of the great king, or whether at this time all traces of the entrance had been obscured. The mummy of Ramesses IX was found in the 1881 cache in DB 320 but it was laid in the later coffin of the princess Neskhons (p. 178).

The reign of Ramesses X has been variously given as ranging from three to nine years, such is the lack of detail available for the period. An inscription from Aniba in Nubia has his cartouche and presumably evidences some continuing small concern with the area; but the great influence and possessions of Egypt to the north-west, into Palestine and Syria, were now things of the past. The king's tomb (KV 18), just beyond Seti I's, has never been properly explored and no mummy has been attributed to him.

RAMESSES XI

With the long 28-year reign of Ramesses XI the 20th Dynasty comes to a close. At least a little more is known about him than his ephemeral predecessors. Some idea of the internal situation of Egypt is given in a papyrus set towards the end of the reign – the Tale of Wenamun, preserved in Moscow. Wenamun was sent by Ramesses XI to Byblos to secure cedars of Lebanon for the barque of Amun at Thebes. In days gone by he would have been an honoured visitor and been given whatever he required for the Egyptian king. Now, not only was it so unsafe

A crude alabaster *ushabti* of Ramesses XI found in the debris of his unused tomb in the Valley of the Kings (KV 4). Luxor Museum.

THE GREAT TOMB ROBBERIES

It was in the reign of Ramesses IX that the first of a series of scandals broke, when it was revealed that the tombs in the Valley of the Kings were being plundered. The robberies mainly took place in Year 16 of the reign, although there had been an earlier incident before Year 9, followed by an attack on KV 9 where Ramesses VI had only recently been buried. The affair in Year 16 largely came to light because of intense rivalry between the mayor of Thebes, Paser, and the mayor of western Thebes, Paweraa, who was responsible for the cemeteries. Reports of the robberies were made to the vizier, Khaemwaset, who ordered a commission to investigate the allegations. Of the ten tombs that were checked, only that of Amenhotep I was said to have been intact. Of the remainder, some had been partly robbed whilst others had been completely despoiled. The verbatim accounts of the trials of several of the culprits have survived in over a dozen papyri, known as the 'Tomb Robbing Papyri', which are now scattered in various museums. One confession by a stonemason, Amun-pnufer, recorded on the 22nd day of the third month of winter in Year 16 of Ramesses IX (c. 1110 BC), related in detail how the tomb of the 17th Dynasty king Sobekemsaf and his queen Nubkhas had been totally pillaged, even to the extent of setting fire to their coffins. The stonemason actually details the extent of the spoils from the two bodies, amounting to '160 deben of gold', which is about 32 lb (14.5 kg). Compare this with the items from Tutankhamun's tomb, where the gold mask alone weighs 22½ lb (10.23 kg) and the inner gold coffin nearly 243 lb (110.4 kg).

to travel that he was robbed on his way to Byblos, but Egypt's stock had fallen so low in the Near East that Wenamun had to pay the princes of Byblos for the wood, and he had lost the payment in the robbery. It is a tale of vicissitudes that reflects the instability of Egypt.

The office of Viceroy of Kush, and hence an interest in Nubia, still existed since a letter to the Viceroy, Panehesy (in Turin), of Year 17 exhorts him to chase up a laggard royal butler who had gone to collect suitable materials for a shrine. Civil war now raged on and off in the Theban region with the king ruling from the north at his capital, Piramesse, whilst the High Priests of Amun held the south of the country. Amenhotep, High Priest of Amun, appears to have over-reached himself, however, since he disappears before Year 12 and Panehesy established himself at Thebes, acting for the king. Some time between Years 12 and 19 Herihor appeared on the scene as High Priest of Amun, having risen through army ranks rather than priestly ones it seems. By Year 19 Panehesy had disappeared. Herihor claimed Panehesy's titles as Viceroy of Kush and other high-ranking offices, and he appears to have taken over the supreme office of vizier, leaving him in a position of unassailable power in the south.

The major monument confirming the might of Herihor is the temple of Khonsu, the moon-god son of Amun, which lies just within the southern temenos wall of the Karnak complex. Reliefs here depict Herihor at the same scale as the king, although not in the same scenes, and in the forecourt Herihor's name and titles appear in the royal cartouche. The implications are obvious. It seems that there might have been as much as a six-year overlap in the reigns of Ramesses XI and Herihor, each ruling in their own northern and southern domain respectively, and with Herihor dying before Ramesses XI. The story is not so much one of blatant usurpation as of a tacit recognition by each of the other's sphere of influence. The documents certainly recognize this with dual dating, where Year 2 of Herihor is equated with Year 25 of Ramesses.

Ramesses XI had a tomb excavated in the Valley of the Kings (KV 4), just outside the main eastern group and a little further up a narrow wadi beyond the tomb of Amenhotep III's parents-in-law, Yuya and Tuya. Although the tomb has been open since antiquity, it was only cleared scientifically in 1980 on behalf of the Brooklyn Museum. A curious story emerged. Apparently, Ramesses XI had not been buried in the tomb and it was, as usual, unfinished. However, from the many fragments of material relating to earlier royal burials found in the debris, it appears that after the tomb was abandoned it became a workshop where some of the royal mummies in process of being transferred to other hiding places (i.e. KV 35 and DB 320, p. 103) were stripped of any valuables that could be used to bolster the country's failing economy; even gold leaf was adzed off coffins such as that of Tuthmosis III. Ramesses XI's mummy has not been found and may well yet be located in a third cache, along with other 'missing persons'.

THE THIRD INTERMEDIATE PERIOD
1069–525 BC

HIGH PRIESTS
(at Thebes)
1080–945

Herihor
1080–1074

Piankh
1074–1070

Pinedjem I
1070–1032

Masaherta
1054–1046

Menkheperre
1045–992

Smendes II
992–990

Pinedjem II
990–969

Psusennes 'III'
969–945

DYNASTY 21
(at Tanis)
1069–945

Smendes I
1069–1043

Amenemnisu
1043–1039

Psusennes I
1039–991

Amenemope
993–984

Osorkon the Elder
984–978

Siamun
978–959

Psusennes II
959–945

DYNASTY 22
(Libyan or Bubastite)
(at Tanis)
945–715

Sheshonq I
945–924

Osorkon I
924–889

Sheshonq II
c.890

Takelot I
889–874

Osorkon II
874–850

Takelot II
850–825

Sheshonq III
825–773

Pami
773–767

Sheshonq V
767–730

Osorkon IV
730–715

Harsiese (at Thebes)
870–860

DYNASTY 23
(Libyan Anarchy)
(at Leontopolis)
818–715

Pedibastet
818–793

Sheshonq IV
793–787

Osorkon III
787–759

Takelot III
764–757

Rudamon
757–754

Iuput 754–715

Nimlot
(Hermopolis)

Peftjauabastet
(Herakleopolis)

DYNASTY 24
(at Sais)
727–715

Tefnakht
727–720

Bakenrenef
(Bocchoris)
720–715

DYNASTY 25
(Nubian/Kushite)
747–656

Piankhi (Piyi)
747–716

Shabaka
716–702

Shebitku
702–690

Taharqa
690–664

Tanutamun
664–656

DYNASTY 26
(Saite)
664–525

Psamtik I
(Psammetichus I)
664–610

Nekau (Necho)
610–595

Psamtik II
(Psammetichus II)
595–589

Wahibre (Apries)
589–570

Ahmose II (Amasis)
570–526

Psamtik III
(Psammetichus III)
526–525

THE LATE PERIOD
525–332 BC

DYNASTY 27
(First Persian Period)
525–404

Cambyses II
525–522

Darius I
521–486

Xerxes
485–465

Artaxerxes I
465–424

Darius II
423–405

Artaxerxes II
405–359

DYNASTY 28
404–399

Amyrtaeus
404–399

DYNASTY 29
399–380

Nefaarud I (Nepherites I)
399–393

Hakor (Achoris)
393–380

DYNASTY 30
380–343

Nakhtnebef (Nectanebo I)
380–362

Djedhor (Teos)
362–360

Nakhthoreb (Nectanebo II)
360–343

DYNASTY 31
(Second Persian Period)
343–332

Artaxerxes III
343–338

Arses
338–336

Darius III
336–332

THIRD INTERMEDIATE PERIOD BEGINS

Herihor
Piankh
Pinedjem I
Smendes I
Masaherta
Menkheperre
Amenemnisu
Psusennes I
Amenemope
Smendes II
Osorkon the Elder
Siamun
Pinedjem II
Psusennes 'III'
Psusennes II
Sheshonq I
Osorkon I
Sheshonq II c. 890
Takelot I
Osorkon II
Harsiese (at Thebes)
Takelot II
Sheshonq III
Pedibastet
Sheshonq IV
Osorkon III
Pami
Sheshonq V
Takelot III
Rudamon
Iuput
Piankhi
Osor

HIGH PRIESTS AT THEBES
DYNASTY 21 (TANIS)
DYNASTY 22
DYNASTY 23
DYNASTY 2

1050   1000   950   900   850   800   750

Psusennes I

Osorkon I

Hakor

Nectanebo I

THE WEAKENING OF PHARAONIC POWER

The Third Intermediate Period 1069–525 BC
The Late Period 525–332 BC

TWO THOUSAND YEARS after its inception, Egyptian civilization began to slide downhill after achieving the giddy heights of the Old, Middle and New Kingdoms. No longer was Egypt, in the eyes of the ancient world, an isolated Shangri La or Land of the Lotus Eaters; no longer were her pharaohs the god-kings manifest on earth as in better times. Economically, around 1000 BC, the country was virtually bankrupt. Outside influences became more evident as other ancient civilizations, Assyrians and Persians, followed by Macedonian Greeks, broke into the fertile valley. Confusion swayed back and forth, even to the extent of Egypt being ruled in the 25th Dynasty by Nubians or Kushites from the once despised lands south of Elephantine. Little could be done about it – the ultimate came with Alexander III, the Great; driving out the hated Persians in 332 BC he was recognized as the son of Ammon in the old traditional way. He at least, in founding Alexandria, brought Egypt fully into the intellectual ambit of the now omnipresent Mediterranean world.

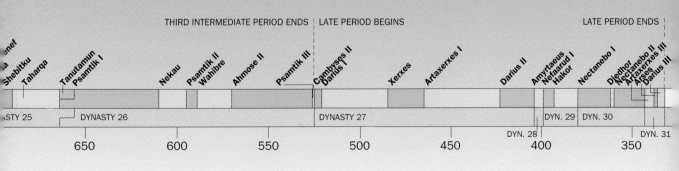

THIRD INTERMEDIATE PERIOD ENDS | LATE PERIOD BEGINS | LATE PERIOD ENDS

...enef
...a
...hebitku Taharqa | Tanutamun Psamtik I | Nekau | Psamtik II Wahibre | Ahmose II | Psamtik III | Cambyses II Darius I | Xerxes | Artaxerxes I | Darius II | Amyrtaeus Nefaarud I Hakor | Nectanebo I | Djedhor Nectanebo II Artaxerxes III Arses Darius III

...STY 25 | DYNASTY 26 | DYNASTY 27 | DYN. 29 | DYN. 30
DYN. 28 | DYN. 31

650   600   550   500   450   400   350

HIGH PRIESTS (at Thebes)
1080–945

 **Herihor** (siamun)
Hemnetjertepyenamun
1080–1074

 Piankh
1074–1070

 **Pinedjem I**
Khakheperre
Setepenamun
1070–1032

 **Masaherta**
1054–1046

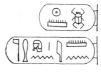 **Menkheperre**
Hemnetjertepyenamun
1045–992

 Smendes II
992–990

 Pinedjem II
Khakheperre
Setepenamun
990–969

no cartouche **Psusennes 'III'**
969–945

DYNASTY 21 (at Tanis)
1069–945

 **Smendes I (Nesbanebdjed)**
Hedjkheperre Setepenre
1069–1043

 Amenemnisu
Neferkare
1043–1039

 **Psusennes I (Pasebakhaen-niut I)**
Akheperre Setepenre
1039–991

 Amenemope
Usermaatre Meryamun
Setepenamun
993–984

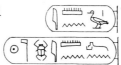 **Osorkon the Elder**
Aakheperre Setepenre
984–978

 **Siamun**
Netjerkheperre
Setepenamun
978–959

Psusennes II (Pasebakhaen-niut II)
Titkheperure
959–945

NEW KINGDOM ENDS | THIRD INTERMEDIATE PERIOD BEGINS

Herihor (Thebes) Piankh (Thebes) Pinedjem I (Thebes) Smendes I (Tanis) Masaherta (Thebes) Menkheperre (Thebes) Amenemnisu (Tanis) Psusennes I (Tanis)

► DYNASTY 20 | HIGH PRIESTS AT THEBES
DYNASTY 21 (TANIS)

1080   1070   1060   1050   1040   1030   1020

ROYAL NAMES (HIGH PRIESTS)

HERIHOR
Birth name + (epithet)
Her-i-hor (Si-amun)
('Horus Protects
Me, Son of Amun')
Throne name
Hem-netjer-tepy-en-
amun ('The First
Prophet [High
Priest] of Amun')
Wife
Nodjmet
Burial
Unknown

PIANKH
Birth name
Piankh
Burial
Unknown

PINEDJEM I
Birth name + (epithet)
Pi-nedjem (mery-
amun) ('He who
belongs to the
Pleasant One
[Horus or Ptah],
Beloved of Amun')
Also known as
Pinudjem I
Throne name
Kha-kheper-re
Setep-en-amun
('The Soul of Re
appears, Chosen of
Amun')
Wives
Henuttawy I
Maatkare
Burial
Mummy in DB 320,
Deir el-Bahari
(Thebes)

MASAHERTA
Birth name
Masaherta
Also known as
Masaharta
Burial
Mummy in DB 320,

Deir el-Bahari
(Thebes)

MENKHEPERRE
Birth name
Men-kheper-re
('Lasting is the
Manifestation of
Re')
Also known as
Menkheperra
Throne name
Hem-netjer-tepy-en-
amun ('The First
Prophet of Amun')
Burial
Unknown

SMENDES II
Known as
Smendes (Greek)
Burial
Unknown

PINEDJEM II
Birth name
Pi-nedjem ('He who
belongs to the
Pleasant One
[Horus or Ptah]')
Also known as
Pinudjem II
Throne name
Kha-kheper-re
Setep-en-amun
('The Soul of Re
appears, Chosen of
Amun')
Wife
Henuttawy II
Burial
DB 320, Deir el-
Bahari (Thebes)

PSUSENNES 'III'
Known as
Psusennes (Greek)
Burial
Unknown

The steadily increasing power of the priesthood of Amun at Thebes had come to a head under Ramesses XI. Homer extolled the wealth of Thebes in the *Iliad*, Book 9: 'in Egyptian Thebes the heaps of precious ingots gleam, the hundred-gated Thebes'. The Amun priesthood owned two-thirds of all temple land in Egypt, 90 per cent of all ships, 80 per cent of all factories, and much else. Their grip on the state's economy was paramount. It was therefore merely a short step for **Herihor**, as mentioned earlier (p. 171), to enforce his supremacy over the last of the Ramessides and create a ruling class of the High Priests of Amun at Thebes.

Herihor ruled alongside Ramesses XI for some six years (1080–1074), and he died about five years before that king. Herihor's antecedents are unknown. He had acquired the high title of Viceroy of Kush and, ultimately, the office of vizier in addition to his priestly functions. His wife, Nodjmet, may have been a sister of Ramesses XI, which helps to explain Herihor's preference. His major building work is at the temple of Khonsu on the south side in the temple complex of Amun at Thebes, where he built the forecourt and the pylons (p. 171), but otherwise the records of him are the pious restorations written on some of the coffins and dockets on the mummies from the royal cache (DB 320). The mummy of Herihor's wife, Nodjmet, was found amongst those in the royal cache in 1881 but their joint funerary papyrus, a magnificent illustrated copy of the Book of the Dead, had come on to the antiquities market some years before the formal discovery. A linen docket on the

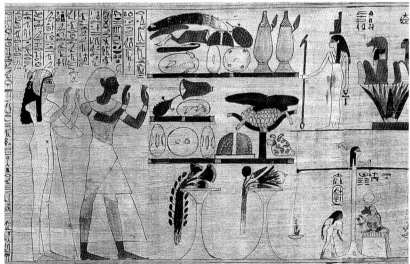

Detail from the joint Book of the Dead of Herihor and Queen Nodjmet. They both make obeisance towards offerings and a Weighing of the Heart scene, and Osiris seated beyond. Removed from the Deir el-Bahari royal cache before 1881. British Museum.

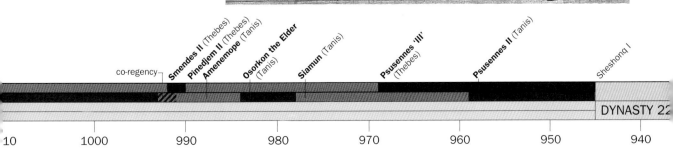

co-regency

Smendes II (Thebes)
Pinedjem II (Thebes)
Amenemope (Tanis)
Osorkon the Elder (Tanis)
Siamun (Tanis)
Psusennes 'III' (Thebes)
Psusennes II (Tanis)
Sheshonq I

DYNASTY 22

10   1000   990   980   970   960   950   940

Detail of a relief of Herihor, his name in a cartouche; from a pillar in the temple of Khonsu at Karnak.

mummy showed that the queen had been embalmed in or after Year 1 of the Tanite king Smendes I (c. 1069: p. 178), indicating that she outlived her husband by some five years. She appears to have been hidden in another cache of mummies before being transferred to her last resting place. Husband and wife were not buried together despite having a joint funerary papyrus. In fact, there is no trace of Herihor's burial apart from this papyrus, no *ushabtis*, canopic jars, or fragments of funerary furniture. There is good reason to believe, from rock-scratched graffiti, that Herihor's tomb may still await discovery in the Theban hills.

Herihor's short-lived successor as High Priest of Amun and de facto pharaoh was **Piankh**, who may have been Herihor's son-in-law. There are records of Piankh fighting some rebels late in the reign of Ramesses XI, but both he and Ramesses appear to have died about the same time in 1070.

Piankh was succeeded by his son, **Pinedjem I**, who is identified as such many times on the restoration dockets on the royal mummies. Pinedjem, although his name later appears in a royal cartouche, did not give himself regnal years (nor had Herihor), but instead on the dockets used those of Smendes I, who ruled in the Delta until 1043. Both coexisted in tranquillity, Pinedjem's sphere of influence being centred on Thebes but also extending south as far as Aswan and north to el-Hiba, just south of the Faiyum.

In the temple of Amun at Karnak, Pinedjem appears on the outer face and entrance of the pylon beyond the first court and his name is on a number of scattered blocks. His major usurpation was to add his name to the colossal standing statue of Ramesses II with a diminutive Queen Nefertari at his knees in the first court of the temple of Amun at Karnak (p. 149).

Relationships between the ruling families of the north and south were cemented in the age-old tradition of marriages. Pinedjem married Henuttawy (I), a daughter of Ramesses XI, by whom he had several sons

Detail from the jointly owned Book of the Dead of Herihor and Queen Nodjmet showing Herihor seated and playing a board game, *senet*. British Museum.

Wooden *ushabti* box and *ushabtis* of Pinedjem I. It was the appearance of these distinctive 'Deir el-Bahari blue' *ushabtis* in the art market in the 1870s that alerted Sir Gaston Maspero to the fact that a major find had been made and was being plundered by the fellahin. Cairo Museum.

and daughters. One son became Psusennes I, the third king in the dynasty at Tanis (p. 180), whilst two other sons, Masaherta and Menkheperre, became successive High Priests of Amun. Their sister, Maatkare, was the 'Divine Adoratrice': God's Wife and chief of the priestesses of Amun (cf. p. 192).

Pinedjem's mummy and a large number of his bright blue faience *ushabti* figures from six *ushabti* boxes were found in the royal cache at Deir el-Bahari (DB 320). Like the mummy of Nodjmet, Pinedjem seems

Examples of blue faience royal *ushabti* figures from the Deir el-Bahari cache. (*Near right*) Queen Henuttawy I (wife of Pinedjem I; (*centre*) Pinedjem II; (*far right*) the Princess Nesitanebashru, daughter of Pinedjem II. Near right Berlin Museum; others, private collection.

ROYAL NAMES (DYNASTY 21)	
SMENDES I *Birth name + (epithet)* Nes-ba-neb-djed (mery-amun) ('He of the Ram, Lord of Mendes, Beloved of Amun') *Also known as* Smendes (Greek) *Throne name* Hedj-kheper-re Setep-en-re ('Bright is the Manifestation of Re, Chosen of Re') *Burial* Unknown **AMENEMNISU** *Birth name* Amen-em-nisu ('Amun is King') *Throne name* Nefer-ka-re ('Beautiful is the Soul of Re') *Burial* Unknown **PSUSENNES I** *Birth name + (epithet)* Pa-seba-kha-en-niut (mery-amun) ('The Star that appears in the City [Thebes], Beloved of Amun') *Also known as* Psusennes I (Greek) *Throne name* A-kheper-re Setep-en-amun ('Great are the Manifestations of Re, Chosen of Amun') *Wife* Mutnodjmet *Burial* Tanis **AMENEMOPE** *Birth name* Amen-em-ope ('Amun in the Opet Festival') *Also known as* Amenophthis (Greek)	*Throne name* User-maat-re Mery-amun Setep-en-amun ('The Justice of Re is Powerful, Beloved of Amun, Chosen of Amun') *Burial* Tanis **OSORKON THE ELDER** *Birth name* Osorkon *Also known as* Osochor *Throne name* Aa-kheper-re Setep-en-re ('Great is the Soul of Re, Chosen of Re') *Burial* Unknown **SIAMUN** *Birth name* Si-amun ('Son of Amun') *Also known as* Siamon *Throne name* Netjer-kheper-re Setep-en-amun ('Like a God is the Manifestation of Re, Chosen of Amun') *Burial* Unknown **PSUSENNES II** *Birth name + (epithet)* Pa-seba-kha-en-niut (mery-amun) ('The Star that appears in the City [Thebes], Beloved of Amun') *Also known as* Psusennes II (Greek) *Throne name* Tit-kheperu-re ('Image of the Transformations of Re') *Burial* Unknown

to have been moved to this cache from a previous one. He apparently had intentions of taking over the unfinished tomb of Ramesses XI (KV 4) but never did so (p. 171). Where he or any of the other priestly, quasi-royal bodies found in the 1881 cache were originally buried – whether in individual tombs or a large, family tomb – is unknown.

After the two successive High Priests of Amun, **Masaherta** (1054–1046) and **Menkheperre** (1045–992), came the latter's son **Smendes II** (992–990) and then **Pinedjem II**, Menkheperre's son by his wife Isiemkheb, daughter of Psusennes I, ruler in the Delta. Pinedjem II's mummy and coffins were found intact in the royal cache (DB 320), suggesting that this was his original place of burial. The king was accompanied by his large blue *ushabtis* (p. 177), together with one of his wives, Neskhons, and their daughter, Nesitanebashru. The fact that other members of the family were also found in the cache suggests that this was the original place of interment.

It was the appearance on the antiquities market in the late 1870s of *ushabtis* and funerary papyri of these members of the 21st Dynasty priestly royal family that alerted Gaston Maspero to the possibility of a new find. He thought that the fellahin had discovered an intact tomb of the period. After intensive local questioning, the Abd el-Rassul family were identified as the culprits and led the authorities to the concealed shaft of DB 320 in the next wadi south of Deir el-Bahari. Here they were amazed to discover not only the 21st Dynasty bodies and equipment but also the mummies of the majority of the great pharaohs of the New Kingdom (see p. 103).

Psusennes 'III' is a shadowy, possibly even non-existent, figure. If the evidence of a doubtfully read docket from Deir el-Bahari tomb 320 is accepted, he would be a son of Pinedjem II, with a reign of at least five years and some have suggested as much as 24 years.

The 21st Dynasty at Tanis

The move of power and control from Upper Egypt to Lower Egypt, especially reflected in the founding of cities in the eastern Delta by kings in the later 19th and 20th Dynasties, made the division of Egypt complete. Whilst the autonomous High Priests of Amun at Thebes paid a nodding allegiance to the kings in the Delta, they were nevertheless a separate entity.

After Ramesses XI died in 1070, **Smendes** proclaimed himself king, ruling from the Delta. With his accession, the 'official' 21st Dynasty may be said to have begun. Manetho is able to present more detail with this dynasty, listing seven kings, each with their length of reign, and allocating a total of 130 years for them. This corresponds well with the overall dates postulated here of 1069 to 945. Since Smendes is known to have lived at Memphis at least for a while, no doubt the crowning ceremony was carried out there as of old. The new king's origins are obscure and he seems to have consolidated his position by marrying one of the many daughters of Ramesses XI.

View of the tomb of Psusennes I within the enclosure of the temple of Amun at Tanis. The group of royal tombs was found by Professor Pierre Montet in 1939 below the temple pavement; that of Psusennes is the only intact royal tomb found in Egypt.

The Delta capital was moved in Smendes' reign from Piramesse to Tanis, which was largely rebuilt, using many monuments of Middle and New Kingdom date transferred from other sites. It was to become a great city of obelisks. Smendes also carried out extensive work at Karnak, which included the restoration of a section of the temple's great enclosure wall that protected it from the waters of the annual inundation.

Smendes died in 1043 and the brief interlude before the accession of Psusennes I in 1039 was filled by **Amenemnisu**, a son of Herihor and

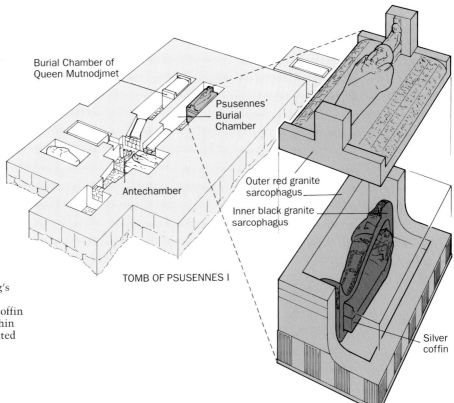

Isometric view of the tomb of Psusennes I at Tanis. Both the king's stone sarcophagi were reused (pp. 180–81) and enclosed a silver coffin with gold embellishments and within that, over the face of the disintegrated mummy, a gold face mask (p. 180).

Burial Chamber of Queen Mutnodjmet

Psusennes' Burial Chamber

Antechamber

TOMB OF PSUSENNES I

Outer red granite sarcophagus

Inner black granite sarcophagus

Silver coffin

(*Above*) One of a pair of rigid gold bracelets, hinged to open. They carry the cartouches of Psusennes but were both found on the arms of King Amenemope at Tanis. Cairo Museum.

(*Right*) The solid silver coffin of Psusennes, its upper half with added gold embellishments. Cairo Museum.

(*Below*) Psusennes' gold face mask is certainly the finest of several found at Tanis, although it does not bear comparison with the earlier one of Tutankhamun (p. 128). Cairo Museum.

Nodjmet. Civil war still raged in the Theban area, and a number of the dissidents were exiled to the western oases, then held by Libyan chiefs. A black granite stele in the Louvre records the banishment of these people and, strangely, their subsequent permit to return under an oracular decree from Amun. It all seems to have been part of a plan between the north and south, the secular and the religious factions. This rapprochement was set in motion by the next king **Psusennes I** in allowing the marriage of his daughter Isiemkheb to the High Priest Menkheperre.

The royal burial chambers at Tanis

Further links between Tanis and Thebes manifested themselves in a temple dedicated to the Theban trio of Amun, Mut and Khonsu at Tanis. It was within the precinct of this temple that Pierre Montet found in 1939–40 the stone-built burial chambers of the 21st Dynasty kings. The rich tomb of Psusennes was found intact, the only pharaonic grave ever discovered thus (the fabulous tomb of Tutankhamun having been robbed twice in antiquity before being resealed, p. 135). A large carved red granite sarcophagus enclosed a black granite anthropoid coffin, which in turn held a silver inner coffin. Over the face of the

(*Above*) The gold funerary mask of King Amenemope from Tanis has little character by comparison with earlier examples. Cairo Museum.

(*Below*) Two gold pectorals from the mummy of King Amenemope at Tanis. The upper with the goddesses Isis and Nephthys supporting Khepri as a beetle, the lower with Amenemope offering incense to Osiris. Cairo Museum.

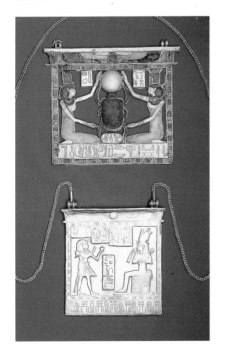

mummy lay a gold face mask, but the mummy had been substantially destroyed by the poor conditions. The large sarcophagus had originally been used 170 years earlier for the burial of Merneptah, successor of Ramesses II, in the Valley of the Kings, as his still readable cartouches on the lid showed. The black granite coffin had belonged to a high-ranking 19th Dynasty noble who could not be identified. The reuse of a Theban sarcophagus shows that there was friendly contact between north and south, and also that the Valley of the Kings was in course of being officially looted or its contents recycled. Other members of the royal court buried at Tanis included Psusennes' wife, Mutnodjmet, and his son and successor, **Amenemope**. Curiously Amenemope was buried in his mother's tomb and not in the one prepared for him. His burial at Tanis produced a fine group of funerary material, including a rather bland-looking gold face mask, but was not so rich as that of Psusennes.

Between the reigns of Amenemope and Siamun there seems to have been a ruler called Aakheperre Setepenre, usually referred to as '**Osorkon the Elder**', who may have reigned for up to six years, but the evidence is very scanty.

Siamun, who came to the throne in about 978 BC, reigned for almost 20 years. He is chiefly represented by his extensive building work in the Delta, at Piramesse but principally at Tanis where he enlarged the temple of Amun. His name, however, is also very prevalent at Thebes, where it occurs several times with different regnal years on the bandages used in the rewrapping of a number of the later royal mummies from the Deir el-Bahari cache of 1881 (DB 320).

The little light that is thrown on the 21st Dynasty comes largely from the Biblical record, since the period coincides with the struggle of David in Israel to unite the tribes and destroy the Philistines, exemplified initially in the story of David and Goliath. Siamun obviously kept a watching brief on the Near Eastern situation and Egypt was able to interfere from time to time to protect her own interests and trade routes. Now, however, there was an evident change in the Egyptian view of diplomatic marriages. Where, hitherto, there had been a stream of foreign princesses coming to the Egyptian court, the process was slightly reversed, with Egyptian princesses 'marrying out'. One princess married Hadad, the crown prince of the kingdom of Edom, when he took refuge in Egypt after succumbing to David's attacks. A son of this union, Genubath, was brought up in the old tradition at the Egyptian court and his father eventually regained his throne after David's death, no doubt still maintaining close family and trade ties with Egypt.

An Egyptian campaign in which Gezer was seized from the weakened Philistines is recorded in the Old Testament. Solomon had succeeded his father David and an Egyptian alliance was sealed by Solomon's marriage to an Egyptian princess. The end of the dynasty came with **Psusennes II** whose reign, lasting 14 years, is little known. His successor, Sheshonq I, the founder of the 22nd Dynasty, married Maatkare, Psusennes' daughter, thus forging another dynastic marriage tie.

DYNASTY 22 (at Tanis)

(Libyan or
Bubastite)
945–712

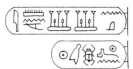

Sheshonq I
(meryamun)
Hedjkheperre
Setepenre
945–924

Osorkon I
(meryamun)
Sekhemkheperre
924–889

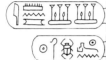

Sheshonq II
(meryamun)
Heqakheperre
Setepenre
c. 890

no cartouche

Takelot I
(meryamun)
Usermaatre
Setepenre
889–874

Osorkon II
(meryamun)
Usermaatre
Setepenamun
874–850

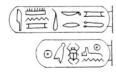

Takelot II
(meryamun)
Hedjkheperre
Setepenre
850–825

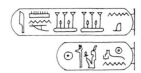

Sheshonq III
(meryamun)
Usermaatre
Setepenre
825–773

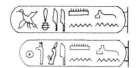

Pami
Usermaatre
Setepenamun
773–767

Sheshonq V
Aakheperre
767–730

Osorkon IV
Aakheperre
Setepenamun
730–715

AT THEBES
Harsiese
(meryamun)
Hedjkheperre
Setepenamun
870–860

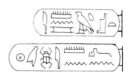

Sheshonq I

Osorkon I

Sheshonq II
*c.*890

Takelot I

► DYNASTY 21 | DYNASTY 22 (LIBYAN OR BUBASTITE)

950   940   930   920   910   900   890

DYNASTY 23 (at Leontopolis)

(Libyan Anarchy) 818–712

 **Pedibastet**
(meryamun)
Usermaatre
Setepenamun
818–793

 Sheshonq IV
Usermaatre
Meryamun
793–787

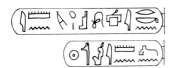 **Osorkon III**
Usermaatre
Setepenamun
787–759

 **Takelot III**
Usermaatre
764–757

 **Rudamon**
Usermaatre
Setepenamun
757–754

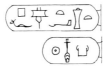 **Iuput**
(meryamun-sibastet)
Usermaatre
754–715

AT HERAKLEOPOLIS **Peftjauabastet**
Neferkare

AT HERMOPOLIS **Nimlot**

DYNASTY 24 (at Sais)

727–715

 **Tefnakht**
Shepsesre
727–720

Bakenrenef
(Bocchoris)
Wahkare
720–715

Often referred to as the Libyan or Bubastite dynasty, the 22nd Dynasty immediately betrays its origins. Manetho lists the kings as all being from Bubastis in the eastern Delta and the Libyan element is evident in the founder, **Sheshonq I**, who inaugurated the sequence of Libyan chiefs who were to rule Egypt for the next 200 years. Sheshonq himself, allied by marriage as the son-in-law of his predecessor, Psusennes II, had the

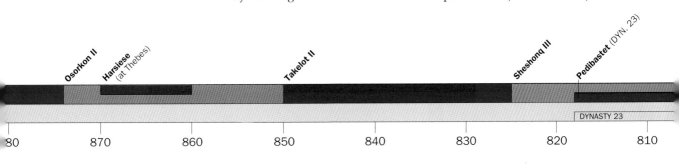

Osorkon II Harsiese (at Thebes) Takelot II Sheshonq III Pedibastet (DYN. 23)

DYNASTY 23

880 870 860 850 840 830 820 810

(*Above*) Sheshonq I's cartonnage coffin from Tanis underlines the Horus iconography in its falcon mask, and his silver coffin was similarly modelled. Cairo Museum.

(*Right*) Gold trinity of Osiris (on a lapis lazuli pillar inscribed for Osorkon II), flanked by Horus and Isis. It probably came from the robbed royal tombs at Tanis but was acquired by the Louvre, Paris in 1872.

strength of the military behind him as commander-in-chief of all the armies. In the Theban records he is noted as 'Great Chief of the Meshwesh', who were originally recruited from Libyan tribes as an internal police force. Like many previous pharaohs, Sheshonq endeavoured to show his right to rule by adopting hallowed titles, in this instance those of Smendes I of almost a hundred years before.

Sheshonq was a strong ruler who brought the divided factions of Thebes and Tanis together into a once more united Egypt. Calculated appointments of his sons to various high offices meant that he exercised specific control over important areas of the country. Uniting the religious and secular spheres, his son Iuput was Governor of Upper Egypt and at the same time both High Priest of Amun and commander-in-chief of the armies. Another son, Djedptahaufankh, supported his brother in the religious field as Third Prophet of Amun. Yet another son, Nimlot, acted as military commander at Herakleopolis, an important garrison that could keep Thebes in check, if need be, to the south. With such a stable power base at home, Sheshonq could then turn his gaze outwards to the old Egyptian Near Eastern possessions.

Sheshonq triumphs in Palestine

Following the death of Solomon in 930 BC, the kingdoms of Judah and Israel under Rehoboam (Solomon's son) and Jeroboam I, respectively,

Sheshonq IV (DYN. 23)
Osorkon III (DYN. 23)
Pami (DYN. 22)
Sheshonq V (DYN. 22)
co-regency
Takelot III (DYN. 23) (sole rule)
Rudamon (DYN. 23)
Iuput (DYN. 23)
Piankhi (DYN. 25)
Nimlot (DYN. 23)
Petjauabastet (DYN. 23)
(precise dates unknown)

▶ DYNASTY 22
▶ DYNASTY 23

800   790   780   770   760   750   740

(Right) Sheshonq I's triumphant relief with captive cities in the temple of Amun at Karnak.

ROYAL NAMES (DYNASTY 22)

SHESHONQ I
Birth name + (epithet)
Sheshonq (mery-amun) ('Sheshonq, Beloved of Amun')
Also known as
Sheshonk I, Shoshenk I, Shishak (Bible)
Throne name
Hedj-kheper-re Setep-en-re ('Bright is the Manifestation of Re, Chosen of Re')

OSORKON I
Birth name + (epithet)
Osorkon (mery-amun) ('Osorkon, Beloved of Amun')
Throne name
Sekhem-kheper-re ('Powerful are the Manifestations of Re')

SHESHONQ II
Birth name + (epithet)
Sheshonq (mery-amun) ('Sheshonq, Beloved of Amun')
Throne name
Heqa-kheper-re Setep-en-re ('The Manifestation of Re rules, Chosen of Re')

TAKELOT I
Birth name + (epithet)
Takelot (mery-amun) ('Takelot, Beloved of Amun')
Also known as
Takeloth
Throne name
User-maat-re Setep-en-re ('Powerful is the Justice of Re, chosen of Re')

OSORKON II
Birth name + (epithet)
Osorkon (mery-amun) ('Osorkon, Beloved of Amun')
Throne name
User-maat-re Setep-en-amun ('Powerful is the Justice of Re, Chosen of Amun')

TAKELOT II
Birth name + (epithet)
Takelot (mery-amun) ('Takelot, Beloved of Amun')
Throne name
Hedj-kheper-re Setep-en-re ('Bright is the Manifestation of Re, Chosen of Re')

SHESHONQ III
Birth name + (epithet)
Sheshonq (mery-amun) ('Sheshonq, Beloved of Amun')
Throne name
User-maat-re Setep-en-re ('Powerful is the Justice of Re, Chosen of Re')

PAMI
Birth name
Pami ('He who belongs to the Cat [Bastet]')
Also known as
Pimay
Throne name
User-maat-re Setep-en-amun ('Powerful is the Justice of Re, Chosen of Amun')

SHESHONQ V
Birth name
Sheshonq
Throne name
Aa-kheper-re ('Great is the Soul of Re')

OSORKON IV
Birth name
Osorkon
Throne name
Aa-kheper-re Setep-en-amun ('Great is the Soul of Re, Chosen of Amun')

HARSIESE
Birth name
Harsiese ('Horus Son of Isis')
Throne name
Hedj-kheper-re Setep-en-amun ('Bright is the Manifestation of Re, Chosen of Re')

were at loggerheads and ripe for strong Egyptian military intervention. Sheshonq – Shishak of the Bible – defeated them both in 925 BC in a highly successful campaign, the like of which had not been seen since the days of Ramesses III in the 20th Dynasty. He moved first against Judah, arriving before the walls of Jerusalem, held by Rehoboam. The city was surrounded but Sheshonq was bought off from entering it by being given 'the treasures of the house of the Lord, and the treasures of the king's house; he even took away all: and he took away all the shields of gold which Solomon had made' (1 Kings 14: 26). All Solomon's treasures, except apparently the most sacred and emotive Ark of the Covenant, fell to Sheshonq. Pharaoh then turned his attention to Israel, pursuing his earlier protégé Jeroboam, who fled over the Jordan. Finally, Sheshonq halted at Megiddo, the scene of Tuthmosis III's victory 500 years before, and erected a suitable victory stele in the manner of his predecessors.

Such success was duly signalled in the appropriate place – on the walls of the temple of Amun at Thebes – and the sandstone quarries at

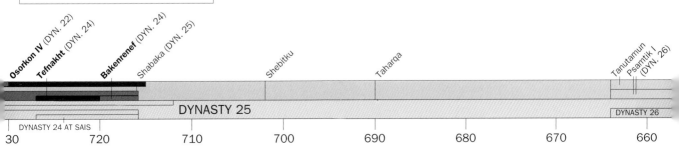

Osorkon IV (DYN. 22)   Tefnakht (DYN. 24)   Bakenrenef (DYN. 24)   Shabaka (DYN. 25)   Shebitku   Taharqa   Tanutamun   Psamtik I (DYN. 26)

DYNASTY 25   DYNASTY 26

DYNASTY 24 AT SAIS

30   720   710   700   690   680   670   660

(*Left*) Granite torso with the cartouche of Osorkon I found at Byblos. A dedication inscription in archaic Phoenician script has been added to it by King Elibaal of Byblos. Louvre, Paris.

(*Right*) The gold funerary mask of Sheshonq II, one of the finer examples from the royal tombs at Tanis. Cairo Museum.

Gebel el-Silsila had to be reopened to provide the building material. Iuput, as High Priest of Amun, was also head of works. A great new court was constructed before the Second Pylon at Karnak, its south outer wall decorated with a huge relief of Sheshonq victorious through the grace of Amun and with captives falling to his might.

Soon after the triumphant Palestinian campaigns, Sheshonq went to join his ancestors in the group of royal tombs at Tanis, his mummy encased in a cartonnage and a silver coffin, both having Horus falcon heads to identify the king with Osiris-Sokar (p. 184).

Osorkon I, who succeeded his father, continued to provide strong patronage for the various leading priesthoods, thereby consolidating his position as well as maintaining a continuous building programme, especially at his native city of Bubastis. The chief priesthood of Amun at Karnak was taken from his brother, Iuput, and given to one of his sons, **Sheshonq (II)**, whom he took as co-regent in 890 BC. Sheshonq, however, predeceased his father by a few months, and both were buried at Tanis. The successor was **Takelot I**, another son of Osorkon by a minor wife. This reign, although 15 years in length, has left no major monuments and saw the beginning of the fragmentation of Egypt once more into two power bases.

Osorkon II succeeded Takelot I as pharaoh in 874 BC at much the same time that his cousin Harsiese succeeded his father (Sheshonq II) as High Priest of Amun at Karnak. Problems arose in Year 4 of Osorkon when Harsiese declared himself king in the south. Although he was only king in name, when Harsiese died Osorkon II consolidated his own position by appointing one of his sons, Nimlot, as High Priest at Karnak and another son, Sheshonq, as High Priest of Ptah at Memphis. Osorkon thereby had the two major priesthoods of Egypt in his family's grasp as a political move rather than from any religious motivation. Major building works were undertaken in the reign, especially at Bubastis in the

Grey granite head of Osorkon II, from Tanis. University Museum, Philadelphia.

(*Right*) Relief of Osorkon II and Queen Karomama I from the great red granite hall the king built at Bubastis to celebrate his *heb-sed*. British Museum.

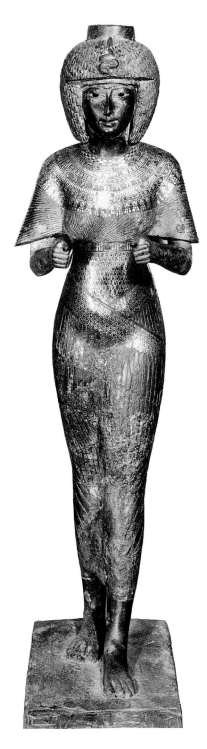

(*Left*) In 1829 at Thebes Champollion acquired a superb bronze standing statue of Queen Karomama II, daughter of Nimlot and wife of Takelot II, almost 2 ft (59.5 cm) high. She is represented in her office as Divine Adoratrice of Amun and details of her elegant features and dress are inlaid in gold and silver. Now in the Louvre, it is one of the finest pieces of its period.

temple of the tutelary cat-goddess Bastet. There Osorkon built a monumental red granite hall decorated with fine reliefs of himself and his wife Karomama I celebrating his jubilee (*heb-sed*) in Year 22. Other buildings in his name were constructed at Memphis, Tanis, Thebes and Leontopolis (to become the seat of the succeeding dynasty).

In the outside world of the Near East a growing menace was coming from Assyria, who turned her attentions towards the Levant after overcoming northern Mesopotamia and Syria, and with an eventual eye for Egypt. The Assyrian king Shalmaneser III (858–828 BC) continued his father Ashurnasirpal II's campaigns into Syria/Palestine. In 853 Egypt was forced to confront the threat by aligning with Israel and neighbouring kingdoms, including her old ally Byblos; together they halted the Assyrian advance at the battle of Qarqar on the Orontes.

Takelot II succeeded his father Osorkon II in 850 and maintained stability in the south where his half-brother Nimlot was still in power at Thebes as High Priest. Nimlot had consolidated his position by extending north to Herakleopolis and placing his son Ptahwedjankhef in charge there. Nimlot then married his daughter Karomama II to Takelot II, thereby cementing a bond between north and south and becoming the father-in-law of his half-brother. Karomama must have been buried

ROYAL NAMES (DYNASTY 23)

PEDIBASTET
Birth name + (epithet)
Pe-di-bastet (mery-amun) ('Wise One of Bastet, Beloved of Amun')
Also known as
Pedubast, Petubastis (Greek)
Throne name
User-maat-re Setep-en-amun ('Powerful is the Justice of Re, Chosen of Amun')

SHESHONQ IV
Birth name
Sheshonq
Throne name
User-maat-re Mery-amun ('Powerful is the Justice of Re, Beloved of Amun')

OSORKON III
Birth name
Osorkon
Throne name
User-maat-re Setep-en-amun ('Powerful is the Justice of Re, Chosen of Amun')

TAKELOT III
Birth name
Takelot
Throne name
User-maat-re

('Powerful is the Justice of Re')

RUDAMON
Birth name
Rudamon
Throne name
User-maat-re Setep-en-amun ('Powerful is the Justice of Re, Chosen of Amun')

IUPUT
Birth name + (epithet)
Iuput (mery-amun si-bastet) ('Iuput, Beloved of Amun, Son of Bastet')
Throne name
User-maat-re ('Powerful is the Justice of Re')

NIMLOT
Birth name
Nimlot

PEFTJAUABASTET
Birth name
Peftjauabastet
Also known as
Peftjauawybast
Throne name
Nefer-ka-re ('Beautiful is the Soul of Re')

ROYAL NAMES (DYNASTY 24)

TEFNAKHT
Birth name
Tefnakht
Throne name
Shepses-re ('Noble like Re')

BAKENRENEF
Birth name
Bakenrenef

Also known as
Bocchoris (Greek)
Throne name
Wah-ka-re ('Constant is the Soul of Re')

(*Opposite*) Relief of Iuput represented as the god Horus seated on a lotus flower, an allusion to the creation legend when the god on his flower arose from the primeval waters. Royal Scottish Museum, Edinburgh.

at Thebes, since her rather poor green-glazed composition *ushabti* figures have been appearing from there in the antiquities market for over 150 years, but her tomb has not been found.

Problems arose, however, in Year 11 of Takelot II with the death of Nimlot. The question of who should succeed him as High Priest of Amun led to open hostilities. Thebes, led by a Harsiese who claimed descent from the king Harsiese, revolted against Takelot's choice of his son Prince Osorkon. Nimlot's son, Ptahwedjankhef, Governor of Herakleopolis, supported Takelot's decision, thereby allowing Prince Osorkon an easy passage south past his fortress to curb the rebellious Thebans. The rebels were relentlessly crushed, the ringleaders executed and their bodies burnt to ensure that there would be no hope of an after-life for them.

For the next four years peace reigned, but in Year 15 of Takelot II civil war once again struck the country. On this occasion, however, the revolt was not so easily put down and lasted for almost a decade. It was probably at this time that further incursions were made into the Valley of the Kings, with 'official' sanction, when the sarcophagus box of Ramesses VI was overturned in a vain search for hidden treasure beneath it (p. 168).

When Takelot II died he was buried at Tanis, where he was found by Pierre Montet in a reused coffin in the antechamber of the tomb of Osorkon II. The Crown Prince Osorkon never succeeded to the throne because his younger brother Sheshonq moved to seize power, proclaiming himself pharaoh as **Sheshonq III**. He was to enjoy an incredibly long reign of 53 years. It was also to be the most confusing period of Egyptian history, with not only an initial split between north and south, Tanis and Thebes, but also a later rift between the east and the central Delta, Tanis and Leontopolis respectively.

There are a number of dates to use as chronological pegs in the long reign of Sheshonq III, but there are also large gaps in between. In Year 6, Harsiese reappeared as Chief High Priest of Amun, apparently without too much commotion at Thebes because Sheshonq had let the Thebans have their own way and choice. In Year 20 (*c.* 806 BC), the usurped Prince Osorkon was appointed to the High Priest's post at Thebes. Unusually, he had not been disposed of by his usurping younger brother. Then, in Year 25 (*c.* 800 BC), Harsiese once again assumed the office of High Priest, only to disappear, perhaps finally dead, in Year 29. Prince Osorkon had not died when Harsiese returned to power and was still evident in Upper Egypt with a controlling hand for another ten years.

The 23rd Dynasty

In Sheshonq III's Year 8 (*c.* 818 BC) he had to contend with a breakaway in the central Delta, at Leontopolis, where a prince named **Pedibastet** proclaimed a new dynasty, the 23rd, with himself as the founding king. Although members of the Tanite royal house held posts at Thebes, the priests of Amun were, as ever, politically very aware and at least two

(*Above*) Bronze statuette of Pami, identified by cartouches on his right shoulder and belt buckle. British Museum.

sons of the new dynasty joined them. Pedibastet reigned for 25 years and was succeeded by **Sheshonq IV** (793–787) and then **Osorkon III** (787–759). For 14 years, Osorkon III at Leontopolis, and Sheshonq III at Tanis, reigned concurrently, but in 773 Sheshonq III died leaving Osorkon III to continue his reign in the central Delta for another 15 years. Osorkon designated his son Takelot as ruler of Herakleopolis while he was also Chief Priest. Around 765 BC Takelot became co-regent with his father, but his sole reign as **Takelot III** after the death of Osorkon six years later lasted only about two years. Meantime at Tanis an obscure king called **Pami** occupied the throne for six years (773–767) before being succeeded by his son, **Sheshonq V**, with his son, **Osorkon IV**, in turn becoming king and officially the last ruler of the 22nd Dynasty.

The coincidence of Dynasties 22 (Tanis) and 23 (Leontopolis) is extremely confusing, especially since not all the relationships between the many rulers, let alone their dates, are clear. At one point, a commander of Herakleopolis named Peftjauabastet married Takelot III's niece, who was also the daughter of Rudamon (Takelot's brother). **Rudamon** enjoyed a brief reign after Takelot, to be succeeded by Iuput, and there arose a situation where three men – **Iuput** (Leontopolis), **Peftjauabastet** (Herakleopolis) and **Nimlot** (Hermopolis) – were all simultaneously claiming to be 'kings'. They merely held sway over small areas of Egypt and it was the growing danger from Nubia that led them to band together for the common good, although in the end it availed them nothing (p. 190 ff.).

The 24th Dynasty

The Nubian influence had indeed been growing in southern Egypt, extending as far north as Thebes. **Tefnakht**, the king of Sais in the Delta, recognized this and attempted to stem the invasion by organizing a coalition of northern kings that included Osorkon IV (Tanis), Peftjauabastet (Herakleopolis), Nimlot (Hermopolis) and Iuput (Leontopolis). Tefnakht became the first of the only two kings of the 24th Dynasty; the other was **Bakenrenef** (better known in Greek myth as the Bocchoris who tangled with Herakles). Tefnakht probably reigned for about eight years and Bakenrenef for six. Initially, the confederation of northern rulers enjoyed a certain success, in that the Nubian king Piankhi (Piyi), allowed them to come south. The two forces met at Herakleopolis and Tefnakht was compelled to retreat to Hermopolis where he, and subsequently the other kings of the coalition, surrendered to Piankhi, who was now personally leading his forces. All four 'kings' were then allowed to continue as governors of their respective cities, a policy which, centuries later, Alexander the Great was to find effective in his world conquest.

DYNASTY 25 (Nubian/Kushite)
747–656

 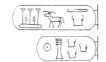

Piankhi (Piyi)
Menkheperre
747–716

Taharqa
Nefertemkhure
690–664

Shabaka
Neferkare
716–702

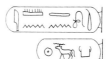

Tanutamun
Bakare
664–656

Shebitku
Djedkare
702–690

ROYAL NAMES AND BURIALS	
PIANKHI *Birth name* Piankhi *Also known as* Piankhy, Piyi *Throne name* Men-kheper-re ('The Manifestation of Re abides') *Burial* el-Kurru	*Throne name* Djed-ka-re ('Enduring is the Soul of Re') *Burial* Napata
SHABAKA *Birth name* Shabaka *Throne name* Nefer-ka-re ('Beautiful is the Soul of Re') *Burial* el-Kurru	**TAHARQA** *Birth name* Taharqa *Throne name* Nefertem-khu-re ('Nefertum is his Protector') *Burial* Nuri
SHEBITKU *Birth name* Shebitku	**TANUTAMUN** *Birth name* Tanutamun *Throne name* Ba-ka-re ('Glorious is the Soul of Re') *Burial* Nuri

Since the days of Ramesses II in the 19th Dynasty, Nubia – the land of Kush south of Aswan – had gone its own way, eventually founding a kingdom, Napata, that was independent at last from its powerful northern neighbour. During the Egyptian presence of the later New Kingdom the cult of Amun had taken a firm hold in Nubia, its major cult centre located at the great rock of Gebel Barkal. Here a major temple was built to the Theban god; the priests engaged in his cult, like their northern counterparts at Thebes, gradually increased their own influence alongside that of the deity until they similarly usurped the kingship. A dynastic succession seems to have been established as early as the late 10th century BC with the use of the traditional pharaonic titles and cartouches.

The Nubian conquest

With the breakdown of Egyptian sovereignty in Egypt the Nubian kings began to look north. They viewed their incursions into Egypt not so much as an invasion but as a restoration of the old status quo and supremacy of Amun. Hence, when **Piankhi (Piyi)** moved north against the coalition of four Egyptian kings in Year 21 of his Nubian reign, about 727 BC, he could take the view that these kings had acted like

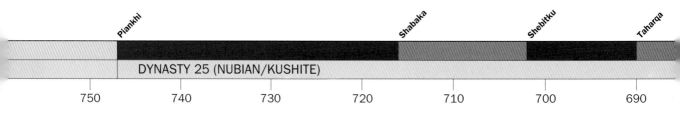

DYNASTY 25 (NUBIAN/KUSHITE)

Piankhi   Shabaka   Shebitku   Taharqa

750   740   730   720   710   700   690

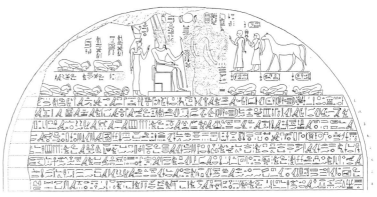

The Victory Stele of Piankhi, 5 ft 10 inches (180 cm) high and 6 ft (184 cm) wide. Its 159 lines are written in the highly rhetorical language of the old tradition. In the lunette relief at the top, Amun, specifically identified as being of Napata, sits enthroned while Piankhi, standing, receives four identified 'kings', each having the royal *uraeus* emblem on their brow, with Nimlot singled out as their leader.

The Nubians' great love of horses is reflected in lines 63–68 which describe how, having successfully besieged Hermopolis, Piankhi had the women-folk of the surrendering king (Nimlot) brought before him, 'but His Majesty turned not his face towards them. His Majesty proceeded to the stable of the horses and the quarters of the foals. When he saw that they had suffered hunger [because of the rigours of the siege], he said: "I swear, as Re loves me and as my nostrils are rejuvenated with life, it is more grievous in my heart that my horses have suffered hunger, than any evil deed thou [King Nimlot] hast done, in the prosecution of thy desire . . . I could not but condemn him on account of it."' Cairo Museum (from Mariette's drawing).

naughty children who needed to be brought into line. After their defeat he treated them with leniency, confirming them as governors, although one, Tefnakht, had fled further north into the Delta where he attempted to regroup and at the same time sent an eloquent address to Piankhi, full of the old rhetoric, seeking a truce.

A remarkably full account of these events is recorded on a large pink granite block found in 1862 in the temple of Amun at Gebel Barkal (now in Cairo). This so-called 'Victory Stele' is obviously the 'home' copy of an inscription that must have been repeated in other major northern sites such as Memphis, still the secular capital, and Thebes itself. Complete details of the campaign are given, from Piankhi's decision to march north and take charge himself (under the guidance of Amun), down to the discussions about how best to invest the fortified city of Memphis. On the way, passing through Amun's Thebes, Piankhi celebrated the Festival of Opet – during which the figure of Amun was carried from Karnak to the Luxor temple – presumably in front of the temple reliefs carved 600 years earlier under Tutankhamun.

Piankhi had legitimized his position in the Nubian succession by marrying the daughter of a king named Alara, the seventh king of Napata. At Thebes, Piankhi took a firm hold on the priesthood of Amun by having the Divine Adoratrice of Amun, Shepenwepet I, 'adopt' as her successor his sister Amenirdis I. The maintenance of the cult of Amun at both Karnak and Gebel Barkal was an important part of the building programme of the successive Kushite kings, to the extent that the latter became a huge southern replica of the former.

Although, curiously, it appears that Piankhi preferred to rule from Napata in the south, since he returned there, he invested himself with the resonant old coronation names of the New Kingdom pharaohs Tuthmosis III and Ramesses II. When he died *c.* 716 BC Piankhi was

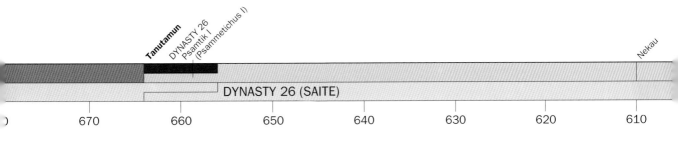

Tanutamun

DYNASTY 26
Psamtik I
(Psammetichus I)

Nekau

DYNASTY 26 (SAITE)

670   660   650   640   630   620   610

THE DIVINE ADORATRICE

During the New Kingdom royal ladies of the court had been invested with a certain theological importance as the God's Wife. This post was held by a royal princess, who – as the wife of Amun – maintained the god's cult on behalf of the king, thus endorsing his divine right to rule. In the late New Kingdom, however, this right was increasingly challenged by the growing power of the priesthood. It may have been partly in response that the role of Divine Adoratrice evolved. Combining the offices of God's Wife and Chief Priestess of Amun, the Divine Adoratrice was dedicated to the service of Amun and held a position of extreme authority, in control of the priesthood and thereby a vast section of the economy. During part of the Third Intermediate Period the celibate priestess 'adopted' her successor, thereby overcoming some of the problems inherent in the transmission of royal power.

Alabaster statue of Queen Amenirdis I, Divine Adoratrice, from Karnak. Cairo Museum.

buried at el-Kurru, just to the north of Gebel Barkal, in the pyramid field that was to include the burials of several of the kings of the 25th Dynasty, as well as other relatives such as two of Piankhi's sisters. The pyramid tombs adopted by the Kushites were very different from their northern antecedents – they were much smaller and their angle of inclination was severely sharper than the true pyramid of 52° 51'.

The Kushite kings wholeheartedly embraced almost all the old Egyptian burial customs – embalming, the provision of splendid carved stone *ushabtis* and other funerary accoutrements. They betrayed their Nubian origins, however, in the practice of laying the royal body on a bed in the tomb and, nearby, burying chariot horses standing in teams of four (for a quadriga) to accompany their master.

Piankhi was succeeded by his brother **Shabaka** (here the Nubian succession was at variance with Egyptian custom), who continued the revival of old Egyptian traditions, delving into whatever temple records could be found, or inventing them if necessary. An important relic of this is the 'Shabaka Stone', a slab of basalt 4½ ft (1.37 m) long, now in the British Museum. Its surface is much abraded and deeply scored from having been used at a later date as a millstone. The text on it states that it is a copy taken from an ancient 'worm-eaten' papyrus discovered at Memphis and recounting the Memphite theology of the creator gods.

The overall control exerted by Shabaka (that is, south of the 24th Dynasty territory in the northern Delta) is indicated by the vast array of building work undertaken in his reign, mainly at Thebes on both east and west banks of the Nile and largely in relation to the Amun cult, but also at other major religious cult centres such as Memphis (Ptah), Abydos (Osiris), Dendera (Hathor), Esna (Khnum) and Edfu (Horus).

After a 14-year reign Shabaka died and, like his brother Piankhi, was buried in a steep-sided pyramid at el-Kurru. He was succeeded, each in turn, by his nephews Shebitku and Taharqa (Piankhi's sons). The Nubian hold on Thebes was maintained through the female line when **Shebitku** married his aunt Amenirdis I (Piankhi and Shabaka's sister), the Divine Adoratrice of Amun. The office was to pass to their daughter, Shepenwepet II.

The threat from Assyria

The history of the period is very much tied in with the rise and expansion of that other great Near Eastern power, Assyria. Whilst Shabaka had kept the Assyrian king Sargon II at bay, thanks largely to that ruler's problems in other areas such as Urartu (Armenia), Shebitku took a different stance and sided with a Palestinian/Phoenician revolt against the Assyrian overlords. The Assyrian king was now Sennacherib, who brooked no such interference, and the Levantine kings were soon brought to heel. Many events of these campaigns, including the siege and capture of Lachish, are graphically represented in the reliefs from Sennacherib's south-west palace at Nineveh (now in the British Museum). In order to save Jerusalem, the Judaean king Hezekiah surren-

MENTUEMHET, PRINCE OF THEBES

Grey granite statue of Mentuemhet with his name and title on his belt. Cairo Museum.

Taharqa's extensive works at Thebes were carried out under the direction of an extraordinary man named Mentuemhet, who held the office of 'Prince [Mayor] of the City [Thebes]' and, in effect, virtually ruled the whole of Middle Egypt. Curiously, he was most proud of his office as 'Fourth Prophet of Amun', a relatively lowly post by comparison with the other offices he held. He is one of the few great officials of whom several very distinctive portrait statues have survived. His tomb in the Assasif at Thebes (TT 34, currently in course of restoration) is among the largest in the necropolis, its great arched brick superstructure rising in front of Deir el-Bahari. From his tomb and inscriptions on his large terracotta funerary cones, we learn that he had three wives. He and his brothers, who also held high-ranking priestly offices, kept the Theban nobility in check for Taharqa.

dered to Sennacherib (Byron's 'wolf') whose opinion of Hezekiah's ally Egypt was to liken it to 'a broken reed'.

A brief respite followed for Egypt. **Taharqa** succeeded his brother Shebitku as pharaoh in 690 BC, and Sennacherib was assassinated in Nineveh in 681 BC, bringing his son, Esarhaddon, to the throne. Taharqa's name is the one most associated with the Kushite dynasty, largely because of his widespread building activities, the best known of which is the splendid re-erected column in the First Court of the temple of Amun at Karnak, just one of a series that formed a great portico kiosk. Not only did Taharqa build throughout Egypt, he was also extremely active in Nubia. At Kawa he virtually resurrected the abandoned site founded under Amenhotep III and dedicated to Amun. A vast complex was inaugurated there that took on important ritual connotations and was second only to the Gebel Barkal complex.

Taharqa's reign was one of confrontations with the Assyrians, the pendulum swinging first one way, then the other. At Ashkelon on the Egyptian/Palestinian border, Esarhaddon was repulsed in 673 by the combined forces of the rebellious city and Egypt. In 671, however, the result went the other way. Esarhaddon then struck deep into Egypt, captured Memphis, the heir apparent and most of the royal family except Taharqa, who escaped south to Thebes. Another uprising in 669 saw Esarhaddon returning to Egypt, but he died on the road and was succeeded by his son, Ashurbanipal, who withdrew shortly thereafter. That was the signal for a renewed uprising, but Assyria exacted swift vengeance on the insurgents in the north of Egypt, executing all the local nobility save one, the future Necho I of the 26th Dynasty. Taharqa lost Memphis again, and then fled south and on past Thebes to his remote capital at Napata. Mentuemhet, Mayor of Thebes, was left to surrender to the Assyrian forces.

Taharqa had not shared power with his predecessor Shabaka, but in 665 BC he recognized his cousin, **Tanutamun**, as his heir and co-regent, and died the next year. Tanutamun's vision was one of the resurgence of Nubian and Egyptian grandeur. The gods were with him, he must have thought, as he swept north, taking Aswan and Thebes and then Memphis itself. The story is inscribed on a stele from Gebel Barkal, narrating how, like Tuthmosis IV before him (p. 114), Tanutamun had a dream of greatness, was crowned at Napata and then realized the dream. The run of good fortune, however, was shortlived. Ashurbanipal reacted swiftly, Memphis fell yet again, and Tanutamun fled south. This time, however, the inconceivable happened: Thebes, jewel of Amun and the ancient world, was sacked and its huge temple treasury laid waste. Its fall was an object lesson to the whole of the ancient Near East, to be quoted for centuries by such as the Old Testament prophet Nahum when he mocked Nineveh's fall in 612 BC. The Assyrians nominally held Egypt but Tanutamun was secure in Napata: Ashurbanipal would not venture beyond the boundary at Aswan. Tanutamun's death in 656 BC extinguished the century-old Nubian domination of its old foe Egypt.

DYNASTY 26 (Saite)
664–525

Psamtik I
(Psammetichus I)
Wahibre
664–610

Nekau
(Necho)
Wahemibre
610–595

Psamtik II
(Psammetichus II)
Neferibre
595–589

Wahibre
(Apries)
Haaibre
589–570

Ahmose II (sineit)
(Amasis)
Khnemibre
570–526

Psamtik III
(Psammetichus III)
Ankhare
526–525

Faience *ushabti* of Nekau (Necho) inscribed with Chapter 6 of the Book of the Dead. The features on many of the later royal *ushabtis* seem to be portraits. Leiden Museum.

Psamtik I
(Psammetichus I)

Nekau
(Necho)

Psamtik II
(Psammetichus

DYNASTY 26 (SAITE)

660   650   640   630   620   610   600

ROYAL NAMES

PSAMTIK I
Birth name
  Psamtik
Also known as
  Psammetichus I
  (Greek)
Throne name
  Wah-ib-re
  ('Constant is the
  Heart of Re')

NEKAU
Birth name
  Nekau
Also known as
  Necho (Greek)
Throne name
  Wah-em-ib-re
  ('Carrying out the
  Wish of Re Forever')

PSAMTIK II
Birth name
  Psamtik
Throne name
  Nefer-ib-re
  ('Beautiful is the
  Heart of Re')

WAHIBRE
Birth name
  Wah-ib-re
  ('Constant is the
  Heart of Re')
Also known as
  Apries (Greek)
Throne name
  Haa–ib-re ('Jubilant
  is the Heart of Re
  Forever')

AHMOSE II
Birth name+ (epithet)
  Ah-mose (si-neit)
  ('The Moon is Born,
  Son of Neith')
Also known as
  Amasis (Greek)
Throne name
  Khnem-ib-re ('He
  who embraces the
  Heart of Re')

PSAMTIK III
Birth name
  Psamtik
Throne name
  Ankh-ka-re ('Re
  gives Life to the
  Soul')

By virtue of the sporadic Assyrian overlordship of Egypt, the end of the 25th (Nubian) Dynasty and the beginning of the 26th (Saite) Dynasty overlapped. After the second uprising against Assyria in 665 BC, Ashurbanipal had confirmed Nekau (I) (Necho (I)) as king of Sais and his son **Psamtik** (better known by the Greek name **Psammetichus**) as king of Athribis – both cities being in the Delta. The Saite family hold on the area was therefore consolidated with Assyrian approval. On the death of Necho in 664, Psammetichus I was recognized by the Assyrians as king of Egypt. His task was to control not only the unruly princes and petty kings of the Delta, but also to come to some reconciliation with the power centre at Thebes. This latter proved to be easier than anticipated. The great noble Mentuemhet was still a major figure there and he allied himself with Psammetichus' daughter, the princess Nitocris, who had been sent south early in 656 BC to be officially adopted as Divine Adoratrice of Amun amidst great celebrations by Shepenwepet II and Amenirdis II, the two current holders of the office. Secular and religious ties were therefore effected that were to hold the state together whilst Psammetichus could turn his attentions to his Delta opponents. He prevailed by conscripting a great army, bringing in mercenaries from the Mediterranean world, many of them Greeks, and including Carians whose inscribed tombstones found at Saqqara have only recently been deciphered.

Renewed prosperity in Egypt

Psammetichus I's reign of over half a century saw a return to stability and the old religious values. Outside influences, both artistic and trade, came into the country as never before but, despite this, there was a great renaissance in indigenous traditions, with many art forms looking back to Middle and Old Kingdom antecedents. It is at times difficult to be absolutely sure whether a statue or relief is a Saite revival piece or something much older. The reliefs in Mentuemhet's tomb at Thebes (TT 34) are prime examples of this.

Status and trade also improved upon a fuller entry into the economy of the ancient Mediterranean. In 653 BC, Psammetichus, profiting from Assyria's internal problems, threw off the foreign yoke, allowing Egypt once more to be a dominant power in the Near East. The gradual Assyrian collapse was, however, leaving a dangerous power vacuum in the area. Like vultures, other nations hovered over the death throes – the Babylonians under Nabopolassar, the Medes and the Scythians particularly. Nabopolassar created havoc in 629–627 BC, advancing as far as

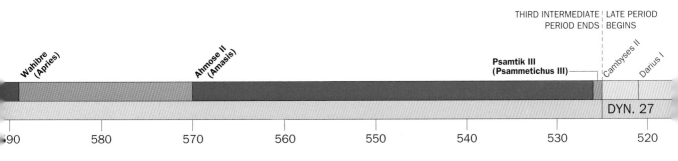

THIRD INTERMEDIATE | LATE PERIOD
PERIOD ENDS | BEGINS

Wahibre
(Apries)

Ahmose II
(Amasis)

Psamtik III
(Psammetichus III)

Cambyses II

Darius I

DYN. 27

90   580   570   560   550   540   530   520

(*Above*) Bronze kneeling statue of Nekau (Necho) in an offering attitude. It is the only known sculpture of the king in the round (cf. his *ushabti*, p. 194). University Museum, Philadelphia.

(*Below*) Black granite head of Apries. Louvre, Paris.

southern Palestine where he was repulsed at Ashdod on the coast by the Egyptians. Psammetichus, realizing the potential danger for Egypt of an Assyrian collapse, actually assisted Assyria against the Babylonians in 616 BC, but did not have sufficient forces to sway the day for them. A joint Scythian and Persian army attacked Assyria a year later, culminating in the fall of its capital Nineveh in 612 BC and the extinction of the royal line.

Nekau (II), better known as **Necho**, continued the foreign involvements of his father Psammetichus, when he came to the throne in 610 BC. Palestine once more became an Egyptian possession and much of the history of Egypt's involvement in the area is enshrined in the Biblical account in the second Book of Kings. It was now, in the late 7th century, that Greece was expanding her trading contacts and Necho took the opportunity of recruiting displaced Ionian Greeks to form an Egyptian navy. This was hitherto unheard of in Egypt because the Egyptians had an inherent distaste for and fear of the sea. Necho's vision was a wide one – he pre-empted the Suez Canal by almost 2500 years when he had a navigable canal dug through the Wadi Tumilat between the Pelusiac branch of the Nile (where the great frontier fortress of Pelusium was located) and the Red Sea. A great entrepôt city, Per-Temu-Tjeku – modern Tell el-Mashkuta west of Ismailia – was built on the canal and its fortunes, like the later Suez, were linked to the prosperity and use of the new waterway.

There is little material evidence of Necho's son, **Psammetichus II** (**Psamtik II**), who reigned for only six years. He was involved with a foray into Nubia in 592, marching as far south as the Third Cataract. A famous graffito scratched in Greek on the left leg of the colossal seated statue of Ramesses II, on the south side of the entrance to the temple of Abu Simbel, records that 'When King Psammetichus came to Elephantine, this was written by those who sailed with Psammetichus the son of Theocles, and they came beyond Kerkis as far as the river permits. Those who spoke foreign tongues [i.e. Greeks and Carians who also scratched their names on the monument] were led by Potasimto, the Egyptians by Amasis.' These two last-named leaders were high military commanders who are known from other sources in the reign. An unexplained outcome of this expedition was the deliberate slighting of monuments of the 25th Dynasty Kushite kings and also of Psammetichus II's father, Necho.

An excursion – it was hardly a campaign – in the following year, 591, into southern Palestine in support of Zedekiah, the Babylonian puppet king of Jerusalem, encouraged a Judaean revolt against Babylonian rule for which Jerusalem paid a heavy price – culminating in a two-year siege by Nebuchadnezzar II. The city fell in 587. This was during the period of the Biblical 37-year Babylonian Exile.

Wahibre, better known as **Apries**, succeeded his father in February 589 and continued his policy of intervention in Palestinian affairs. His reign, however, was fraught with military problems at home as well as

The superb black basalt lid of Ankhesneferibre's sarcophagus (one of the treasures of the period in the British Museum) is carved in low relief, and shows her standing figure clad in a pleated gown. She wears the royal queen's vulture headdress topped by plumes, a solar disc and Hathor horns, whilst she holds the royal emblems of flail and sceptre. Around her are texts from the Book of the Dead and the underside of the sarcophagus lid is carved with a naked figure of the goddess Nut, her arms extended above her head, just as she occurs on a number of New Kingdom sarcophagi and painted ceilings of royal tombs in the Valley of the Kings.

abroad. A mutiny by the strategically important Aswan garrison was contained, but when Apries' army – sent to aid Libya against Dorian Greek invaders – was heavily mauled by the aggressors, civil war broke out upon the survivors' return, pitching the indigenous Egyptian army against foreign mercenaries. As was to happen so often under the Roman empire, the army turned to a victorious general, in this case a veteran of the Nubian campaigns, **Amasis** (**Ahmose II**), and when the two sides met in 570 Apries was killed. The victor nevertheless observed the proper rituals and had the body of Apries buried at Sais, probably the royal cemetery for the 26th Dynasty.

The Delta site of Sais (modern Sa el-Hagar) is heavily waterlogged and has never been properly investigated. Although it is thought to be the royal burial ground, it is strange that little evidence remains of the royal burials themselves apart from a few *ushabtis,* most of whose known provenances are other than Sais. The ten *ushabtis* in the name of Psammetichus are difficult to assign specifically to one or other king of that name. There is also a splendid *ushabti* (p. 194) and a heart scarab of Necho II, three *ushabtis* of Apries and six of Amasis.

The Greek historian Herodotus is one of the best sources for details of this period; he visited Egypt in about 450 BC, only a century after the events of the later 26th Dynasty. Amasis attempted to restrict the internal racial conflicts by granting specific trading rights and privileges to foreigners settled at Naukratis in the Delta, making it a free zone rather like Delos was in the Greek world. Petrie's excavations there in the late 19th century produced interesting evidence of the city's cosmopolitan nature and its temples to 'alien' deities. Mediterranean trade was a keynote of the reign of Amasis; links were forged with many other nations, especially the Greeks. Amasis even underwrote the rebuilding of the great oracular sanctuary of Apollo at Delphi after a disastrous fire destroyed it in 548 BC.

Although the essential focus of the dynasty was its seat at Sais, the family hold over Thebes was maintained through most of the dynasty by a great lady, the princess Ankhesneferibre, daughter of Psammetichus II by Queen Takhut. She had been adopted by the Divine Adoratrice Nitocris (who was closely associated in the administration with Mentuemhet) and succeeded her in 584 BC. She held the office for almost 60 years until the Persian Conquest in 525 BC. Her sarcophagus (*left*) was reused in the Ptolemaic period by a royal scribe, Amenhotep, who had the feminine suffixes altered to masculine ones.

Assyrian followed by Babylonian expansion and military activity had in turn threatened and subdued Egypt. Now there was a new contender on the scene, Persia. She had waged war against the Greeks; Egypt was no match for her. Within a year of succeeding to the Egyptian throne, **Psammetichus III** (**Psamtik III**) had to face the Persian army in 525 BC at Pelusium, the eastern gateway into Egypt. The inexperienced king eventually fled, defeated, to Memphis, only to be captured and transported to Susa, the Persian capital.

DYNASTY 27
(First Persian Period)
525–404

Cambyses II
Mesutire
525–522

Darius I
Setutre
521–486

Xerxes
485–465

Artaxerxes I
465–424

no cartouche

Darius II
423–405

no cartouche

Artaxerxes II
405–359

ROYAL NAMES AND BURIALS	
CAMBYSES II *Birth name* Cambyses *Throne name* Mesut-i-re ('Offspring of Re') *Burial* Takht-i-Rustam (Iran) **DARIUS I** *Birth name* Darius *Throne name* Setut-re ('Likeness of Re') *Burial* Naqsh-i-Rustam (Iran)	**XERXES** *Birth name* Xerxes **ARTAXERXES I** *Birth name* Artaxerxes **DARIUS II** *Birth name* Darius **ARTAXERXES II** *Birth name* Artaxerxes

The Persian conquest of Egypt in 525 BC was not so traumatic an occurrence as the biased contemporary accounts would have us believe. The Saite dynasty had collapsed, Psammetichus III had been captured and the Achaemenid Persians, led by **Cambyses II**, simply took charge of the country. At the beginning of Book 3 of his *Histories*, Herodotus, writing only three-quarters of a century after the event, tells three curious stories as to why Cambyses invaded Egypt: all concern women. One was the king's request for an Egyptian princess for a wife (i.e. in reality, a concubine), and his anger when he realized he had been fobbed off with a second-rank lady. The second saw Cambyses as the Persian king Cyrus' bastard son by Nitetis (daughter of the Saite king Apries), thus making Cambyses half Egyptian anyway. The third tale concerns a promise Cambyses, aged ten, made to his mother (this time Cassandane) that he would 'turn Egypt upside-down' to avenge a slight paid her. Herodotus expresses doubt concerning all three stories, but they do reflect the later Greek propaganda that was to colour views of the Persian dynasty. More to the point, and more accurately, Herodotus notes how the Persians easily entered Egypt across the desert, having been advised by the defecting mercenary general, Phanes of Halicarnassus (Herodotus' own home city), to employ the bedouin as

LATE PERIOD
BEGINS

DYNASTY 27 (FIRST PERSIAN PERIOD)

530　　　　520　　　　510　　　　500　　　　490　　　　480　　　　470

(*Right*) Cylinder seal of Darius I, said to have been found at Thebes, and presumably used by a high official. It shows the king hunting lions in a palm plantation and is inscribed with his name in Persian, Susian and Babylonian. British Museum.

(*Below*) Darius I represented as an Egyptian pharaoh before Horus on the door from a wooden shrine. British Museum.

guides. The Egyptian revenge on Phanes for betrayal was dire: as the two armies confronted each other, his sons, who had been left behind in Egypt, were brought out in front of the Egyptian army, where they could be seen by their father, and their throats were slit over a large bowl. When they had all been killed, Herodotus tells us, water and wine were added to the ghastly contents of the bowl and drunk by every man in the mercenary force.

The Egyptians were routed in the subsequent battle and fled back to Memphis. Herodotus gives at length the tribulations suffered by the captive Psammetichus and his family, as well as the outrages perpetrated by Cambyses. Not least among them were the desecration and deliberate burning of the embalmed body of Amasis, ripped from its tomb at Sais, and the stabbing by Cambyses of the sacred Apis bull of Memphis, leading to its subsequent death. The high propaganda level of such stories may be judged from an inscription in the Serapeum (the burial place of the Apis bulls at Memphis/Saqqara) recording the burial of a bull with full honours in Cambyses' sixth (Persian) year, 523 BC.

After his initial military success in Egypt, Cambyses had little further luck. Legend tells of his losing an entire army in the desert on its way to Siwa Oasis, and alleged traces of the 'lost army' are still reported from time to time in the press.

Although Cambyses had his name written in a cartouche, he remained a Persian and was buried at Takht-i-Rustam, near Persepolis. Only the ruined platform of his tomb survives. Cambyses and the rest of the Persian dynasty ruled Egypt from Susa like absentee landlords, leaving a satrap in control.

Darius I succeeded Cambyses in 522 and took a closer interest in the internal affairs and administration of Egypt. He had one satrap (Aryandes) executed for overstepping his office, built a temple at Khargah Oasis and repaired others as far apart as Busiris in the Delta and at el-Kab just north of Aswan. Not least, he recorded on a large stele

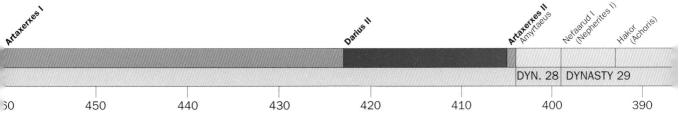

Artaxerxes I

Darius II

Artaxerxes II
Amyrtaeus

Nefaarud I
(Nepherites I)

Hakor
(Achoris)

DYN. 28 | DYNASTY 29

50   450   440   430   420   410   400   390

THE TESTIMONY OF AN EGYPTIAN COURTIER

A standing green basalt statue of a man named Udjahorresne (now in the Vatican) is one of the most important records of this first period of Persian occupation. The head and shoulders have been restored but the rest of the statue is literally covered in a long autobiographical inscription. Udjahorresne, a chief physician and priest of Neith at Sais, had served

Green basalt statue of Udjahorresne.

under both Amasis and Psammetichus III as a naval officer and, subsequently, like many of the nobility and upper classes of Egypt, supported the Persian administration. He became a courtier and, it would seem, a personnel officer: 'I furnished them with all their staffs consisting of the wellborn, no lowborn amongst them.' He records how he had composed the Egyptian titulary of Cambyses (Mesutire), was summoned to Susa by Darius I, drew the attention of both rulers to the traditions of Egypt, and was able especially to help his home city of Sais in having the important temple to the goddess Neith reconsecrated.

(*Left*) An alabaster storage jar found at Susa with the cartouche of Darius (also shown here in Champollion's rendering of it) and a bilingual inscription of cuneiform around the shoulder. Louvre, Paris.

now in Cairo his completion of the canal from the eastern Delta at Pelusium to the Red Sea, begun by Necho II.

The 35-year reign of Darius I – who, like Cambyses, wrote his name in a cartouche – was one of essential prosperity for Egypt, despite her now being subject to many outside influences and the politics of the Mediterranean world. In 490 the Greeks had, against all odds, defeated the Persian army at the battle of Marathon. Darius' attentions were elsewhere and, in 486, the Egyptians took the opportunity to revolt. Before Darius could suppress the insurgents he died and was buried in a great rock-carved tomb in the cliffs at Naqsh-i-Rustam at Persepolis. The revolt was put down with great severity by the next Persian king, **Xerxes**, who himself had to contend with the Greeks again, but this time at sea, at Salamis in 480 BC. The cruelty of the Persian satrap Achaemenes (Xerxes' son) only served to rouse the Egyptians to revolt once more when Xerxes was assassinated. His successor, **Artaxerxes I**, thus found himself opposed by the princes Inaros of Heliopolis (son of Psammetichus III) and Amyrtaeus of Sais. The former became a legendary 'crusader' in later folklore, recorded in several damaged demotic papyri; the latter's grandson was to be the sole king of the 28th Dynasty. Despite initial successes with the aid of Greek allies, the Egyptians were defeated and Inaros executed in 454 BC. Relative tranquillity then ensued for the next 30 years and the reign of Artaxerxes I, 465–424, left little mark in Egypt.

Revolt broke out again with the advent of **Darius II** (423–405 BC), although he did endeavour to woo the nationalistic elements by selected building works. The trouble spots were still concentrated round the Delta families, Sais being a particular centre (much as el-Kab had been centuries before, in the Second Intermediate Period). The Egyptians relied heavily on Greek mercenaries and, curiously, centuries later the Athenians were to recognize Sais as being particularly associated with Athene (an Athene of Sais even appeared on the *nome* coinage in Roman times). The Egyptians were able to take advantage of the murderous internal family problems of the Achaemenid royal house and maintain a quasi-independence during the reigns of the last two Persian kings, Darius II and **Artaxerxes II** (405–359 BC).

DYNASTY 28
404–399

no cartouche ## Amyrtaeus
404–399

DYNASTY 29
399–380

 ## Nefaarud I
(Nepherites I)
Baenre Merynetjeru
399–393

 ## Hakor
(Achoris)
Maatibre
393–380

DYNASTY 30
380–343

 ## Nakhtnebef
(Nectanebo I)
Kheperkare
380–362

 ## Nakhthoreb
(Nectanebo II)
Snedjemibre
Setepeninhur
360–343

 ## Djedhor
(Teos)
Irmaatenre
362–360

DYNASTY 31
(Second Persian Period)
343–332

no cartouche ## Artaxerxes III
343–338

 ## Darius III
336–332

no cartouche ## Arses
338–336

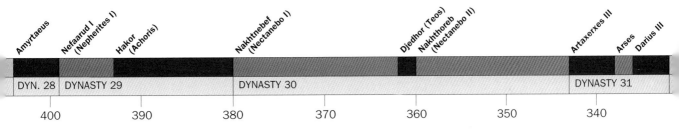

With the death of Darius II in 405, **Amyrtaeus** Prince of Sais, who had been fighting a guerrilla action against the Persians for at least six years, declared himself king. Somehow he managed to assert his authority as far south as the old Egyptian border at Aswan, but he is otherwise virtually unknown and was the sole king of the 28th Dynasty. In the next dynasty, founded by **Nepherites I (Nefaarud I)**, the northern Delta capital moved from Sais to the more centrally placed Mendes, indicating perhaps a stronger royal line arising from that city and the ousting of the previous one. To strengthen his claim and position, Nepherites I, like many before him, cast backwards to underline his legitimacy, associating himself with the Saite Renaissance policies. Certainly there is far more evidence of building work and inscriptions in Egypt during his reign, largely located in the northern sphere, than during those of his immediate predecessors. He also maintained the cult of the sacred Apis bull at Memphis and is recorded in a Serapeum inscription. As the capital was at Mendes the presumption was that Nepherites was buried there, but no royal tombs had been found until it was located in late 1995. The torso of a glazed composition *ushabti* inscribed for him was found in a plundered sarcophagus at Mendes, and the other three examples of his *ushabtis* (one complete but repaired, and two upper halves) have no known provenances.

(*Left*) *Ushabtis* of Nepherites I (*above*) and Achoris (*below*). Both are inscribed with Chapter 6 of the Book of the Dead, and their distinctive features may well be portraits of their respective owners. Louvre, Paris.

(*Right*) A bronze kneeling statue of a king that has been identified as Achoris from the indistinct hieroglyphs on his belt. Nelson-Atkins Museum, Kansas.

Detail of a basalt relief from Alexandria showing Nectanebo I kneeling and making an offering. British Museum.

ROYAL NAMES

AMYRTAEUS
No hieroglyphic writing extant of his name

NEFAARUD
Birth name
Nef-aa-rud ('The Great Ones Prosper')
Also known as
Nepherites I
Throne name
Ba-en-re Mery-netjeru ('Soul of Re, Beloved of the Gods')
Burial
?Mendes

HAKOR
Birth name
Hakor
Also known as
Achoris (Greek)
Throne name
Maat-ib-re ('Justice is the Heart of Re')

NAKHTNEBEF
Birth name
Nakht-neb-ef ('Strong in His Lord')
Also known as
Nectanebo I (Greek)
Throne name
Kheper-ka-re ('The Soul of Re Abides')

DJEDHOR
Birth name + (*epithet*)
Djed-hor (setep-en-inhur) ('Horus Says [he will live], Chosen of Onuris')
Also known as
Teos (Greek)
Throne name
Ir-maat-en-re ('Carrying out the Justice of Re')

NAKHTHORHEB
Birth name + (*epithet*)
Nakht-hor-heb (mery-hathor) ('Strong is His Lord Horus, Beloved of Hathor')
Also known as
Nectanebo II (Greek)
Throne name
Snedjem-ib-re Setep-en-inhur ('Pleasing to the Heart of Re, Chosen of Onuris')

ARTAXERXES III
Birth name
Artaxerxes

ARSES
Birth name
Arses

DARIUS III
Birth name
Darius

For about a year after the death of Nepherites (in 393) there was confusion, his son and a usurper, Psammuthis, struggling for power. Both were overcome by an unrelated man, **Achoris** (**Hakor**) who disregarded their year and dated the start of his own reign from the death of Nepherites. Achoris too was concerned to present legitimate continuity and associated himself with Nepherites in such a blatant way on his monuments, naming his son after him into the bargain, that he must have been trying to consolidate a relationship that had no factual basis. Nevertheless, Achoris' 14-year reign stands out amongst those of the later kings as one in which an enormous amount of building and refurbishing took place. Achoris took more than a hand in Near Eastern politics as well. The Greeks, initially the Spartans and then the Athenians, were the main protagonists in the struggles against Persia; by comparison, Egypt was merely a flea bite in the Persian arm. Achoris concluded a treaty with Athens in 389, but it lasted only three years in the face of internal squabbling amongst the Greeks which was settled by the Persian king Artaxerxes II's edict of 386, giving him the cities of Asia Minor and Cyprus and declaring the other Greek cities (with a few exceptions) autonomous, so long as they did not make war on him. The Greeks had been quietened and Egypt was isolated, thus attracting the attentions of Persia. Achoris repulsed several attacks between 385 and 383, largely with the use of renegade Greeks in the now considerably strengthened Egyptian navy, and Persia turned away and moved against Cyprus.

Achoris died in 380 but his son did not succeed him, being ousted by **Nectanebo I** (**Nakhtnebef**) of Sebennytos who founded the 30th Dynasty. A combined Persian and Greek force entered Egypt from the western (Mendes) side of the Delta, bypassing the strongly fortified and usual access through the eastern Delta fortress of Pelusium. Fortunately for Nectanebo, after being defeated, the strange allies delayed in their march on Memphis, distrusting each other, which gave him time to regroup, launch a successful counter-attack and fling them out of Egypt. Local conditions played a big part in his success – the inundation gave the Egyptians the advantage in a flooded landscape they knew well.

Nectanebo I achieved much in his stable 18-year reign, restoring dilapidated temples throughout the land and, in particular, erecting the small kiosk on the sacred island of Philae that was to blossom into one of the most sacred and delightful sites of later Egypt. He was succeeded by his son, **Teos** (**Djedhor**) (by his wife Udjashu), who immediately began to move against Persia, supported by Greek mercenaries, and hoping to gain Syria. Because of heavy tax impositions to pay for the mercenaries, Teos was unpopular in Egypt. In his absence Teos' son Tjahepimu declared his own son (i.e. Teos' grandson) king as **Nectanebo II** (**Nakhthoreb**) and Teos fled to sanctuary at Susa after a short two-year reign.

The first eight years of Nectanebo II's reign were protected from Persian aggression by that country's own dynastic squabbles and conse-

PAYING THE GREEK MERCENARIES

The Greek mercenaries employed in Egypt had to be paid, although Egypt was not at this time a monetary society. Special gold staters seem to have been struck (probably at the only recently identified mint of Memphis) to pay the Greeks. A unique example from the reign of Teos is a small gold stater found at Memphis that copies the Athenian coin-types with obverse the head of Athene and reverse an owl, but it has the king's name in place of the usual ΑΘΕ for Athens. Gold staters from the time of Nectanebo II had a different design.

One side bore a device the Greeks could identify with – a prancing horse; the reverse had two hieroglyphic signs reading *nfr nb* – 'good gold'. Less than three dozen examples are known and,

strangely, many have provenances from south of Aswan down to Abu Simbel where, of course, occurs the Greek graffiti referring to mercenaries marching south (p. 196).

Athenian gold stater compared with the stater of Teos that copies it. British Museum.

(*Below*) A diminutive Nectanebo II is sheltered by an impressive Horus falcon, the statue itself being a rebus of the king's name, 'Strong is His Lord Horus'. Metropolitan Museum, New York.

quent problems. By 350 BC, however, the new Persian ruler Artaxerxes III had sufficiently re-established authority over most of the empire to contemplate attacking Egypt – but the expedition failed. Word of this spread and soon Greek and Levantine cities were once more militarily challenging the Persian might, at first with a degree of success.

Nectanebo II's reign is characterized by a definite return to the old values and stability brought by the gods. Temples were built or refurbished and the king was presented as the pious one under the gods' protection. This is well exemplified in a superb large stone statue in the Metropolitan Museum, New York of Horus the falcon, wearing the Double Crown. Between its legs it has a diminutive figure of Nectanebo wearing the *nemes* headdress and carrying a curved harpesh and a small shrine. Not only is it a striking statue, it is also an icon reflecting the age-old clash between Horus (i.e. good, the king and Egypt) and Seth (evil and Persia). Not least, it is also a clever pun or rebus since it symbolizes the king's name as 'Strong [the harpesh] is Horus of Behbeit [the shrine]', the latter being a temple, now much ruined, dedicated to the goddess Isis in that Delta city.

Greek mercenaries fought for both Egypt and Persia and it was with some 20,000 Greeks, forming about one-fifth of his army, that Nectanebo II stood at Pelusium, the eastern Delta fortress entrance to Egypt, in 343 BC against the latest Persian advance. Greek generalship on the Persian side outflanked the Egyptians; Pelusium fell, followed by other Delta strongpoints, and Memphis itself soon afterwards, forcing Nectanebo to take refuge in Nubia. Persian rule was established in Egypt once more.

What became of Nectanebo II is unknown. A splendid large and complete faience *ushabti* figure of the king (unprovenanced, acquired by Turin Museum in the 19th century), plus ten other known fragments, are all that remains and point to preparations being made for his royal burial, presumably at Sais. His tomb was probably destroyed under the Ptolemies. In the British Museum is a huge black granite sarcophagus, finely carved all over with texts and scenes from the Book of What is in the Underworld, inscribed for Nectanebo II. It was never used and was found in Alexandria where, having had holes cut through its lower walls into the interior, it was later employed as a bath, often called 'Alexander's bath'. Curiously, in medieval legend (recounted in the 'Alexander Romance'), Nectanebo is said to have fled to the Macedonian court (i.e. to the anti-Persian faction). There he was recognized as a great Egyptian magician, attracted the attentions of the Macedonian king's (Philip II's) wife Olympias and became the father – unbeknown to Philip II – of Alexander the Great, thus continuing in due course the pharaoh-bred line legend for Alexander.

The Second Persian Period

When Egypt fell to the Persians in 343 BC, the reign of Nectanebo II, the last Egyptian pharaoh, came to an end; he was also the last Egyptian to rule Egypt for 2300 years until General Neguib and the 1952 Revolution. The Persian reaction, according to later Greek accounts which are obviously biased, was severe. Cities were slighted, temple treasuries robbed, sacred animals such as the Apis, Mnevis and Buchis bulls were slain, and the people enslaved with taxes. Once more a Persian satrap (this time Pherdates) ruled for an absentee king in Susa.

Whereas the first Persian dynasty had lasted from 525 until 404 BC, this time the occupation was for only a decade. **Artaxerxes III** was poisoned in Persia in 338 and his young successor, **Arses**, survived for only two years, to be murdered and succeeded by **Darius III**. There is little evidence of this period of Persian hegemony in Egypt. Artaxerxes struck Athenian-style silver tetradrachms at Memphis with an inscription in demotic (a cursive and difficult-to-read script derived from hieroglyphs) giving his name, and only two specimens survive. Mazaeus, who was satrap under Darius III, struck similar copies of Athenian tetradrachms but with his own name on them in Aramaic. He it was who wisely opened the gates of Egypt to Alexander the Great in 323 BC, saving the country and his own skin, and was transferred to high office in Babylon.

(*Right*) Silver tetradrachm that copies the Athena head and owl of Athens (*opposite, above*) but with a demotic inscription on the reverse showing it to have been struck by Artaxerxes III, presumably at the Memphis mint. British Museum.

MACEDONIAN KINGS
332–305

Alexander the Great
(Alexander III)
Meryamun Setepenre
332–323

Philip Arrhidaeus
Meryamun Setepenre
323–317

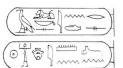

Alexander IV
Haaibre Setepenamun
317–305

Posthumous portrait of Alexander the Great with the ram's horn of Ammon, adopted after his visit to the god's temple at Siwa. Silver tetradrachm of Lysimachus, 323–281 BC.

ROYAL NAMES	

ALEXANDER III
Birth name
  Alexander
Also known as
  Alexander the Great
Throne name
  Mery-amun Setep-
  en-re ('Beloved of
  Amun, Chosen by
  Re')
Burial
  ?Alexandria, Egypt
 	
PHILIP ARRHIDAEUS
Birth name
  Philip Arrhidaeus
	Throne name
	  Mery-amun Setep-
	  en-re ('Beloved of
	  Amun, Chosen by
	  Re')
	
	ALEXANDER IV
	Birth name
	  Alexander
	Throne name
	  Haa-ib-re Setep-en-
	  amun ('Jubilant is
	  the Heart of Re,
	  Chosen of Amun')

When Philip II was assassinated in Macedonia in 336 BC, his 20-year-old son **Alexander** took up his father's intended attack on the crumbling Persian empire. Marching and fighting southwards over the next few years, and onwards through Asia Minor and the Levant, Alexander decisively defeated Darius III at Issus in 333 and entered Egypt in 332. Making his way to the oracle of Ammon in the Oasis of Siwa, he was hailed as the god's son, pharaoh incarnate. The Egyptians looked upon him as a divine being and saviour. At the mouth of the Nile he founded Alexandria, the first, and greatest, of the many cities that were to bear his name. Although his sojourn in Egypt was short, his influence was immense and lasting. On his orders restorations and repairs were carried out at the temples devastated in the Persian attack of 343. At Luxor temple the holy of holies was rebuilt and the best reliefs of Alexander in Egypt, carved on its outer walls, show him offering to Amun-Min. Egypt was now truly part of a much wider Mediterranean world of culture and religion, and could no longer hide within the sheltering cliffs of the Nile Valley.

From Egypt Alexander moved into Asia where, in an extraordinary series of campaigns, he overcame first Babylon and then Susa and Persepolis. Within just a few years he had extended his empire all the

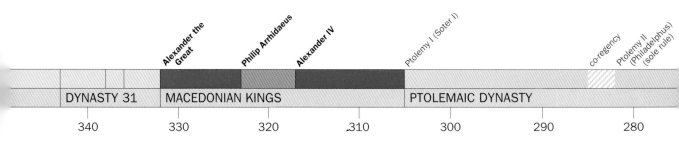

Alexander the Great | Philip Arrhidaeus | Alexander IV | Ptolemy I (Soter I) | co-regency | Ptolemy II (Philadelphus) (sole rule)

DYNASTY 31	MACEDONIAN KINGS	PTOLEMAIC DYNASTY

340 330 320 310 300 290 280

way to the Indus River. Alexander died of fever in Babylon in 323 BC and was succeeded by his half-witted half-brother **Philip Arrhidaeus**. Philip left a relief on the outside wall of the granite central shrine at Karnak, of the priests of Amun carrying the sacred barque of the god on their shoulders. He was murdered in 317. Alexander's posthumous son by his Persian wife Roxane, who became **Alexander IV**, was similarly despatched, together with his mother, in 311 BC by Cassander, now General of Europe. Although he was dead, Alexander IV is listed as nominally ruling from 317 to 305 BC, but it was Ptolemy son of Lagus who was the de facto king.

(*Below*) Alexander the Great offers a libation to the ithyphallic god Amun-Min on a relief on the outer wall of the sanctuary in the temple of Amun at Luxor.

PTOLEMAIC DYNASTY

305–30 BC

Ptolemy I (Soter I)

Meryamun
Setepenre
305–282

Ptolemy II (Philadelphus)

Userkaenre
Meryamun
285–246

Ptolemy III (Euergetes I)

Iwaennetjerwysenwy
Sekhemankhre
Setepamun
246–222

Ptolemy IV (Philopator)

Iwaennetjerwy-
menkhwy
Setepptah Userkare
Sekhemankhamun
222–205

Ptolemy V (Epiphanes)

Iwaennetjerwy-
merwyitu
Setepptah Userkare
Sekhem-ankhamun
205–180

Ptolemy VI (Philometor)

Iwaennetjerwyper
Setepenptahkhepri
Irmaatenamunre
180–164, 163–145

Gold stater of Ptolemy I with the deified
Alexander the Great on the reverse.

When Alexander left Egypt to conquer the rest of the known world, he left the Persian infrastructure in place and appointed as the satrap one Cleomenes, a banker of Naucratis. This post was next taken over by **Ptolemy I**, the son of Lagus – Alexander's boyhood friend at Pella who later became one of his trusted generals. When Alexander died in 323, Ptolemy acted, nominally at least, as satrap for Alexander's two successors in Egypt. Cleomenes, in Alexander's name, had extorted money from the people, robbed temples and, worse, embezzled the soldiers' pay. Ptolemy had little option when he found out but to try, sentence and execute him.

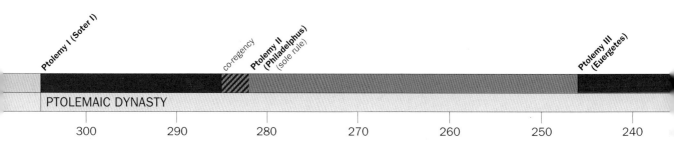

PTOLEMAIC DYNASTY

ROYAL NAMES

PTOLEMY I–VI
Birth name (I–VI)
  Ptolemy
Throne name (I)
  Mery-amun Setep-
  en-re ('Beloved of
  Amun, Chosen of
  Re')
Throne name (II)
  User-ka-en-re Mery-
  amun ('Powerful is
  the Soul of Re,
  Beloved of Amun')
Throne name (III)
  Iwa-en-netjerwy-
  senwy Sekhem-
  ankh-re Setep-amun
  ('Heir of the Twin
  Gods, Chosen of
  Amun')
Throne name (IV)
  Iwa-en-netjerwy-
  menkhwy Setep-
  ptah User-ka-re
  Sekhem-ankh-amun
  ('Heir of the [two]

Benificent Gods,
Chosen of Ptah,
Powerful is the Soul
of Re, Living Image
of Amun')
Throne name (V)
  Iwa-en-netjerwy-
  merwyitu Setep-
  ptah User-ka-re
  Sekhem-ankh-amun
  ('Heir of the [two]
  Father-loving Gods,
  Chosen of Ptah,
  Powerful is the Soul
  of Re, Living Image
  of Amun')
Throne name (VI)
  Iwa-en-netjerwy-per
  Setep-en-ptah-
  khepri Ir-maat-en-
  amun-re ('Heir of
  the [two] Houses of
  the Gods, Chosen
  of Ptah, Truth is the
  Form of Amun-Re')

With the break-up of Alexander's empire and no strong and obvious heir his generals, known as the *diadochi* ('followers'), pursued their independent interests. Ptolemy moved to Egypt, answerable in name only to the Council of State that had been set up in Babylon after Alexander's death, and to Perdiccas, the regent who held Alexander's signet ring.

At Babylon, Alexander's body had been prepared for the long journey back to Vergina, the royal burial ground in Macedonia, where Philip II's tomb has been found in recent years. On the journey, at Damascus, Ptolemy made his most astute move: he kidnapped the body on the pretext that Alexander had wanted to be buried in the shrine of Ammon at Siwa. The body was taken first to Memphis – where, nine years earlier, Alexander had been crowned pharaoh – pending the completion of the Siwa tomb. In the event the tomb was built at Alexandria. According to Strabo it was located in the area of the royal palaces known as the 'Sema'. Although Octavian/Augustus visited the tomb, it has never been found and the site is now probably under the sea, the coastline having shifted since then.

With Alexander's body under his control, Ptolemy had an immense political and religious advantage, and Perdiccas realized this. In the spring of 321 BC he marched against Ptolemy with an army of 5000 cavalry and 20,000 infantry, but was repulsed near Memphis and then murdered by his own officers.

The diadochi continued to war amongst themselves, although Antigonus Gonatus, Commander-in-Chief of the Grand Army, endeavoured to keep them under control by a firm policy of repression, replacement and execution where necessary. To ward him off three of the diadochi, Ptolemy, Lysimachus and Cassander, entered into an uneasy alliance that was to pay handsome dividends. When Antigonus prepared to attack Cassander in Macedon, Ptolemy marched against Antigonus' son Demetrius Poliorcetes and defeated him at Gaza in 312. A peace treaty the following year confirmed Ptolemy as satrap in Egypt.

Wars amongst the diadochi continued. Ptolemy lost the sea battle of Salamis in Cyprus against Demetrius in 306 BC but held Antigonus back on land the same year at Gaza. At the battle of Ipsus in 301 Antigonus was killed and the three allies divided the spoils of empire between them. Ptolemy added Palestine and lower Syria to his Egyptian empire and under his rule they prospered.

Ptolemy had secured his link back to the pharaonic line by marrying a daughter of Nectanebo II, but she had been set aside in 320 for

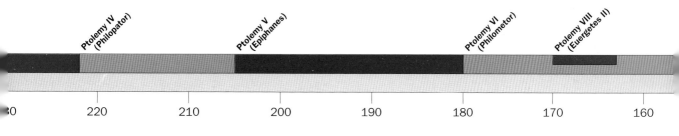

THE MARRIAGES OF PTOLEMY II

The fortunes and possessions of the Ptolemies in the Mediterranean world swayed back and forth, some being more adept than others in the military game of chess. Their family history is so complex that it reads like exaggerated pulp fiction.

Ptolemy II, Philadelphus, made a dynastic marriage with Arsinoe, daughter of the powerful Lysimachus of Thrace, one of Alexander's foremost generals. They had three children: the eldest son was Ptolemy Euergetes (later Ptolemy III); the second was called Lysimachus for his grandfather; and the third, a daughter named Berenice, was to marry Antiochus II of Syria in 252. About 279 BC, rumours of treason associated with Queen Arsinoe's name led to her being banished with her children to Coptos in southern Egypt. In her place, Ptolemy married his sister, also Arsinoe. She had been married, as a girl of 17, to Lysimachus of Thrace, but he was killed at the battle of Korupedion in 281. The brother-sister, husband-wife relationship of earlier Egypt and of the legends (e.g Isis and Osiris) was thus continued. Queen Arsinoe II reigned for about seven years during her husband Ptolemy II's 38-year reign. She enjoyed great influence and took her namesake's three children into her care. After her death, the king deified her and dedicated temples in her honour.

Portrait statues of Ptolemy II and Arsinoe II. Vatican Museum.

Eurydice, daughter of Antipater, Regent of Macedon. By her Ptolemy had four children, and then another three by Berenice, a widowed lady-in-waiting to Eurydice, who had already borne three children (one of whom, Magus, was later to become king of Cyrenaica).

The Ptolemies were monarchs in the great outside world of Hellenistic rulers whilst in Egypt they continued the line of god-kings, paying lip service to the prominent priesthood that, with an excellent civil service, kept the country stable and prosperous. The Ptolemies, and also many of their queens, appeared on the coinage portrayed in fine Hellenistic royal style; at the same time, in Egypt, they appeared on temple reliefs with full pharaonic trappings, essentially in the old styles tempered by Mediterranean artistic influences of more rounded limbs and fleshier bodies. Generally, only the cartouches make it possible to identify them individually, so bland are the representations on the reliefs. Problems arise with some reliefs where the cartouches were left empty of a name, there being uncertainty as to who would be on the throne at completion.

During Ptolemy I's reign were laid the beginnings of the many vast building projects of temples and towns that were to follow throughout the Ptolemaic dynasty. Chief amongst them was the Pharos (lighthouse) of Alexandria, actually completed in Ptolemy II's reign, that became one of the Seven Wonders of the Ancient World, and the Library that became one of the great centres of learning. The finest extant temples in Egypt are all of the Ptolemaic period – Dendera, Edfu and Philae – and many of them, like European cathedrals, were added to and embellished by several rulers over a long period. Most of these temples seem to have been built exactly over the sites of earlier structures, which makes it extremely difficult to ascertain their previous building history.

In 285 Ptolemy I took as co-ruler one of his sons by Berenice, who became sole ruler as **Ptolemy II Philadelphus** on his father's death in 282. His was a successful reign which saw the expansion of Ptolemaic possessions around the Mediterranean and internal stability in Egypt.

Ptolemy III Euergetes had been brought up by his stepmother, Arsinoe II (see box), and succeeded to the throne at the age of 30. He married Berenice, the daughter of his half-uncle Magus, king of Cyrenaica. Shortly after taking the throne, Ptolemy was called to the support of his sister Berenice, wife of Antiochus II, in Syria. Court intrigues there by the king's first wife, Laodice, had led to his death by poisoning and, before Ptolemy could reach Antioch, the death of his sister Berenice and her son, his young nephew.

Ptolemy sacked Antioch in revenge for their deaths and then continued campaiging into Babylonia for the next five years, leaving his wife, Berenice, as head of state with a panel of advisors. When trouble erupted in Egypt he returned rapidly to put down the dissidents. Ptolemy III began building the great temple dedicated to Horus at Edfu in the tenth year of his reign (237) but the main structure was not finished until 231 BC, in the reign of his son. The temple was formally opened in 142 under

Black diorite statue of Ptolemy IV or V. Without an identifying inscription it is often difficult firmly to attribute later Ptolemaic royal portraits. Yale University Art Gallery.

Ptolemy VIII, although the reliefs on the great pylon had to wait until Ptolemy XII to be completed.

Like his father, Ptolemy III's reign of 25 years saw Egypt prosper and expand and he was succeeded by his eldest son, **Ptolemy IV Philopator** in 222 BC. Unlike his ancestors, this Ptolemy led a dissolute life, aided and abetted by Sosibius, an Alexandrian Greek who had ingratiated himself into high office and made sure that he was indispensable. Acting on a wild rumour that Sosibius may well have started, Ptolemy agreed to have his mother Berenice and his brother Magus respectively poisoned and scalded to death within a year of his accession. There was one military excursion during Ptolemy IV's reign when Antiochus III of Syria, led to believe that Egypt would be easy prey under its dissolute monarch, moved through Phoenicia taking Egyptian vassal cities. Fortunately for Ptolemy, Antiochus held back from the fortress city of Pelusium, which could not have withstood him, and agreed to a four-month truce that Ptolemy, with Sosibius' aid, used to recruit foreign mercenaries and train an Egyptian levy army. At the battle of Raphia in 217 Ptolemy triumphed over Antiochus, but the Egyptian recruits had realized their own strength and there were revolts in the Delta.

Ptolemy IV married his sister Arsinoe in 217, and she produced an heir seven years later. The king then turned his affections to another woman, Agathoclea, who, with her brother Agathocles, encouraged his excesses. They were probably the cause of his death at the age of 41, leaving his sister-wife Arsinoe, who was soon poisoned by Sosibius and Agathocles, and his young son who became **Ptolemy V Epiphanes.** The conspirators then appointed themselves the five-year-old king's guardians, but suspicion about the events had been aroused. Matters came to a head when the popular general Tlepolemus, who held Egypt's eastern frontier fortress Pelusium, rescued the king and the mob broke into the royal palace at Alexandria and lynched Agathocles and his sister Agathoclea.

The map of Ptolemaic possessions and naval bases around the Mediterranean was shrinking as other rulers took advantage of Egypt's internal weaknesses to seize them. As an endeavour to settle the civil commotions, it was decided to crown the now 12-year-old **Ptolemy V** as king at the old capital of Memphis and make grants of land and tax remissions. Much of this is recorded in the decree of the priests of Memphis in 196 BC and inscribed in three scripts (hieroglyphs, demotic and Greek) on the Rosetta Stone found in 1799 (p. 10).

An uneasy peace was made with Syria in 192 when Ptolemy V married Cleopatra (I), the daughter of Antiochus the Great. In the last 13 years of his reign they had two sons and a daughter, of whom the elder boy became **Ptolemy VI, Philometor**, at roughly the same age as his father had become king. His mother acted as regent, but when she died five years later two greedy officials, Eulaeus and Lenaeus, appointed themselves guardians, much as had happened under the previous Ptolemy. They were foolish enough to declare war on Antiochus IV in

170 and were soundly beaten near Pelusium. The young Ptolemy was now Antiochus' prisoner and so the Egyptians declared Ptolemy's younger brother, also Ptolemy, and his sister Cleopatra, king and queen.

The curious situation thus arose of there being two Ptolemies, brothers, both nominally declared rulers of Egypt. Both sides – the Egyptians on behalf of the younger brother (Ptolemy Euergetes), and Antiochus (holding Ptolemy Philometor, his own nephew) – appealed to Rome as the major power for aid. The outcome was that Ptolemy Philometor ruled in the old capital of Memphis, and his younger brother Euergetes in Alexandria with his sister Cleopatra.

Antiochus IV returned to Syria in 169, but he was still a dominant power in Egypt by virtue of his protection of Ptolemy VI, which was an anathema to the brothers and sister alike. They, therefore, joined forces and appealed to Rome for help against Antiochus. Antiochus for his part marched to Pelusium, where he demanded control not only of this frontier fortress, but also Cyprus, an Egyptian possession. Both were denied him so he marched on Memphis and then turned north to Alexandria. At that moment Rome's hands were tied because of her involvement in the Macedonian war with Perseus, but on 22 June 168, at the battle of Pydna, Perseus was defeated. Rome was now free to respond to the Ptolemaic plea and a three-man mission sailed for Alexandria, led by Caius Popilius Laenas.

The confrontation between the Senate's representatives and Antiochus IV took place in July outside Alexandria at Eleusis. The Senate's decree was that Antiochus should vacate Egypt and Cyprus immediately. He asked for time to consider. Popilius refused and, taking his stick and drawing a circle in the sand around Antiochus' feet, demanded his answer before he left the circle. Antiochus realized that Rome was now the major state in the Mediterranean; he had no option but to comply with the Senate's demand. Ptolemy VI was confirmed as ruler in Egypt and his younger brother, Euergetes, was made king of Cyrenaica.

The next quarter-century of Ptolemy VI's reign passed quietly with Egypt prospering. In 145, however, he was mortally wounded in battle in Syria, where he had gone in support of his daughter, Cleopatra Thea, who was married to the dissolute Alexander Balas (150–146 BC). Alexander was to be removed (and subsequently beheaded by his own soldiers) and Demetrius II became king, similarly marrying Cleopatra Thea.

Silver tetradrachm portrait of Cleopatra I, Thea, the daughter of Ptolemy VI, who in a series of dynastic marriages was successively married to Alexander I Balas, Demetrius II and Antiochus VII, becoming the mother of Antiochus VIII of Syria. British Museum.

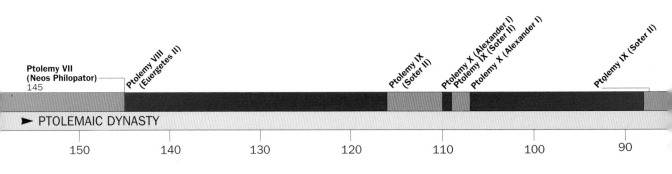

Ptolemy VII
(Neos Philopator)
145

Ptolemy VIII
(Euergetes II)

Ptolemy IX
(Soter II)

Ptolemy X (Alexander I)
Ptolemy IX (Soter II)

Ptolemy X (Alexander I)

Ptolemy IX (Soter II)

► PTOLEMAIC DYNASTY

150   140   130   120   110   100   90

PTOLEMAIC DYNASTY

305–30 BC

no cartouche

Ptolemy VII (Neos Philopator)

145

Ptolemy VIII (Euergetes II)

170–163, 145–116

Ptolemy IX (Soter II)

116–110,
109–107,
 88–80

Ptolemy X (Alexander I)

110–109, 107–88

no cartouche

Ptolemy XI (Alexander II)

80

Ptolemy XII (Neos Dionysos)

Iwaenpanetjernehem
Setepptah Irmaat

80–58, 55–51

no cartouche

Queen Berenice IV

58–55

Queen Cleopatra VII

(netjeret-merites)

51–30

Ptolemy XV (Caesarion)

Iwapanetjer
entynehem
Setepenptah
Irmaatenre
Sekhemankhamun

36–30

ROYAL NAMES	
PTOLEMY VII–XII	of Her Father')
Birth name	
Ptolemy	PTOLEMY XV
Throne name (XII)	*Birth name*
Iwa-en-panetjer-	Ptolemy
nehem Setep-ptah	*Throne name*
Ir-maat ('Heir of the	Iwa-panetjer-
God that Saves,	entynehem Setep-
Chosen of Ptah, in	en-ptah Ir-maat-en-
the form of Truth')	re Sekhem-ankh-
	amun ('Heir of the
	God that Saves,
CLEOPATRA VII	Chosen of Ptah,
Birth name + (epithet)	Carrying out the
Cleopatra (netjeret	Rule of Re, Living
mer-it-es)	Image of Amun')
('Goddess, Beloved	

The widowed Cleopatra was left in Alexandria with the young heir, **Ptolemy VII Neos Philopator**, and little protection since her late husband's army, largely composed of mercenaries, had joined Demetrius II in Syria. Ptolemy Euergetes, king of Cyrenaica, saw his chance and returned to Egypt, driving the queen and heir to take refuge in Memphis. A reconciliation was arranged and Euergetes married his sister Cleopatra, she agreeing to the match to protect her son's interests. However, as soon as she produced an heir for Euergetes, he had Ptolemy VII, his stepson and nephew, killed.

Ptolemy VIII Euergetes II, repulsive and nicknamed 'physon' (potbelly), was captivated by his niece, also Cleopatra, the daughter of his

Ptolemy XI (Alexander II)
80

Ptolemy XII (Neos Dionysos)

Queen Berenice IV

Ptolemy XII (Neos Dionysos)

Queen Cleopatra VII

Ptolemy XV (Caesarion)

ROMAN EMPERORS

80 70 60 50 40 30 20 10

Black diorite head of Ptolemy VIII.
Brussels Museum.

Two clay sealings from Edfu with
portraits of Ptolemy IX (top) and
Ptolemy X (above). Royal Ontario
Museum.

sister-wife Cleopatra. The niece agreed to the liaison so long as she could also become queen – so mother and daughter, sister and niece of Euergetes, became joint queens as Cleopatra II and III, generally differentiated as Cleopatra the Sister and Cleopatra the Wife. The former was much beloved by the people since her late husband Ptolemy VI's reign was such a shining example and memory compared to their present situation. Public resentment against Ptolemy VIII grew to such a point that he fled to Cyprus, taking the younger Cleopatra (III, the Wife), their two children and the young boy Memphites (his son by Cleopatra II) with him. His flight was not a moment too soon, for the mob broke into the palace seeking his blood.

In Cyprus, Euergetes plotted his return to Egypt where his sister, Cleopatra II, reigned as Cleopatra Philometor Soteira. In a fit of maniacal revenge against his sister and the Alexandrian mob which had been busy destroying his statues and memories of him, he murdered Memphites, his own son by Cleopatra II, and sent the child's dismembered body to her as a present on her birthday.

In 129, now strong enough to invade Egypt, Euergetes returned from Cyprus and in 128 Cleopatra II fled for protection to her daughter Cleopatra Thea, now married to Demetrius II of Syria. Strangely, she was to return to Egypt, and Euergetes survived until 116. What happened to his sister-wife Cleopatra II after her return is not known, but she presumably predeceased him as her daughter, Cleopatra III, inherited Egypt by Euergetes' will.

Cleopatra III, now queen-mother and regent for her two young sons, soon proved that she was as strong-willed as any of her ancestors. Although the younger son, **Ptolemy X Alexander I**, was her favourite, the two boys had, by popular pressure, to be seen to rule jointly with her so the elder, **Ptolemy IX Soter II**, was associated with them. He began building the temple of Hathor at Dendera, to which many of his successors added, including Cleopatra VII (below) and several of the Roman emperors. In 106 BC Ptolemy IX, whose nickname was 'lathyrus' (chickpea), fled to Cyprus because he had been accused of plotting to murder his mother. Since Cleopatra had always favoured Ptolemy Alexander, there is a strong possibility that the charge was false in an attempt to dispose of Ptolemy Soter. Cleopatra took her younger son, Ptolemy Alexander, to be her consort, and he may well have had a hand in her death at the age of 60 in 101 BC.

Ptolemy X practised the gross excesses of his immediate forebears and was so huge that he was incapable of walking on his own without support. As with Ptolemy VIII, the Egyptians eventually turned against him; he fled but was killed at sea between Lycia and Cyprus. The older brother, Ptolemy IX, was therefore able to return and claim his throne, dying in 80 BC aged 62.

Ptolemy IX had no legitimate male heir so he left the throne to his daughter Berenice. She needed to have a male consort and a nephew, **Ptolemy XI Alexander II**, was found to marry her; but Ptolemy disliked

Black basalt slab with Ptolemy XII adoring the god Heh who holds notched palm ribs signifying 'millions of years' (cf. p. 80). Louvre, Paris.

Berenice, who was older than him. Foolishly he decided to reign alone and had her murdered within a month of their wedding. However, the queen had been a popular choice with the people, and he was lynched after a 19-day reign. This left a royal vacuum on the throne again. The only male descendants of Ptolemy I available, albeit illegitimate, were the sons of Ptolemy IX by an Alexandrian Greek concubine whose name is not even known. They were then living in safe exile at the court of Mithridates VI of Pontus at Sinope. The eldest of the boys was proclaimed king as **Ptolemy XII Neos Dionysos** and, to complete the royal pair, he married his sister Tryphaena.

Rome was now the major factor in all Mediterranean politics and Ptolemy XII sought to legitimize his rule not only by an Egyptian coronation but also with Roman approval. Like his predecessors, his habits were not to the liking of the populace – he earned the nickname 'auletes' (the flute player) – and his heavy taxes and fauning attitude to Rome made history repeat itself. He fled to Rome, driven out of the country by the people.

Once more the throne of Egypt was vacant with only a female heir, Ptolemy XII's daughter **Berenice**. She needed a male consort and was married to a Seleucid cousin. As strong-willed as her female forebears, she had him strangled within a week of their wedding and then took as her husband Archelaus, whom she knew as a friend from her exile at the court of Mithridates VI. They ruled for a brief period of four years whilst Ptolemy XII plotted in Rome to regain his throne. He needed two things initially to achieve this: recognition by the Roman Senate, and an army. A large bribe to Julius Caesar (underwritten from Egyptian revenues) secured the first, and a similar large bribe to the pro-consul of Syria, Gabinius, secured the use of his three legions. They marched on Alexandria and in the conflict Archelaus was killed, Berenice captured, imprisoned and then murdered. Ptolemy XII had returned but ruled Egypt only by virtue of the backing of the Roman legions. His second reign lasted just four years. History records that Ptolemy XII was neither valiant nor religious, despite the fact that he is so represented in the reliefs he completed on the temple pylons at Edfu and Philae.

(*Right*) The temple of Horus at Edfu is the finest preserved of Egyptian temples. It was begun under Ptolemy III in 237 BC, added to by Ptolemy IV, VIII and IX, and the pylons finally decorated by Ptolemy XII in 57 BC with figures of himself smiting the enemy.

(*Above*) Cleopatra VII presents her son, Caesarion, and offerings to the gods in a large-scale relief on the rear wall of the temple of Hathor at Dendera.

(*Below*) Although there are some sculptures identified as Cleopatra, she is best seen on the coin portraits, particularly those issued at Antioch where she appears as a bejewelled eastern queen along with a portrait of Mark Antony, who was to take Caesar's place after the latter's assassination on the Ides of March in 44 BC.

Cleopatra and the last of the Ptolemies

Egypt was bequeathed to Ptolemy XII's daughter, **Cleopatra VII**, aged 17, with the injunction that she should marry the elder of her two brothers, Ptolemy XIII. He, with the aid of ever-scheming palace courtiers, this time Pothinus and Achillas, attempted to dispose of her, but she was warned in time and fled to safety in Syria. However, Cleopatra was soon back with an army at the gates of Egypt at Pelusium where a stand-off between her and her brother took place, neither side being willing to make a move.

Rome now entered the scene with Julius Caesar pursuing his defeated adversary Pompey after the battle of Pharsalus in 48 BC. Pompey, seeking sanctuary with Ptolemy XIII, landed at Pelusium and was immediately assassinated by the conspirators Pothinus and Achillas, who were backing the Caesarian faction. When Caesar arrived at Alexandria, and was presented with Pompey's severed head, he had Pothinus executed (Achillas met his death later at the hands of Arsinoe, Cleopatra's younger sister). At Alexandria Caesar summoned the young king and queen before him. He favoured the queen, Cleopatra, as history and so many plays and novels recount. Ptolemy, with Achillas, unsuccessfully besieged the Romans on the Pharos island and Ptolemy was drowned in the attack.

In order to maintain the necessary dual rule on the throne, Cleopatra now married her younger brother, Ptolemy XIV. She simultaneously became Caesar's mistress and bore him a son, **Ptolemy XV Caesarion**. Cleopatra is shown in a relief on the rear wall of the temple of Hathor at Dendera presenting the young boy to the gods. It is the only relief of her in Egypt. Although her beauty has been fabled in literature, Cleopatra was above all things a very clever, intelligent and political woman – she had to be to captivate two such men as Caesar and Antony in turn and endeavour to use them to maintain her kingdom. She was said to be the only one of the Ptolemies who could understand and speak Egyptian. Egypt was now simply a rich pawn in the great struggle for power after Caesar's death between Octavian, Caesar's heir, and Antony. It came to a head at Actium on the west coast of Greece on the afternoon of 2 September 31 BC. The sea battle swung first one way and then the

(*Above*) On the outer southern wall of the Ptolemaic and Roman temple at Esna, the 3000-year-old motif of pharaoh smiting (cf. p. 24) is repeated by the Roman emperor Titus, AD 79–81.

(*Below*) The reliefs on the Roman *mammisi* (birth house) beside the Ptolemaic temple at Dendera continue the ancient Egyptian iconography with, here, Trajan (AD 98–117) as pharaoh offering to Isis as she suckles her son Horus.

other when, for some unaccountable reason – some say a mutiny, others say misunderstood orders – Antony broke off the engagement and sailed for the open sea after Cleopatra's ships and followed her to Egypt. Octavian was left master of the field.

The following year Octavian took the fight to Egypt and entered Alexandria on 1 August 30 BC. Cleopatra, as is well known, committed suicide rather than be an ornament in a Roman triumph. Antony fell on his sword, and Octavian had them buried together in the royal mausoleum in the Sema at Alexandria that Cleopatra had prepared.

Roman Egypt

Although Rome conquered Egypt with the defeat of Antony and Cleopatra, the country did not become a Roman province in the normal manner. Octavian (who became Augustus in 27 BC and the first emperor of Rome) took Egypt as his personal estate. It was ruled by a prefect, answerable to the emperor, and no member of the Imperial family or the Senate was allowed to visit the country without the express permission of Augustus. Egypt's production of vast quantities of grain was an important factor in the maintenance of stability in Rome – 'Give them [the mob] bread and circuses', Juvenal wrote, and Egypt provided the bread with the annual grain fleet that sailed from Alexandria .

Successive Roman emperors after Augustus maintained the pharaonic fiction, appearing in Egyptian dress on reliefs or statues and carrying out the old rituals. Without the provision of an identifying cartouche they can rarely be recognized. From Augustus until the reform of the mint at Alexandria under Diocletian in AD 294 coinage was struck on the Greek module, mainly tetradrachms (four-drachm pieces) that bore the emperor's likeness as a Roman, an inscription identifying him around his head in Greek, and often with a reverse type that harked back to ancient Egyptian themes or deities.

Roman Egypt was immensely prosperous and many new cities were founded, especially in the Faiyum area, with the classic Roman buildings of baths, basilica and agora. Some temples were still built following the old plans; for example, Esna reflects the layout of the earlier Ptolemaic temple at Dendera and has several 1st-century AD emperors represented in reliefs on its walls. One of the best known buildings in Egypt, Pharaoh's Bed or Trajan's Kiosk, on the island of Philae, was built by Trajan (AD 98–117) and was intended to be a grand monumental entrance to the temple of Isis, but it was never finished. On Philae occurs the latest known firmly datable hieroglyphic inscription, carved in AD 394. Pompey's Pillar at Alexandria has nothing to do with him but was erected in the reign of Diocletian (AD 284–305). Generally, however, Roman period monuments, apart from the sand-swept town sites, are few in Egypt. Although paying lip-service to the old ideas and religion, in varying degrees, pharaonic Egypt had in effect died with the last native pharaoh, Nectanebo II in 343 BC, a thousand years before the rise of Islam and the fall of Egypt under its sway in AD 641.

THE FIVE ROYAL NAMES OF THE PHARAOHS

From the Middle Kingdom, the 11th and 12th Dynasties, an Egyptian king was given a unique combination of five names. The first was his actual birth name, the other four were conferred on him at his enthronement. The sequence of the five names was:

Name		Accompanying Title
HORUS		Horus
NEBTI OR TWO LADIES		He of the Two Ladies (Wadjet and Nekhbet)
GOLDEN HORUS		Golden Horus
THRONE NAME OR PRENOMEN		He of the Sedge and the Bee (King of Upper and Lower Egypt)
BIRTH NAME OR NOMEN		Son of Re

To take an example, the five names of Tutankhamun are listed below, and read from right to left in the hieroglyphs:

HORUS NAME
Ka-nakht tut-mesut
'Strong bull, fitting from created forms'

NEBTI NAME
Nefer-hepu segereh-tawy sehetep-netjeru nebu
'Dynamic of laws, who calms the Two Lands, who propitiates all the gods'

GOLDEN HORUS NAME
Wetjes-khau sehetep-netjeru
'Who displays the regalia, who propitiates the gods'

THRONE NAME
Nesu-bity: Nebkheperure
King of Upper and Lower Egypt: Lord of Manifestations is Re

BIRTH NAME
Sa-re: Tutankhamun (heqa-iunu-shema)
Son of Re, Living Image of Amun, Ruler of Upper Egyptian Heliopolis

Before the 4th Dynasty the king was generally known only by his Horus name. Written in a *serekh* panel (p. 21) it is easily identifiable by the Horus falcon standing on its top. The first occurrence of the *serekh* is on the Narmer Palette (p. 18) at the beginning of Egyptian history. During the 2nd Dynasty political troubles seem to have forced the king Sekhemib to change his name to Peribsen, thereby moving from the nominal protection of Horus to that of the god Seth (p. 27). The Horus falcon on the top of the *serekh* panel is supplanted by the Seth animal. Khasekhemwy, the next king, appears to have appeased both factions by having Horus and Seth above his *serekh*.

Occasionally in the early dynasties the king might have secondary titles. The *nebti* sign of the Two Ladies is used by Hor-Aha in the 1st Dynasty, but not as part of his royal titles. The Two Ladies, the cobra and vulture, are respectively the goddesses Wadjet of Buto in Lower Egypt (the Delta) and Nekhbet of Nekheb (el-Kab) in Upper Egypt. Later in the dynasty Semerkhet included the Two Ladies as part of his honorifics, but it is not until the 12th Dynasty that the *nebti* title became a standard part of the five-fold sequence of names.

The title He of the Sedge and of the Bee (i.e. King of Upper and Lower Egypt) was first used by Den in the 1st Dynasty, and he also associated his Horus name with the sign for gold (a necklace with pendants). The third part of the royal titulary, the Golden Horus, became standard with the Middle Kingdom.

The best known and immediate recognition of a royal name is by its enclosure in an oval cartouche (originating in a loop of rope with tied ends). It was Snefru, first king of the 4th Dynasty, who introduced the use of the cartouche to enclose royal names and the cartouche name thereafter supplanted the Horus name in identifying the king. A second cartouche name was added in the 5th Dynasty by Neferirkare, the first being his name given on his accession to the throne (his prenomen), and the second containing his birth name (nomen). Confusion between kings of the same name can arise when they share a common prenomen, e.g. Sobekhemsaf or Ramesses, and the second cartouche is not present.

Although the sequence of five names or titles was a necessary requirement for the king, rarely are they actually seen used together except on the occasion of his coronation. Of the five names, those most frequently used are the first (Horus), fourth (throne) and fifth (birth) names.

SELECT BIBLIOGRAPHY

The following list is indicative of some of the main literature; the individual titles themselves contain further bibliographies (especially Grimal, pp. 404–83).

Aldred, A. *Akhenaten King of Egypt*. London and New York 1988.
– *The Egyptians*. Revised ed. London and New York 1984.
– *Jewels of the Pharaohs: Egyptian Jewellery of the Dynastic Period*. London 1971.
Andrews, C. *Ancient Egyptian Jewellery*. London and New York 1990.
Bagnall, R.S. *Egypt in Later Antiquity*. Princeton 1993.
Baines, J. and Malek, J. *Atlas of Ancient Egypt*. Oxford and New York 1980.
Bowman, A.K. *Egypt after the Pharaohs, 332 BC–AD 642 from Alexander to the Arab Conquest*. London 1986.
Breasted, J.H. *Ancient Records of Egypt*. 5 vols. New York 1906 (repr. 1962).
Daressy, G. *Cercueils des cachettes royales*. Cat. Gen. du Musée du Caire, nos 61001–61044. Cairo 1909.
David, R. and David, A.E. *A Biographical Dictionary of Ancient Egypt*. London 1992.
Dodson, A. *The Canopic Equipment of the Kings of Egypt*. London 1994.
Edwards, I.E.S. *The Pyramids of Egypt*. Revised ed. Harmondsworth and New York 1991.
–, Gadd, C.J. and Hammond, N.G., eds. *Cambridge Ancient History*. I and II. Cambridge 1971, 1973.
Emery, W.B. *Archaic Egypt*. Harmondsworth 1961.
Gardiner, Sir Alan. *Egypt of the Pharaohs*. Oxford and New York 1961.
– *The Royal Canon of Turin*. Oxford 1959.
Gautier, H. *Le Livre des Rois d'Egypte, Recueil des titres...* 5 vols. Cairo 1907–17.
Glanville, S.R.K. *The Legacy of Egypt*. 2nd ed. edited by J.R. Harris. Oxford 1971.
Grimal, N. *A History of Ancient Egypt*. Oxford and Cambridge, Mass. 1992.
Habachi, L. *The Obelisks of Egypt; Skyscrapers of the Past*. London 1978.
Hall, H.R. *Catalogue of Egyptian Scarabs in the British Museum*. I. *Royal Scarabs*. London 1913.
Harris, J.E. and Wente, E.F., eds. *An X-ray Atlas of the Royal Mummies*. Chicago 1980.
Hayes, W.C. *Royal Sarcophagi of the XVIII Dynasty*. Princeton 1935.
– *The Scepter of Egypt*. 2 vols. New York 1953.
Herodotus. *The Histories*. Harmondsworth 1972.

Hodges, P. *How the Pyramids Were Built*. Shaftesbury 1989, Warminster 1993.
Hornung, E. *The Valley of the Kings: Horizon of Eternity*. New York 1990.
Josephus. *Contra Apionem*. London 1926–65.
– *Jewish Antiquities*. London 1926–65.
Kitchen, K. *The Third Intermediate Period in Egypt (1100–650 BC)*. Warminster 1973.
Lichtheim, M. *Ancient Egyptian Literature*. 3 vols. Berkeley, Calif. 1973, 1976, 1980.
Manetho (trans W.G. Waddell). London 1940.
Mendelssohn, K. *The Riddle of the Pyramids*. London 1974, New York 1986.
Murnane, W.J. *Ancient Egyptian Coregencies*. Chicago 1977.
– *The Penguin Guide to Ancient Egypt*. Harmondsworth and New York 1983.
Peet, T.E. *The Great Tomb Robberies of the Twentieth Egyptian Dynasty*. 2 vols. Oxford 1930.
Petrie, W.M.F. *Scarabs and Cylinders with Names*. London 1917.
Porter, B. and Moss, R.L.B. *Topographical Bibliography of Ancient Egyptian Hieroglyphic Texts, Reliefs and Paintings*. I. *The Theban Necropolis*. Part I. *Private Tombs*. Oxford 1960.
– Part II. *Royal Tombs and Smaller Cemeteries*. Oxford 1964.
Quirke, S. *Who Were the Pharaohs? A History of Their Names with a List of Cartouches*. London 1990.
– and Spencer, J., eds. *The British Museum Book of Ancient Egypt*. London and New York 1992.
Reeves, C.N. ed. *After Tut'ankhamun: Research and Excavation in the Royal Necropolis at Thebes*. London 1992.
– *The Complete Tutankhamun: The King, The Tomb, The Royal Treasure*. London and New York 1990.
– *Valley of the Kings: The Decline of a Royal Necropolis*. London 1990.
Saleh, M. and Sourouzian, H. *The Egyptian Museum Cairo*. Mainz 1987.
Smith, Sir Grafton Elliot. *The Royal Mummies*. Cat. Gen. du Musée du Caire, nos 61051–61100. Cairo 1912.
Spencer, A.J. *Early Egypt: The Rise of Civilisation in the Nile Valley*. London 1993.
Thomas, E. *The Royal Necropolis of Thebes*. Princeton 1966.
Winlock, H.E. *The Rise and Fall of the Middle Kingdom in Thebes*. New York 1947.
Yoyotte, J. et al. *Tanis: L'or des Pharaons*. Paris 1987.

ACKNOWLEDGMENTS AND ILLUSTRATION CREDITS

a: above; t: top; b: bottom; c: centre;
l: left; r: right.

Very special thanks are owed to Dr
Richard Parkinson, Curator in the
Department of Egyptian Antiquities in
the British Museum, for making
available the cartouches he drew for Dr
Stephen Quirke's book (see
Bibliography) and then adding many
more for use here. Thanks also to my
old photographer friend John G. Ross for
making many of his splendid portrait
photographs available.

The following abbreviations are used
to identify sources and locate
illustrations: IB – Ian Bott (illustrator);
BM – courtesy of the Trustees of the
British Museum; BMFA – Boston
Museum of Fine Arts; BrM – Brooklyn
Museum; PAC – Peter A. Clayton; EAO
– Egyptian Antiquities Organization;
EES – Egypt Exploration Society; HM –
Hirmer, Munich; KT – Kodansha Ltd,
Tokyo; LP – Louvre, Paris; MMA –
Metropolitan Museum of Art, New
York; AP – Annick Petersen (illustrator);
JP – James Putnam; JGR – John G. Ross;
AS – Albert Shoucair; UMP – University
Museum Philadelphia, Pennsylvania.

half-title, Camera Press; frontis, PAC;
pages: 5t&cb EAO, ca JGR; 6 George
Ortiz Collection, Geneva; 7a Bildarchiv
Preussischer Kulturbesitz, b Jon Abbot,
courtesy WONDERS, The Memphis
International Cultural Series; 8 AP; 10a
BM, b AP; 11a Museo Nazionale
Palermo, b PAC; 12-13 JGR; 14l&r JGR,
c BM; 15 JGR; 17 AP; 18 EAO; 19 AP;
20a AP, b PAC; 21 AP (after W.B.
Emery); 22 AP; 23a EES, bl W.M.F.
Petrie, *Royal Tombs of the First
Dynasty* (1900), br Documentation
Photo, Paris; 24 BM; 25a JGR, b RMN,
Paris; 26 JGR; 27 JGR; 28 after W.M.F.
Petrie, *Royal Tombs of the Earliest
Dynasties* (1901); 29tl PAC, r EAO, b
after Petrie, *Royal Tombs*; 30-31 JGR;
32a HM, b BM; 33a PAC, b EAO; 34a JP,
b PAC; 35 JGR; 36l EAO, r AP; 37a after
Kurt Mendelssohn, b PAC; 38a PAC, b
John Freeman; 39 PAC; 40a PAC, b
EAO; 41a PAC, b PAC; 42l JGR, r HM;
43 HM; 44a PAC, b A.J. Spencer; 45 JP;
46 BMFA; 47 Pelizaeus Museum,
Hildesheim; 48a PAC, b Alberto Siliotti;
49a PAC, b JGR; 50 LP; 51 PAC; 52
George Hart; 53a JGR, b PAC; 54 EAO;
55a PAC, c AP; 54b-55b AP (after
Mendelssohn); 56 PAC; 57a&b PAC; 58a
Hirmer, b BMFA; 59 EAO; 60 JGR; 61
AP (after Borchardt); 62 MMA; 63 A.F.
Kersting; 64 BrM; 65al Chris Scarre, ar
Oriental Institute, Chicago, b JGR; 66
EAO; 67 BrM; 68l-r Michael Duigan,
PAC, JGR, PAC; 69l-r JGR, JGR, JGR,
PAC; 73a PAC, b JGR; 74 Archives
Photographiques; 75 BrM; 76l Marburg,
r PAC; 77 PAC; 78 Marburg; 79a
Michael Duigan, b HM; 80a AS, bc PAC,
bl PAC, br AS; 81al PAC, ar HM, bl
MMA; 83t LP, c EAO, b Ian Shaw; 84
HM; 85l JGR, r BM; 86t AS, c EAO, b
HM; 87 PAC; 88a EAO, bl EAO, br
Costa Cairo; 89a PAC, b BM; 92l HM, r
RMN Paris; 93 Numismatic Fine Arts
International Inc; 95 Professor Manfred
Bietak; 96a PAC, bl BM, br BM; 98l-r
JGR, JGR, EAO, PAC; 99l-r PAC, KT,
JGR, BM; 100 JGR; 101 BM; 102 PAC;
103 from G. E. Smith, *The Royal
Mummies* (1912); 104 MMA; 105a HM,
b EAO; 106a PAC, c PAC, b EES;
107a&b PAC; 108a HM, bl EAO, br
PAC; 109 EAO; 110a PAC, b PAC;
111a,c&b PAC; 112 EAO; 113a PAC, b
MMA; 114a HM, b PAC; 115a JGR, b
BM; 116a PAC, b NFA International Inc;
117a&b PAC; 118a PAC, b EAO; 119a
Berlin Museum, b EAO; 120 PAC; 121
PAC; 122a BMFA, b HM; 123a HM, b
EAO; 124a&c PAC, b JGR; 125a PAC, b
AP; 126 PAC; 127a&b PAC; 128 KT;
129a PAC, bl C.N. Reeves, br KT; 131a
PAC, c AP; 132a KT, b JGR; 133a PAC,
b JGR; 134a Griffith Institute, Oxford, b
EAO; 135 IB; 136 PAC; 137 HM; 138a
MMA, b PAC; 139a Leiden Museum, b
PAC; 140 R. H. Wilkinson; 141 t-b G.E.
Smith, *The Royal Mummies*; 142
Girodias Paris; 143a&b PAC; 144a R.H.
Wilkinson, b BM; 145 PAC; 144-5 IB;
146l Staatliche Sammlung Ägyptischer
Kunst, Munich, r JGR; 148l Alberto
Siliotti, c PAC; 149l PAC, r Cyril
Aldred; 150 JP; 151 Thames and Hudson
Ltd, London; 152 PAC; 153 PAC; 154a
PAC, b AP; 156 MMA; 157a R.H.
Wilkinson, b & r EAO; 159a JGR, bl & r
AS; 160 BM; 162a HM, b PAC; 163a, c, b
Oriental Institute, Chicago; 164a PAC, b
Fitzwilliam Museum, Cambridge; 165
G.E. Smith, *The Royal Mummies*; 166
PAC; 168a from A. Piankoff, *The Tomb
of Ramesses VI*, b Marburg; 169a JGR, b
AS; 170a Royal Scottish Museum, b
PAC; 173 l-r PAC, PAC, JGR, PAC; 175
BM; 176a&b PAC; 177a&b PAC; 179a
PAC, b IB; 180 al AS, ar PAC, b PAC;
181a PAC, b AS; 184a&b PAC; 185
Gaddis Luxor; 186al RMN Paris, ar J.
Mortimer, b UMP; 187l LP, r BM; 189a
BM, b Royal Scottish Museum,
Edinburgh; 191 from A. Mariette,
*Monuments divers Recueillis en Egypte
et Nubie* (1889); 192 HM; 193 Girodias
Paris; 194 Leiden Museum; 196a UMP,
b RMN Paris; 197 BM; 199a BM, b PAC;
200l Vatican, r M. Chuzeville, Paris;
202a&bl PAC, r Nelson-Atkins
Museum; 203 BM; 204a PAC, b MMA;
205 PAC; 206 PAC; 207 PAC; 208 PAC;
210 Mansell London; 211 Peabody
Museum, Yale University; 212 PAC;
214a ACL Brussels, b Royal Ontario
Museum; 215a LP, b PAC; 216a&b PAC;
217a&b PAC; 218 Tracy Wellman.

INDEX

Numbers in *italic* script refer to illustrations on the relevant pages.

(gd) god; (gds) goddess; (k) king; (q) queen